# Sharing

# Sharing
## *Self Discovery in Relationships*

**Kathy Oddenino, R.N.**

*Joy Publications*

**SHARING**
**SELF DISCOVERY IN RELATIONSHIPS**

by KATHY ODDENINO, R.N.

**Copyright © 1990 by Kathy Oddenino**

CURRENT PRINTING (last digit)
10 9 8 7 6 5 4 3 2 1

Printed in the United States of America by:

**Joy Publications**
**133A Lee Drive**
**Annapolis, MD 21403**

Front cover art entitled—*The Boating Party* by Mary Cassatt
Front cover design by Deborah Daly
Back cover photo by Wallace F. Rollins
Text design by Anita Crouch

**ISBN 0-923081-02-X**

# Dedication

This book is dedicated to my granddaughter,
Nicole Oddenino,
who shared our lives for fourteen months.


**NICOLE**

With your choice

You made me listen

until I could hear.

You made me look

until I could see.

I love you.

*A percentage of the
profits from this book
is dedicated to the:*

Nicole Oddenino Memorial Burn Research Fund
Marshall United Methodist Church
P.O. Box 144
Marshall, VA 22115

# Acknowledgements

As I receive the information that you find in my books, I realize that I am the first pupil of the spirit energy within me. This is the third complete text that I have accepted from the source of enfinite knowledge within. This knowledge is available to all of man from the spirit energy within himself. I call my spirit energy "HS" for Heavenly Spirit. This energy of the spirit self is an energy that most of man denies because he does not understand that it is always within and available to him. Having integrated the energy of my Heavenly Spirit into my life is the most peaceful and joyful gift that I could ever give myself.

It is my wish to publicly acknowledge the source of this information as the energy of the Heavenly Spirit within me. It does not come from my physical intellect but it is integrated with my intellect. We are, as man, body (intellect), mind (soul memory), and spirit (enfinite knowledge of love, truth, and perfection). I gratefully acknowledge, accept, respect, and value the energies within me that I can access and integrate into my daily life. Man is forever searching for the balance of these energies within himself. I feel total humility at having found them.

As I receive the information within our books, I find myself living the dramas, the experiences, the traumas, and the multiple lessons of my own life. My understanding of self allows me to accept, with more insight than I have ever imagined possible, the events that I cannot change. Each new challenge allows me to see and to appreciate my own internal balance that I have worked a lifetime to create. What I can do each of you can do, if you want to do it badly enough to commit yourself to the physical, mental, and spiritual work that is involved.

A loving thank you to my six beautiful children and their partners who have shown the support and love that is within them: Gloria Oddenino Moren and John Moren, Lynn Oddenino and Jim Hackney, Sarah Oddenino Pernell and Carl Pernell, Chuck Oddenino and Ann Knipper, Diana Oddenino and Jonathan Moss, and John Oddenino and Adair Whitehouse Oddenino.

Last but not least, I want to acknowledge all of my wonderful friends that support and love me. When you have friends that "do," you can see the truth within them. A special message of peace and joy to Anita Crouch, Ron Shurie, Beverly Malnar, Linda Bruce, and Bob Heiss who live their truth in our daily relationship. Without their loyal support I would not be able to do the numerous speaking engagements, seminars, radio and television shows, books, and private readings that I do. To them, HS and I are enfinitely grateful.

Kathy Oddenino

# Contents

# A Message
# To The Reader

Thank you for reading Sharing. As you read you will begin to understand yourself with a different perspective and in understanding yourself, you will love yourself. As a human being you were created as an expansive, magnificent, and loving integrated energy. It is from the focal point of your energy that you relate to yourself, your life, your friends, your family, and all others within your world.

**Sharing: Self Discovery in Relationships,** is the third book in a series of books that have been, and are being written to teach and guide you into a deeper and more profound understanding of self. Sharing is an overview of how you relate to yourself and the rest of the world in which you live.

**The Joy of Health: A Spiritual concept of Integration and the Practicalities of Living,** is an overview of who you are. It relates the integrated interaction of the body, mind, and spirit of you to self and to the world in which you live.

**Bridges of Consciousness: Self Discovery in the New Age,** is an overview of the twelve most influential consciousness energies. Your consciousness energy creates what you are in life.

Our books are an integrated work that are designed to help you expand your understanding of who you are, what you are, and how you relate in the physical world. Future books will expand this information into a more complex explanation of why you were created and when this creation occurred.

When you understand yourself, you will understand the Universe. In understanding yourself you will go beyond the intellectualization of your physical perception and see the wisdom and ingenuity of your soul and spirit within. You will accept the truth of eternal life and in accepting you will validate the relevance of self.

Life is an experience of self-discovery. Each and every relationship is an experience of self-discovery. Self-discovery is our path of learning. The path of learning is the way of soul evolution or self-realization.

Every time that we begin to feel comfortable in our world something happens to get our attention. The events or experiences of our lives are created by us as part of our life design. Each event of your life is relative to your relationship with self.

Experiences will occur within your relationships that may not have an active impact upon your physical body but they can have a dramatic impact upon your mind and your perception of reality. The degree of the impact will depend upon you and your attachment to the relationship. The consequences of the relationship will depend upon your actions that follow your thoughts, words, and feelings after the experience of the event.

It is our responsibility to understand these events and learn the lessons they represent. Discovering the expansiveness of the experience within an event or relationship is many times overwhelming. Your vision is controlled by the openness of your mind and your physical belief system to perceiving the relationship of the experience relative to self.

Our growth as individuals, families, communities, cultures, the world, and the Universe is controlled by our ability to gain insight into the lesson of the experience of sharing. We are a complex network of interwoven energy which we share consciously, subconsciously, and unconsciously. This is true in all aspects of our lives from the most dramatic event to the commonplace, daily life experience. The experiences of life are understood relative to the image or vision projected by the conscious mind into our life activities.

Truth is the living spirit of consistency between the thoughts of man, the words of man, and the actions of man. We live truth when we are no longer afraid to acknowledge, accept, respect, and value that consistency from the moment of inspiration to the moment of creation.

If we think one thing, say another thing, and then do something totally different, we are not BEING truth within our lives. All of us are affected by our truth in relationships and our truth is then impacted upon ourself, our life, and upon the energy of the world in general.

First of all our truth will impact upon us. Our first relationship is with ourself. If we create confusion and conflict within our mind by not being truth, we will create depression, anger, fear, denial, and resistance within ourself and our life. We will create an internal climate within ourself of confusion, of not being able to understand what we want. This confusion is the result of inconsistences between our internal thoughts and feelings, and our external words and actions.

Thoughts and words are in reality the same thing with the exception that thoughts are internal perceptions, and words become the external symbols. Actions are always seen by us as physical happenings.

Have you ever felt that someone is speaking to you with words that they think you want to hear and not with the words that are within their mind? This is the creation of confusion and conflict. This is the discrepancy between what you think and what you say.

This inconsistency of internal thoughts and external words is the beginning of untruth. Chances are the actions that follow these words will also take a different path. When your actions are not consistent with your words, you create another level of untruth, conflict, and confusion.

In relationships we frequently find inconsistency in the way we think, the way we speak, and the actions that we achieve. In the world of corporate business, science, education, medicine, religion, law, and all other occupations, we find inconsistencies that are glaring between the thought behind the intention, the words of the intention, and the physical result of the action.

It is the individual that creates. Each and every individual creates according to his inner truth being balanced with his external truth. This external truth is subjected to a belief system that has been created by the ego of man.

When I was close to completion of this book, an event occurred in my life that seized my attention. My youngest grand-child, Nicole, was accidentally burned when she fell into a tub containing a small amount of hot water.

This accident occurred during the preparation of her bath, which she loved. Thirty-six percent of her body was burned with primarily second degree burns. On the surface this does not sound fatal, although ultimately it was.

My experience as a nurse coached me to understand that burns are many times fatal with a child under two. As a nurse I am also familiar with the protocol for burn therapy. None of this prepared me for the horror of burn therapy to a baby that I loved. I was daily exposed to the self-hypnotic focus that exists in the world of science.

Science defines a particular way to deal with a particular problem. These are known in medicine as medical protocols. Protocols are "beliefs" that are created by man.

Sometimes protocols work and sometimes they do not work. In the scientific world there are accepted ways of treatment which the medical world accepts as "scientifically" proven. When you focus upon the "science" of action, you remove from that action the creativity of inspiration and motivation.

Inspiration and motivation are the art of medicine. The art of medicine treats the patient as a whole being. No one part of the patient is ignored. The focus of the treatment is on balancing the body, mind, and spirit of the patient. We, as patients, are all totally different with different physical responses, different mental and emotional responses, and we have different lessons to learn.

Today patients are treated by bigger and better machines and more powerful medications. The quantity of machinery, chemicals, protocols, and statistics have mushroomed. The quality of care has become focused on caring for the machines, giving the medications, and creating the statistics. The patient becomes only another part of the scientific process and another part of the belief system.

The focus is upon the science of medicine and not upon balancing the body, mind, and spirit of the patient. The patient is forgotten in the focus of adhering to the protocol or the belief in the statistics of the medical world.

Focusing upon the physical belief system is more of a self-hypnotic trance for the medical world than the spiritual world could ever induce. Focusing within the spirit world acknowledges that we are capable of many areas of focus for knowledge. Focusing within the physical belief system excludes, resists, and denies all other areas of focus for knowledge.

Burns are viewed within the world of science as a "surgical problem." This is a "belief system" that has been honored for many years. The focus of surgeons has always been to perform surgery. This focus maintains truth for the surgeon but not for the patient.

When medicine as a science focuses only upon what it "believes" is right instead of staying open to change, we as patients and family must inspire and motivate change.

It has been 39 years since I graduated from nursing school. In those 39 years nothing has changed the focus of burn therapy away from surgery as the primary treatment. The physicians and nurses continue to do what they have learned to do by following the accepted approach.

To a lesser degree the nurses and physicians suffer the same agonies that the family suffers when they lose a life. Their intention is to save lives and they try very hard, using all of their "scientific" knowledge. Many are now expanding their understanding of the need to change, but they do not understand the path of change.

Scientific knowledge is based upon the creations of man from the ego and the intellect of man. Past "facts" are analyzed and statistics are formed. Therapy is then directed towards supporting the belief created by the statistics. The "belief" then becomes the "gospel" of the scientific world.

This cycle of focus and refocus is a self-fulling prophesy that catapults man and science into an energy of ever increasing problems. It allows man to go further and further beyond the support of the cells within man, to the support of the belief system itself. This belief then creates an octopus energy within the world reaching out to affect all aspects of the individual, the community, the world, and the Earth around us.

Since my books are written from the spirit energy within me, my integrity is involved in BEING and understanding the words that I am given. My own experience of self-discovery has been in motion since the day that I was created. My truth is creating total consistency between my thoughts, my words, and my actions.

It is not by accident that I became a nurse. I have known since birth that it was my choice to see and to live in a world that is opposite to my own personal belief system. By seeing the opposites, I can define the opportunity to change.

Science is a study of past fact, which is analyzed and hypothesized. Billions and billions of dollars have been spent to study disease and death. Little has been gained with that knowledge except the ability to add a few more years to life. If you remove the quality of life, is the living worth the personal suffering that results? Indeed, the focus of our world is on "disease" not on health and happiness. It is on quantity of life not on quality of life.

Physicians focus upon treating disease and trauma. This is their profession and it is a valuable profession within our world. It is our responsibility as members of the human race to personally focus upon our health and happiness. The medical world is there to bridge the gap between disease and health. Bridging the gap between disease and health gives each of us the opportunity to change our life and to restore our health.

My vision is to create prevention of disease and a humane and supportive therapy for accidents that facilitates and allows the body to heal itself.

To do this we need to integrate the world of science with the world of inspiration and motivation. The world of inspiration and motivation is the world of creation from within. It is utilizing the information of soul memory and spirit genetics to create positively within the physical world.

As man we are one. In caring and loving man in the world of science we must Be one. The medical community has a responsibility to treat the human body as a whole BEING rather than only physical matter.

During the two weeks that Nicole was in the Intensive Care Burn Unit at Children's Hospital in Washington, D.C., I saw with my spiritual vision as clearly as I saw with my physical vision. My visions were simultaneous as I saw in minute detail what was happening and what could happen.

During this time, I was given a formula by HS that will support tissue growth from cellular memory. I was shown ways to clean the burns and to consistently keep them clean while stopping the pain. I saw visions of the equipment that would be needed to use the formula. I saw healing occurring within a matter of weeks with no scarring, no surgery, and no additional emotional trauma.

It is my belief that physical life and physical death are both choices of the soul and spirit within. Because we are focused on loving people physically, we are saddened by physical death. I am no different than any other grandmother in this respect. But in my sadness, I have been given a message from Nicole for all of mankind.

The visions that I experienced for those two weeks are continuing and in those visions are new and creative methods of treating many patients. They are focused not upon past experience but upon the enfinite knowledge of HS.

There are no accidents within the Universe, and therefore, I accept that Nicole's death was the free choice of her spirit. The experiences of life show us the truth of life and our relationship to life. Each event has within it the lesson that it was designed to relate to the world. I have looked carefully at this event within my life to understand the lesson for me in the experience.

Nicole's message by her choice of death clearly means to me that I must listen until I can hear, and I must look until I can see the ways in which we can integrate the science of medicine with the art of medicine. Medicine itself has reached a state of imbalance.

Each time that I can understand the way to integrate the art of medicine into the science of medicine, then I am committed to creating that action within our world. This action will be the final step in creating truth in the words of HS as he gives them to me in our books.

Each of us deserve the opportunity for supportive, humane, and therapeutic care that touches us as whole and integrated people. Machines and medicines cannot reach the heart and soul within us. It is within the energy of your heart and soul that your healing capabilities are found.

This is a crystal clear message for me to Be truth in action. HS can give me his spiritual wisdom in the form of thoughts, words, and images. It is my responsibility as his physical body to put those thoughts, words, and images into action. That is my commitment to creating the truth of his messages.

My theories will challenge those who feel that suffering is a choice of the spirit. This perspective can be viewed in a number of ways. Suffering is a need of man, not of God. If we create suffering for burn patients, we may return to Earth and be burned to capture the attention of someone else. Lessons that are not learned become Karmic in our spirit energy and will indeed be lessons of other embodiments.

Spirits who choose active participation in suffering of any type are offering those who are passive participants the opportunity for another level of active participation that creates change. Indeed, Jesus accepted crucifixion to prevent other men from having the same "need" to make a statement in the same way. When man chooses "crucifixion" or suffering, he chooses it to create a challenge for the rest of man.

The roles of active and passive participation repeat themselves in countless ways in our daily experience. These roles create the opportunity for each of us to accept the challenge for change.

> *Our participation in life events defines the relationships that each of us have with others and with self.*

When we think of disease and accidents, we think in terms of it happening to another, never to ourself. We view ourself as invincible because if we did not we would be subjected to panic or anxiety attacks of absolute fear.

HS in his wisdom has told me that we as a nation and as a world have created the possibility for massive burn injuries. This could be a potential disaster to our world because medical science does not know how to care for burn victims humanely, efficiently, and economically.

The pain of burns is so profound that it can scar a person emotionally for a lifetime. The burn therapy that is used today recreates the pain several times each day. This agony of pain remains within the subconscious memory to create fear and agony within us for life.

The current burn therapy often requires years of in-patient care with multiple surgical grafts. This is emotionally, physically, and economically traumatic to the patient, the family, and our entire economy.

We have, as a world, created the potential to expose our own self-hypnotic, scientific focus to a personal challenge. When massive burns occur within our world the energy wave will be of tidal force. This force will send out energy vibrations that will affect billions of people on many different levels.

In the text of **Sharing: Self Discovery in Relationships,** relationships are clearly defined as the fiber of our learning experience. All relationships begin with the relationship to self and to life, but without the interaction of others we suppress self and life.

When we care about self and others, we are inspired by the love of the spirit and motivated through soul memory to create with new ideas, new concepts, new perspectives, and new levels of conscious awareness. It is time we expand our creative abilities to help ourselves in disease prevention and treatment.

It is evident within our world that physicians and nurses are not always comfortable with the outcome of therapy. It is also evident by the expanding liabilities that patients and families are not comfortable with medical care.

Physicians are facing a world of people that are not happy with the care they are receiving. But from the perspective of the medical world they are doing all that they were taught to do. The medical world has become a "victim" of the cyclic energy of instant gratification. The more science focuses upon scientific gratification, the more the public focuses upon self-gratification.

This phenomena of the "quick fix" creates an energy that is captured between the judicial and medical system. Feeding upon this system is the supporting energy of self-gratification for the pharmaceutical business, all the supporting businesses of the medical world, the insurance companies, and the government.

There are more and more instances occurring where medical judgment is based upon the beliefs and self-gratification needs of the physician and patient, and not upon correcting the balance within the body. The beliefs of the patient are many times manipulative and unethical in the world of science. In turn, science can be manipulative and unethical in the world of mankind.

The reasons for opposite focuses are multiple and they are always influenced by all sectors of society that support and expand the phenomena of self-gratification and dissatisfaction. Instant gratification is publicized by all avenues of the media, the family, the schools, and the business world.

Blaming is a disease of negative energy. Creating change is a challenge of positive energy. It is my intention to commit my positive energy to researching the HS information for burn treatment until we find the way to support and restore health in a humane manner.

Death can never be avoided in all instances because the spirit uses death as its method of change. But it is our responsibility to create an atmosphere of healing and loving support regardless of the choice of the spirit.

When the challenge of burn treatment has been met, we will continue to research other medical therapies that are given to me from the Heavenly Spirit within. Change will occur more rapidly when multitudes of people understand the need for change and are willing to support change.

Medicine is an art. Protecting and healing the body is an art. Science has made many advances that can be integrated with the art that is within the soul and spirit of us. Now we need to open our minds to new perspectives, new ideas, new inspirations, and integrate them with the intellect that has expanded within us.

Integrating art and science will give us the opportunity to provide for ourselves the love and support that we all may need at some point in our lives. This challenging endeavor will benefit from the loving energy of each and every person who understands the importance of self.

It is through actively sharing ourself that we can truly discover self. My truth in thoughts, words, and actions will be the burn research that I am actively involved in creating with my family and with Joy Publications.

The words within this book will define for you the relationship between each of us with the other. We are inseparable as human beings in the same way that the art and the science of medicine are inseparable.

Many of us do not have a clear understanding of the unity that exists within our world. Not seeing the unity of the world and the individual does not mean that the relationship does not exist. That unity within you begins with the inseparable energy of your body, mind, and spirit.

Self creates life, and life creates the world. When you accept and change self, you change life. When you change your life, you change your world and you grow. As you read the text of this book, you will see yourself many times over and you will be able to grow if you can accept change.

You are energy and energy by its very nature will move and change.

Be in peace and joy.

Kathy Oddenino

OTHER BOOKS by KATHY ODDENINO, R.N.

**THE JOY OF HEALTH:** *A SPIRITUAL CONCEPT OF INTEGRATION AND THE PRACTICALITIES OF LIVING*

**BRIDGES OF CONSCIOUSNESS:** *SELF DISCOVERY IN THE NEW AGE*

These books by Kathy Oddenino are presented to the world as the beginning of a series to help man to understand himself. **Joy of Health** answers the question of who man is. **Bridges of Consciousness** answers the question of what man is. Sharing answers the question of how man relates to himself and the world.

The books build one upon the other, providing man with a comprehensive view of self. Each book can stand alone and each commentary can stand alone, but the maximum benefit for each of you will be to study the books as a perspective.

**Discovering Self: The Path of Soul Evolution** is the next book to be published in January 1991 and it will address the other questions that man has about himself—why is man on Earth and when did he arrive.

# Introduction

Man is energy. All of man's thoughts, words, and actions are energy. The physical body is a creation of the energy of man's thoughts, words, and actions. The physical world of man is the energy of the thoughts, words, and actions of man. The thoughts, beliefs, and understandings within the mind of man structure the life, health, and happiness of man.

It is through the energy of the mind that man creates his reality. The energy of the mind is interwoven in an intricate web of being, believing, and learning. This inseparable web of energy creates energy points that intersect with other energy points to create relationships.

**The connection of energy points creates the inter-action of man within relationships that is understood as sharing.**

Relationships are an energy of consciousness. Not all relationships exist within your conscious awareness. Many exist within your subconscious soul level and others exist within your unconscious spirit level. As you expand your conscious awareness to the level of self-realization, your mind energy will expand until you consciously understand the multitude of relationships that you have on all levels.

**Multiple relationships that exist on all levels, creates sharing your energy on all levels.**

The energy of relationships creates the energy of multiple events within your lives. These events are understood by you as the daily happenings that you are familiar with. These happenings begin for you at the moment of your birth and they continue for you until you choose to leave the physical world.

Sharing the energy of the events in your life will have a focus of positive energy or negative energy. The focus of the energy will depend upon the lesson that you have chosen to learn and the way in which you have designed the learning experience.

**Experiences will always be designed by you to get the attention of yourself, and the attention of other people within your world.**

You can be a passive participant in the energy of an event or you can be an active participant. Either role will allow you a vision, an image of the lesson. When you experience a lesson as an active participant, you may choose to be a passive participant in the next lesson. Your chosen role will create a different image of the lesson in each and every instance.

*Each and every experience of life is created by the soul and spirit for the purpose of learning. To learn from the experience, you must understand, accept, acknowledge, and value the lesson from your physical state of conscious awareness.*

Until this level of conscious awareness has been reached, you will repeat your lessons over, and over, and over again. You will repeat lessons within the same lifetime as you recreate the experience with different people, and you will repeat lessons in different physical embodiments if you fail to learn in a single lifetime.

When a lesson is "left over" from one physical embodiment to another, it is known as Karma within your world. The spirit of you will design Karmic energy into your lifetime by choosing to approach the lesson from a different focus.

For example, if you focus intensely upon only the intellect in your life, you may choose your Karma of balancing the intellect by coming into a physical embodiment with a "compromised" intellect in your next life. If you focus upon the physical to the extreme in one life, you may choose in your next life to be physically handicapped. If you focus upon being totally spiritual in one life, you may design excess physical activity or excess intellectual activity into your next life with an ego denial of the spirit world.

Life is a lesson in balancing the physical, as ego, body, and intellect, with the soul and the spirit.

*You are not one to the exclusion of all others. You are integrated as one in total unity. And you are separate in your own energy. You must learn to be conscious of that integration, to acknowledge the integration, and to function from the energy of the integration.*

Your individual world is structured in the same way that the Universe is structured. There is one primary source of energy that is created by GOD that is relative to the individual world of self in levels of seven relative to seven.

You relate first to yourself, then to your life, and then to the seven major levels of relationships. In each major level of relationship there are seven levels of relating. From each of these levels there are seven levels.

> *Each level of consciousness within relationships*
> *is interwoven, intermingled, and inseparable.*
> *Each level also exists within the physical, the soul,*
> *and the spirit energy on a conscious, subconscious*
> *and unconscious basis.*

As the levels exist within themselves, they do not need names. It will be sufficient at the moment for you to simply understand the structure of the energy. The structure of the energy is your structure of BEING.

> *When you understand yourself, you will under-*
> *stand the Universe.*

In your world each thought is an internal energy. Each word and each action is an external physical manifestation of the internal energy of thought. Each thought can be from a different cycle of development, awareness, understanding, and integration, as well as a different level of acceptance, acknowledgement, respect, and value.

Each cycle and each level can then be found in the other 147 levels of consciousness that exist within each of the three consciousness states that surrounds the physical body of man. Other consciousness levels exist within the infinite energy of the soul and within the enfinite energy of the spirit.

> *These multiple levels of consciousness exist*
> *within man as an aware consciousness of physical*
> *understanding, as a subconscious understanding of*
> *soul memory, and as an unconscious understand-*
> *ing of spirit knowledge.*

There are multiple examples of these consciousness energies that occur on a microsecond basis within your concept of time. For instance, if you are angry with yourself, you will be angry with other people. If you hate yourself, you will hate other people. Your anger and hate will be manifested within your physical world as harmful acts toward your fellow man and toward yourself. These harmful acts will occur as rejection, dishonesty, lying, stealing, verbal and physical abuse, property damage, war and/or killing.

If you love yourself, you will love other people. Your love will be manifested within your physical world by caring, sharing, compassion, serving, honesty, protection, teaching, and healing. These examples are limited by physical space and are intended only to create a structure within your mind. Here again, all energy is relative to seven into infinity.

Indeed, within your physical world you will see emotions and events occur that seemingly have no similarity to each other. But in the reality of energy they are all created by love or fear as the case may be. You will fragment your emotions and slide from one energy to the other in the space of less than a second. Your focus will change dramatically from one moment to the next and from one day to the next.

> *This change in focus occurs for you because you do not understand the magnitude of your different consciousness energy levels or how to focus your physical mind into an energy level.*

As you learn the capabilities of the mind, you will learn to control your mind. You have allowed your mind to control you because you do not understand how to direct it to the place that you choose to be. Not understanding that it is choice for you, creates the victim consciousness within your mind.

> *You as human beings live your life from your accepted level of consciousness. If you deny your ability to change your level of consciousness, you are choosing to live in ignorance of all that is not currently known and accepted by your belief system.*

The belief system of man is the ego energy of man. The ego and the spirit live in a continual tug-of-war in the lesson of balance that man is forever learning in his Earth embodiments.

> *Love or fear is the primary energy of self.*

Your belief system creates the primary energy of fear within you. You must learn to understand, accept, acknowledge, and value your primary energy of love before you can BE love.

Allowing fragmentation of the mind creates confusion within your physical world. Confusion interferes with the self-worth that you create when you love yourself.

*When you love yourself, you will love your
Universe.*

We have given you an overview of yourself and how you
relate to the energies of your mind and body in our book, **The Joy
of Health: A Spiritual Concept of Integration and the Practicalities of Living.**

We have given you an overview of the major energies or
consciousnesses that affect your mind and your development in
our book, **Bridges of Consciousness: Self Discovery in the New
Age.**

**In Sharing: Self Discovery in Relationships,** we are going
to show you as clearly as we can how you create your world by
sharing your interactions within your relationships with other
people.

*SHARING IS THE MENTAL, PHYSICAL, AND
SPIRITUAL ENERGY OF INTERACTION IN
RELATIONSHIPS.*

*Nothing in your world is ever a singular energy
response. Every thought, every word, and every action sets up its own vibrational path of energy that
reaches further and further into the Universe.*

In the expansion of this energy vibration, your energy inter-
mingles, interweaves, and interpenetrates the energy of countless
other physical, soul, and spirit energies. This integration creates
an inseparable web of energy that binds each of you together for
enfinity.

*The strength of the soul and spirit binding be-
gins with the twin soul that shared your creation
and continues in diminishing levels similar to the
family structures that you understand.*

As human beings you are integrated as one trilocular energy.
These three energies of you reside within your left brain, your
right brain, and your cerebellum as mind energy.

The physical is the intellect and ego energy of the external
mind in your left brain.

The soul is the internal energy of the inner, rational mind
in your right brain.

The spirit is the internal energy of the higher intuitive mind
in your cerebellum.

Integration is the reality of energy movement. Energy will integrate whether or not you have a conscious awareness that it is happening. Like energy will integrate with like energy.

In your world you could compare this to the way oils will blend together if you pour them into the same container. Water will also integrate thoroughly if you mix it together. If you try to mix oil and water together, you will find them both settling at their own levels.

> **The energy of human consciousness will attract like to like, if you are seeking a bonding together.**

Indeed, as your energy moves along its vibrational path it creates new and different vibrations as it attaches to, reflects from, or intersects with other energy paths. In all instances a certain element of energy absorption will occur that changes the vibrational tone.

It is this accumulation or interpenetration of energies that creates mass energies or consciousnesses within your world. Yet each individual has a unique energy within the mind that has been created as a result of individual energy experience.

> **The energy of thought is the POWER of CREATION given to you by GOD. This energy exists within you as the GODSELF. The power of creation is the spirit energy of you. The spirit of you is manifested within your physical world as inspiration. In the spirit world inspiration is defined as "the spirit in action."**

If you take a pebble and drop it into a body of water, you will see the vibration of energy that spreads out from the force of the pebble coming in contact with the water. The interaction of the pebble and the water has created an individual path of energy. This path of energy continues to repeat itself, over and over, and over again.

Water is symbolic of the consciousness energy within you. The original energy was released by you when you held the pebble in your hand over the water and made your decision to drop it.

You created the energy of interaction mentally, which was manifested in physical form when the pebble was dropped and the pebble and water met physically. The meeting of these two energies then created a new path of vibrational energy that spread out over the water.

At this moment a mosquito within the area made a decision to ride the energy of one of the vibrational waves. As the mosquito made contact between his body and the water, a new wave of vibrational energy began.

Do you see how this mingling of energy occurs in your physical world? This vibrational energy that occurs on a physical level in your physical world also occurs within the energy of you, in your mind, and in your body.

The above example is symbolic of the birth of you into the physical world. The waves that you generate within your world spread out from the weight of your energy and impact on all other energy that you touch or that touches you.

> *Each thought, each word, and each action that you create for your entire life creates an individual pattern of energy waves within the energy of your soul and spirit and within the Universe.*

Some of the energy interactions within your life will be the direct result of your birth (existence of the pebble); others will be the direct result of your consciousness (existence of the water); others will be the touch of you to other energies (the impact of the pebble and the water); some will have a large impact (weight of the energy or pebble); and others will have a small impact (weight of the energy or mosquito).

> *The vibrational energy that occurs within you and your world from relationships will depend upon the energy of the two souls involved.*

If you have an expanded consciousness level and an energy of less conscious awareness enters into your world, the impact of the energy points will not create expanded vibrational energy for you. This energy will create the vibrations within you that the mosquito created within the water of the pond.

In the example of the mosquito, if a mosquito comes into contact with an ocean wave, the mosquito will not change the energy vibration of the ocean wave to a measurable vibration within your world. If the energy of a mosquito comes in contact with the glassy surface of a puddle of water, it will create noticeable energy waves upon the water.

If your consciousness level is equal to the water in a teacup and you encounter an expanded consciousness energy, you will reject the energy because contact would destroy you as you see yourself. You would cling to your nice teacup that has solid limits created to protect you.

Having an energy that is open and expanding join you in your teacup would be like dropping a huge bolder into your teacup. The teacup would undergo total change back to the original form of sand. All structure of the cup would be lost.

In you this would be equivalent to releasing all of your belief systems at once that provide structure to your life. Unless your consciousness is ready to awaken, this experience would be rejected by you because the ego structure that you have created would be too fragile for the new energy.

> *As you live your life you will find yourself interacting in relationships that teach you nothing. These relationships will be the resting mosquitos of your world. They will create an image of learning but the image is a reflection of a consciousness level that you fear leaving. You will not experience soul and spirit expansion in terms of energy growth.*

In other instances you may meet energies that are harmonious and expansive, and that will allow you to grow and learn. Your acceptance and understanding of these relationships will again depend upon your conscious awareness. If you at this moment try to remember all that you have learned in previous relationships, you will be focused upon growth and you will acknowledge and accept the challenge of the energy.

> *A willingness to grow is choosing to be the pebble in the water that is willing to expand your energies and allow them to reach out and touch others.*

If you are focused on the physical and intellectual energy of your world, you will be focused on the external energies of life. You will not accept, acknowledge, respect, or value the energy of the relationship.

Your understanding will be focused upon the teacup not the pebble, and the vibrational energy of your consciousness will not be accepted, understood, or used. Indeed, you will ignore the water and the vibrations as you make your conscious choice to

If you create within your intellectual world but your private world is full of drama, you are not creating from a balanced energy. If you create within your physical world but you cannot create peace and joy in your world of relationships, you are not creating from a balanced energy. If you create a world that appears to be perfect but you are not at peace within, you are not creating from a balanced energy.

In your world of today when you think of balance, you think of the scales in your bathroom. Balance is more than the physical you.

**Balance is more than what you are, it is who you are, and how you are.**

As you expand the energy within, you may also expand your energy without as you seek balance. As you restrict your energy within, you may restrict your physical self without. When you are balanced within and without, you will know perfect health.

You chose your planet Earth to cleanse and heal your soul and spirit within. Healing within is manifested as healing without for you within the physical world.

In healing self you must first understand what needs to be healed. If you do not understand, accept, acknowledge, respect, and value self, you cannot understand, accept, acknowledge, respect, and value other men.

**When you look with your physical eyes, you do not see the energy of the drama of life. When you hear with your ears, you hear only what you are prepared to receive.**

Therefore, the energy of self is reflected from other souls and spirits that you are in relationship with. This reflection of self will frequently be acknowledged by you as unacceptable within your life. You do not see it as your own reflection. You do not hear it as your own vibrational energy.

**If you look at another man and judge him, you are judging yourself. You perceive in others what is within you.**

This mirror image of "images of self" creates the "school" of relationships within your physical world. Your perception of your physical world is limited by your understanding of who you are, your relationship to self, others, the world, the Earth, and the Universe.

> *Your perception of who you are, creates the reality of how you act. How you act, mirrors your level of consciousness.*

If you love yourself, you love all of man. If you do not love yourself, you can love no other person.

The challenge for you is to accept the totality of self without fear. If you create only from the physical perspective of intellect, you will create from the facts that you think you understand. If you are open to your soul memories, you will create from the energy of all your experiential learning. You will know how to do many things that you have not learned intellectually in this lifetime.

If you are open to your spirit energy, you will understand yourself and the Universe from the intuitive energy of the spirit which is the love, truth, and perfection of God. When you create from spirit energy you are love, truth, and perfection in all facets of your life. In your world today there is a need for you to integrate your spirit energies.

Throughout the period of Earth energy, you have used all facets of self because you are inherently integrated. You have used the energy of soul and spirit without a conscious physical awareness of how the phenomena occurred. You have only a limited understanding that something outside of the physical, influences the physical.

As your soul and spirit are accessed on a subconscious and unconscious basis, they are triggering an awakening within. Indeed, they are seeking balance with your physical self. Your soul and spirit within are inviting you to be all that you can be within the physical world. It is their mission to help you discover who you are.

For many, the concept of a soul and spirit within is accepted as fact. Fact is an intellectual belief, not an energy of faith. When you intellectualize the soul and spirit energy, you create the walls of your belief system as your own resistance and denial. You place the perspective of your soul and spirit in the realm of judgment.

> *Judgment is created by fear.*

Your soul and spirit energy are created by the love of God for man. Your soul and spirit energies cannot be understood or accessed through fear. Therefore, your fear of the unknown becomes your denial of your soul and spirit. When you deny your soul and spirit, you deny what you cannot intellectually understand. You deny love, truth, and perfection of self, when you deny your soul and spirit. You deny your power of creation, which is your power of love.

*In the image of self as reflected in relationships, you can see your soul and spirit energy. Accepting your soul and spirit energy will allow you to heal all fear.*

The fear within you is based in your fear of the separation from God which you subconsciously and unconsciously understand. You fear a total separation in the integration that you refuse to accept. Your fear is acted out in your physical world by your resistance to loving all of mankind, the world, and your Earth.

*Fear is your ego's struggle for survival.*

The challenge for you is expanded because of your energy of love and fear. Love and fear are not tangible in the sense that you can feel them with your physical hands, taste them with your tongue, see them with your eyes, and hear them with your ears.

*Love and fear are not physical in your physical world. Love and fear are energies that are created by you and exist without physical form.*

You have created the act of love to remind yourself to love. When you search for physical love, you are searching for your love energy within yourself.

*When man reflects love within himself, he can give himself as a gift of love.*

Because you can only experience self through the relationship of others, you have created a design of life that allows you to interact with others. This is the reality of your schoolroom of life on Earth. If you deny the love of self, you will deny the friendship of others.

The level of your denial can be seen in the number of true friends that you have in your physical world. Friends are created through the interaction that occurs with other persons within your physical world. If you fear interaction, you fear friends because you fear yourself. This is your cycle of physical energy.

*Fear is a creation of your ego. Ego fear is at-tached to beliefs, identities, victim energies, and judgments of your physical world. It is these fear energies that create resistance, denial, and fear of the soul and spirit energies which are identified by the ego as the unknown.*

Energies that are unknown to the physical senses must be acknowledged and accepted upon faith. Faith itself cannot be defined by the logic of science because it is the non-physical energy of the subconscious and unconscious minds. Therefore, in your intellectual/ego mind, faith does not exist.

The spirit and soul of you is indeed eternal as energy. It is a shining golden light that creates a circle of energy within the Universe. It is all that you can imagine and more. Your soul and spirit has been since eternity, for eternity.

*All of man IS. He IS the energy of the Godself. There is nothing without. There is everything within. What IS, has always been and will always BE.*

You create external avoidances to justify your focus of attention upon your external world. You search for your energy in external elements. This is your understanding of self relative to your belief system. You create yourself as self-centered, not self-realized.

Self-centered has to do with your external direction. Self-realized has to do with your internal direction. The self-centered you, seeks self-gratification, not self-realization.

When I say to you, "Look within. Listen to the silence. Be in peace and joy." I am saying to you, "Realize that you, as SELF, are spirit and soul. I AM. As I AM, you are. These are the words of GOD."

TODAY is your moment of energy. In your moment of energy you are as I AM. We are one. But we are separate. NOW IS your energy of conscious awareness. All else is the illusion of what will be tomorrow.

*Illusion is the belief of man in another time and space, the illusion of another Universe which he believes to be his hereafter.*

What God has created, IS. What He has not created does not in reality exist. TODAY man IS BEING. Today man IS GOD. Today man IS with GOD. Today man IS BEING GOD.

To understand, accept, acknowledge, and value the God within, man must first forgive and love the man without. That is the Law of God.

There are no limits within the Universal energy. There are no beliefs, no restrictions, no denial, no judgment, no anger, no hate, and no fear. It is the love of spirit energy that nurtures you. It is the love of spirit energy that nurtures relationships. Without spirit energy, love is only an illusion of your belief. Love IS. Love is BEING. I AM LOVE.

Be in peace and joy.

HS

*Minds sleep*
*restlessly searching*
*fearing what is in life*
*as they hide*
*from the vision of self.*

## Sharing
# Self

*Souls reflect*
*the image of you*
*attached as mind to body*
*infinite*
*in the beauty of self.*

*Spirits change*
*joyful in eternal love*
*peaceful in enfinity*
*forever one*
*with all in self.*

*Thoughts*
*soar and glide*
*rainbows of imagination*
*sharing a harmony and rhythm*
*in loving self.*

Self is the inherent integration of the three facets of the mind. You are a triad of energy. You consist of physical energy, soul energy, and spirit energy. The strength of one energy over the other creates a vortex of energy from which you function. You begin your life on Earth from the energy of the spirit. As your attachment to Earth increases, you begin to spin with the force of your physical energy.

Imagine within your mind a top, a toy that you played with as a child. The physical part of you is the point, the rigid end of self, from which you spin around and around, faster and faster. The spirit energy of you is the expansive top, the soul energy is the middle of your toy that is sandwiched between the rigid physical base and the expansive top.

To understand self you must understand the vortex of your energy and balance it to the point, the physical you, to keep yourself from falling over and losing your rhythmic spin. As you pull the soul and spirit energy of self down into the physical vortex you provide a broader, more stable base from which you spin. Gradually your energy will assume the shape of a rapidly spinning disc that is totally balanced in energy and impossible to "topple." To topple in your world is to lose your balance, to "fall."

Loving self is the energy of self-realization. Self-realization is the energy of balance. It is acknowledging all facets of self. It is understanding self, acknowledging self, accepting self, respecting self, and valuing self.

### *When man understands himself, he will understand the Universe.*

In this understanding you will recognize the relative relationship of all things, and the creation of all events.

You do indeed find yourself in very hectic situations at times. Many times these situations are pure drama that challenge you with your ability or inability, as the case may be, to remain balanced and to remain in total love of yourself.

### *Self-realization comes to man naturally when he learns to integrate the three facets of the mind.*

The external mind is the intellect/ego. This is the mind that controls your physical body and your physical life. The intellect functions by gathering facts from your past physical perceptions and building upon these facts through the process of repetitious experience. This is acknowledged within your world as your intellectual, logical, or scientific mind.

You focus on understanding by repetitious hard work, structure, discipline, and the re-creation of known facts. The ego part of your mind then accepts these facts as truth. These accepted "truths" in turn create your belief system. Your beliefs in turn create within your life self-fulfilling prophecies or continued repetition.

*You spin faster and faster in the vortex of your daily life, repeating cycle after cycle of repetitious dramas. You spin faster and faster in your vortex of physical creation, repeating cycle after cycle of physical lives.*

You create your physical vortex of energy within you from the understanding that you have of self and your relationship to life, family, friends, lovers, other people, the world, the Earth, and the Universe. This vortex of personal energy becomes the reality of yourself and your life. You have total control over the restriction or expansion of your energy and your life in your physical world.

The inner mind is known to man as the rational mind. The inner mind is the internal mind of soul memory. Within this memory bank is the accumulation of all experiences that you as a spirit have lived and learned.

*Your soul memory source is the energy of millions of years of existence in spirit energy and many thousands of "lifetimes" of living within the physical world.*

Your lives were spent in numerous cultures, ethnic groups, worlds, and families. The lessons that you have learned as a soul are different than the facts that you have accumulated in your external intellect of today. When you experience a rush of energy motivation, you are experiencing a rush of soul memory.

The higher mind is known to man as the intuitive mind. This higher mind is the eternal mind that is the energy of the Creator that dwells within you. Within your eternal higher mind is found the accumulation of all that is love, truth, and perfection. These energies are being remembered through the soul experience as your inherent birthright from the God energy that is your Creator.

*Your inherent birthright is your power of cre-
ation through the positive energy forces of love,
truth, and perfection.*

When you experience inspiration within, you are feeling the
energy of your power of creation.

In self-realization you maintain an open channel, an energy
flow between the three facets of your mind. Your spirit inspiration integrates with the soul memory for motivation and with the
intellect of the external mind for physical creation. Your intellect
provides the structure and discipline to create by working within
the physical world.

You can always recognize a self-realized person because
they will have a creative attitude. They will have no ego connection to their creation. They will know no fear. Indeed, they will
be open, innocent, totally unselfconscious, accepting, peaceful,
humble, and happy.

*A self-realized person will not be stuck within
the limitations of scientific fact but will integrate
all knowledge from all facets of the mind and will
create from the love, truth, and perfection within.*

You will create because you acknowledge and accept your
power of creation, and allow the continual flow of inspiration
and motivation to become part of your physical world.

Your creative experience of integration will be an experience
of joy, not "work." The experience of energy integration has been
defined in your world as peak experience, ecstasy, rapture,
inspiration, channeling, psychic communication, intuition, and
on and on.

*Words are unimportant except as they focus
your belief system. You attach yourself to a linear
identity of words and then focus on becoming the
identity rather than the integrated experience.*

In self-realization you will have access to the inner mind
and the higher mind but it must integrate with the intellect and
be manifested into action within the physical world.

If you access the inner mind of soul memory and then
become "psychic," you must continue the integration into the
higher mind and the physical intellect to experience self-
realization.

If you focus on the higher mind and find yourself accessing information intuitively, you must continue the integration into the soul memory and the physical intellect to integrate all facets of the mind before you can reach the level of self-realization.

If you focus on the physical you, you cannot become self-realized until you can integrate the energy of the soul and spirit. One facet of self cannot experience integration without the balanced unity of all.

It is when you reach the point of self-realization that you can truly love yourself. In accepting that you are more than a physical body and a physical intellect/ego, you have acknowledged the soul and spirit self.

*Acknowledging self validates self, and creates*
*an unconditional love within. When you accept, ac-*
*knowledge, respect, and value self, you no longer*
*judge yourself as unworthy. You know who you are.*

You must learn to love yourself before you can learn to love your neighbor and your God. The reason that it is necessary to love yourself is because there is a God within you. When you learn to love yourself, loving the image of God that lives within you is acknowledged. When you learn to love yourself, loving all of man is acknowledged, because your energy is the same energy that all other humans share.

*When man denies that he is God within, he de-*
*nies his ability to love himself.*

If you love yourself, TRULY love yourself, the question of loving your neighbor will not be an issue. The question of loving God will not be an issue. Because you will realize that you are, indeed, ALL within. You are yourself, your God, and your neighbor within as well as without. You are separate, but you are one.

In acknowledging your love of self in your physical world, you must not fear looking at yourself, and you must not fear looking at the dramas in your life. When you can objectively look at each and every drama that exists within your world, you will understand that you have created each and every one of them. You will understand that you have created them in order to learn.

It is also important to understand that you created each and every drama, with more insight than you are aware of, for the express purpose of learning the lessons that you came to Earth

The friends that you had at 16, may not be the friends that you would choose today unless they have matched your intellectual, soul, and spirit growth.

### *Growth is a personal responsibility. No one else can create growth for you.*

When you focus only upon the external world from which you have formulated your beliefs, your relationships will be chosen relative to your "concept of need" at that moment. This concept of need will be a physical belief that you hold about yourself.

Therefore, if you feel unworthy, you will choose relationships that mirror your feelings of unworthiness. If you feel unloved, you will choose a partner that is unloving. If you are angry at the world, you will choose a partner that supports your anger. If you believe that you must marry someone of status, money, or fame, you will seek a partner that fulfills your belief system. If you are dishonest, distrusting, introverted, and on and on, you will choose your relationships to support the energy of self.

Externally there will be obvious differences but the energy within will be the same. The focus of the belief can be directed toward a totally unrelated energy. For example, if a man is totally self-focused and directed toward his own self-gratification his focus may be on making money.

The partner that he chooses will be self-focused and directed toward her own self-gratification, but her focus will be on spending the money her husband makes. He may receive his money by dishonest means or legitimate means, and she will receive her share of his money by being what he wants her to be.

This is a drama that repeats itself from the street levels of prostitution to the penthouses of your world. This drama reflects the mirror image of each within the other.

When you are comfortable with seeing only a mirror image of your external beliefs in your relationships, your will avoid the challenge to grow and to expand into the soul and spirit energy. Seeing the mirror image of the soul and spirit energy of self in another, will create denial and resistance to the relationship.

Indeed, you will use relationships as your focus of resistance in your own growth. You will focus upon the external physical "needs" as you see them, because you fear what you "feel" internally. You will fear acknowledgment and acceptance of the soul and spirit within you. Your fear is the survival energy of your ego self.

When the focus is external the energy is negative. When the focus is internal the energy will be positive. The internal focus will allow you to grow and expand more rapidly because there will be more of the loving self that is acknowledged.

Fear is created within man by the core belief in original sin. This belief is so expansive within your world that it has reached critical mass energy. When a belief reaches critical mass energy it is accepted by the soul energy of all of humanity. The belief may be denied within the intellect, but this does not prevent the subconscious fear energy from effecting your life.

***Your core belief in original sin creates the fear
of separation from God.***

Your beliefs have taught you that you are guilty, sinful, unworthy, and distrusting. These beliefs are the fiber from which you create your world.

For example, if you are dishonest and acknowledge that you will lie and cheat in your relationships, you will expect that all other men will be dishonest in their relationships with you. You will trust no one, not even yourself.

The combined energies of this negative belief system create a poor self-image within all humans. You learn not to trust love, to be angry, to be dishonest, to be deceitful, to cheat, and to lie. Indeed, you are being truthful and supportive of your belief system relative to your understanding of self. Examples of this distrust can be seen in your governments, your corporate boardrooms, your businesses, your marriages, and all other relationships.

***This negative energy is the reflection of man at
his lowest level of development which begins with
the development of his physical world and his
value system.***

In each and every embodiment of the spirit within physical form, man is required to pass through the cycles of development, awareness, understanding, and integration. If the physical mind remains open to the memory of development, the dramas of development will be of little consequence in your physical world.

*It is the inner life force or spirit of you that is searching to trigger your soul memory that focuses the dramas within your physical life.*

Many souls will spend thousands of lifetimes captive of the physical forces of development. They create their intellects and egos to such an expansive degree that they find it impossible to grow beyond what they believe as physical reality.

For these souls to acknowledge the eternal spirit while in physical form is a true challenge in the physical sense. They will choose handicapped lives and long-lasting terminal disease in life, which is their lesson in patience with themselves. These life paths will be repeated thousands of times until memory of the soul and spirit within can be acknowledged.

Indeed, these are physical beings who view God as a Savior who will someday "carry" them home. They do not acknowledge that the responsibility for "going home" remains with the individual soul and spirit and its willingness to grow.

*Growing is living the spirit energy of truth within the physical world. The spirit energy of truth is living with consistency of your thoughts, words, and actions within the physical world.*

You cannot profess to love God while you are stealing, lying, cheating, killing, committing adultery, and wallowing in your guilt and sin energy. Truth is found in BEING love, truth, and perfection in your thoughts, words, and actions of the physical world.

You have not learned the lesson of responsibility of self. You do not understand who you are and why you have chosen to be on Earth. Your vision is clouded by your belief system which is the resistance and denial that is found within the cycle of development on Earth.

*In reality, each and every human is created in the image of God. You are love, truth, and perfection. You have the power of creation. Having lived a life as a captive of the fear of separation from God, you believe in your own unworthiness. It is a challenge for you to be acknowledged as the son of God and to acknowledge the love, truth, and perfection that is within you.*

THE EXTERNAL WORLD OF MAN HAS BEEN PROMOTED BY MAN AS THE SOURCE OF LOVE, JOY, AND HAPPINESS.

All physical realities in your world are external, such as schools, education, intellect, religion, churches, science, and on and on. Within you is infinite knowledge, infinite understanding, infinite love, infinite truth, and infinite perfection. These infinities will not be recognized or acknowledged if you focus only upon your finite, intellectual understanding of your physical world.

**The energy of love, truth, and perfection are the energies of the soul and spirit within.**

If you believe that you can find love, joy, and happiness only within the material, external world, you will be forever searching for happiness within the physical world. Love, joy, and happiness are within the heart and soul of you. Love, joy, and happiness are the actions that occur within you when you are love, truth, and perfection.

If you were the only man on a desert island, how much would you learn? Do you think that you would be able to learn sitting on that island by yourself? You would indeed, because you would begin to look within yourself, and you would learn from the soul and spirit within.

You would of necessity develop a relationship to self and to your life, or you would choose to leave the physical world. This relationship would be valuable but it would be restrictive of energy points to trigger soul memory, and it would be restrictive of energy interaction to create drama from which to learn. Your interaction would be focused upon the interaction of the different facets of self.

You would integrate the physical intellect and ego with the expansive soul memory and the enfinite spirit energy. This would create within you inspiration from the life force of spirit energy and motivation from the source of soul memory. This internal energy would combine with the external physical energy of the intellect to create a plan to be rescued. This would be accepting responsibility for self by the interaction of the total self.

But you see, you are not on a desert island. You are a spirit energy focused upon a physical, material world. When you find yourself in the physical world obsessively attached to the activity of the physical world, you will slow down your soul evolution.

You will not stop your evolution completely, but you will slow it down as you ignore the tug of the soul and spirit within.

As you expand your focus upon the external world, you will ignore the internal world. You will fail to see the "need" to look beyond what you know and accept. You will become a captive of your physical belief system. You will accept what you believe and you will refuse to open your mind to the inner self.

> *It is through the interaction of other souls and spirits that you invite your soul and spirit to be triggered to wakefulness. Isolation without deprivation does not inspire you to look within.*

It is forever important for you to learn to love yourself by interacting with many types of other souls and spirits on the physical level. If you are afraid, what are you afraid of? You see, fear is the opposite of love. When you are captured by fear, fear becomes a resistance to interaction, to taking risks, to living to your fullest.

Have you ever met someone who is afraid to drive across a bridge? There are millions of people in your world who are afraid to drive across a bridge. Now, how do they conquer their fear? They must look within themselves. They must understand what created the fear.

Always when there is fear it is of your creation, secondary to your belief in original sin. Physical fear is symbolic of the fear of separation from God. When you fear crossing a bridge, your are acknowledging your fear of death. In death, you fear separation from God because you see yourself as unworthy of being loved by God. You feel that since you are "unworthy" you will be cast aside, or separated from God.

> *It is your belief system that allows you to fear a separation from God. God is within you as the spirit of you. The spirit of you is eternal. If you are attached to the physical concept of self, then you fear for the physical being that you believe yourself to be. You are one with God, you cannot be separated.*

Your physical body is a creation of the spirit. It is finite and was created by the spirit to give the spirit physical power within the physical world. If the spirit did not create the physical body it could not function within the physical world except as I function through my conduit.

For you, as man, to function from the integration of your spirit energy you must be an open and advanced soul upon Earth. Allowing the spirit to act within the physical body is the action of integration. Therefore, in the cycles of development the spirit will choose a physical body as a platform for learning.

Once the spirit enters into the physical body, it becomes overshadowed by the physical reality of Earth. As the physical body enters into the cycle of development, the beliefs of the physical world are being absorbed by the intellect and the ego. The physical mind then becomes dominant as it attaches itself to the physical belief system. As the physical body becomes your focus, you will find yourself suffering more disease and more traumas in your creation of opportunities to change.

> **When you identify your physical body as your connection to God, you will perceive physical death as a separation from God.**

When you fear separation from God, you restrict your freedom to live. Your fear of death will be manifested in multiple physical realities as the soul and spirit create dramas to capture the attention of the physical intellect.

Your soul and spirit are attempting to change your physical attachment to fear by balancing the energy of the physical with the inspiration and motivation of the spirit and soul. Fear can only be released by love.

If you are afraid to drive across the bridge, you are afraid the bridge will fall and you will drown. Do you see that the ultimate fear in this individual would be the fear of death?

When you focus upon the finiteness of the physical body and you believe in only one physical life, you will find fear to be an intimate part of your living. The ultimate fear in all individuals is the fear of separation from God, because in life they relate to God intellectually. The intellect is part of the physical body which is understood and accepted as finite.

When death is viewed as a finite experience, your fear becomes a fear of the unknown. You do not understand and acknowledge that there is never a separation from God. Your belief focuses upon the finite body, not on eternal life. You feel

that you can only return to God if in His judgment you are worthy
of being in His presence.

*Your belief in the separation of yourself and*
*God in your physical reality, creates the belief in*
*your separation from God for eternity.*

You create your "truth of belief" from your fear of the
unknown. The "unknown" spirit energy within you is an external
belief that is learned as an element of your belief in original sin.
The unknown is not a spiritual reality. All spirit energy is known
as one with God. You are God within. You are totally acknowledged and loved by God. You are separate, but you are one with
God.

If you see yourself only as a physical being, without eternal
life; if you see yourself as dying and being buried, and that is the
end of you, of course you do not want to fall off the bridge, because
that would end a beautiful existence.

If you see yourself as eternal, as a spirit who changes bodies
when it has learned all there is to learn in that body, you will no
longer fear death. Death itself is not real. It is an illusion created
by the spirit and soul within. You will understand that when
death comes in the physical sense for you, it will be your choice.
Your choice will be made to create change for the soul and spirit
within.

The one negative emotion that keeps you from loving yourself is fear. In your world fear is divided into many other negative
energies such as guilt, sin, anger, hostility, resistance, denial, and
rejection. Do you see how it works?

Fear is an energy. It is the energy of fear that is the direct
opposite of the energy of love. Think of your emotions and you
can visualize the energy that holds you captive within your
physical world.

*The energies of love and fear create within you*
*a level of conscious awareness from which you*
*will in turn structure your entire life.*

Fear that is created and focused toward any issue in your
world will affect your entire world. In the identical concept, love
created toward any issue in your world will affect your entire
world. This becomes the creation of a consciousness energy.
From this energy you create an awareness of self, your world,

your relationships, your work, your love life, and all aspects of self.

You must first understand and love self to conquer fear. It is the inclination of the intellect to immediately fear what it does not understand. In this energy of intellectual fear, man will refuse to hear, to see, and to understand. When the intellect refuses to be open to understanding it is protecting the ego that is accepted as its protection from death.

> *Your focused belief in your intellect is your most expansive denial of loving self.*

Self is the physical body, ego, and intellect as one external facet. The soul and the spirit are the inner and higher energies or facets of you. If you are focused only upon the intellect, you are denying the soul and spirit. You will never understand yourself until you can integrate the three facets of self into a balanced energy.

> *Man cannot love himself until he can understand himself, because he will subconsciously and unconsciously fear what he does not understand.*

If you are married and your wife or husband leaves the house, do you have a fear that they are seeing someone else?

You see, this fear would be translated into jealousy, anger, hate, and hostility. These emotions would then affect every other aspect of your daily world. Do you see how fear works?

It is important to understand how the mind uses fear, and how it literally subdivides it into the other elements that you recognize as something else. These elements of fear will totally control your life and your living. You will not escape them until you understand them and the role that you have assigned them.

When you see an individual that focuses on the negative energies of life, you are seeing an individual who is overwhelmed by fear. They may have fears that are very common; a fear of being fired from their job; a fear of oversleeping in the morning; a fear of driving a car; a fear of not being dressed properly; a fear of eating too much; a fear of not being wanted; a fear of not being as "good" as another person.

Fear wears many faces in your physical world. When you fear, you cannot love yourself. If you do not love yourself, you cannot love another person or your world.

When you do not love yourself, you will attach great importance to the physical act of sex in your desire to capture "love." Sexual promiscuity will create dramas within your world. These dramas will be focuses of negative energy that you create to capture your attention and the attention of mankind. When you create attention-getting dramas, you create physical symbols of your challenges and your opportunity to change.

*Physical love should always be a celebration of the communion between the soul and spirit within. Until sex is understood in the beauty of sharing the physical, soul, and spirit energy with unconditional love, it will remain a source of disease and anguish within your physical world.*

You must explore and search to understand how you can change fear to love. There are some techniques that can be used in this instance. The most important way to overcome fear is to overcome the belief system that created the fear.

If you think that you are not beautiful, stand in front of the mirror and repeat to yourself, "I AM beautiful. I AM beautiful."

Do you know what you do when you do this? You change your belief system. You reprogram the mind to a new understanding of self.

If there is someone in your life that you feel that you hate—we will call him George—stand in front of your mirror and say, "I love George." This statement needs to be repeated several times each time you say it, and you should say it several times each day.

Repetition is the method of learning for man on Earth. This simple technique will change your belief system. Indeed, you will be creating a new belief system so you should be careful where you send your love energy. Being IN LOVE is also a challenge for man.

You could begin by standing in front of the mirror and saying, "I love me. I love me." When you say "I love me" many times each day, you will suddenly realize that you have a different energy toward yourself. You will begin to be nice to yourself. You will begin to accept and acknowledge yourself on a physical basis.

You will find that the "concept of need" that you had, the concept of needing attachments, the concept of needing other people, the concept of needing jobs, indeed your total "concept of need" will disappear. You will lose your attachment because you will suddenly begin to enjoy the energy of accepting yourself.

When you accept yourself you will begin to love yourself. You will lose this "concept of need" and the "concept of attachment," and you will begin to live in total freedom. You will begin to work because you WANT to work. You will begin to be with people because you ENJOY being with people. You will begin to love WITHOUT CONDITION, because as you learn to accept and love yourself, you will be able to accept and love everyone else in the same way.

When you love without condition, you are loving in the same manner that Christ loved man when He was crucified. You see, Jesus did not have to be crucified. Crucifixion was His choice to show you that from all things you can grow. His growth was manifested in the Resurrection.

It was through His choice that Jesus as the Christ Consciousness demonstrated for man that when you love yourself, you can love your neighbor, despite his actions, and your God without a concept of needing a gift, a favor, or your life as a condition. You will love on an unconditional basis without judgment and without seeking anything in return for the love that you are willing to give.

You do not say, "I would love you IF you were rich, I would love you IF you were thin, IF you were fat, IF you were beautiful, IF you had red hair; I would love you IF you were short, IF you were tall, I would love you IF you were a professional, I would love you IF you were a race car driver...." You see, you do not place conditions on love. Love, to be love, is unconditional.

*Just as the Christ Consciousness did not say to His persecutors, "I will love you, IF you do not crucify me...." He showed us by His actions that He could love Himself, AND His persecutors, AND His Father in an equal energy that was not dependent in any way upon physical circumstances.*

This does not mean that you should allow people to persecute you. You see, Christ agreed to persecution because He was showing us a lesson in the extreme.

> **Man has a way of not seeing, not hearing, and not understanding unless the event is truly extreme and can capture his attention.**

The Crucifixion was a path of teaching man unconditional love by capturing man's attention with the extreme.

Today when man is feeling totally unloved by himself and all others, he will create dis-ease or disease to capture his attention. He will create self-persecution to capture his attention. Or he will steal, cheat, lie, have affairs, kill, fight, and hate, to get the attention of the rest of the world. Inside he is crying for help because he is lost in his ability to search for understanding of himself.

When we love ourselves the energy of us will be such a beautiful magnet, that each and every soul that comes within our energy will love us. That sounds very simple, doesn't it? It is indeed very simple. If someone comes into your energy and they do NOT like you, understand that it is the spirit energy within you that is pushing their buttons.

Understand that it is okay for them to have their buttons pushed. Pushing their buttons then becomes a choice of theirs. If they recognize that they are reacting to you because of what is within them, they will choose to deal with the issue. If they blame their reaction upon you, they will not want to be with you.

You can either become a teacher to this individual and help them through their own lesson of unconditional love, or you can choose to allow them to learn it in another way. If you are not advanced enough in your own soul evolution to help them without traumatizing yourself, remove yourself from their physical presence.

Let me assure you that unless you have learned this lesson very well, it will be difficult for you to remember the lesson if you get into a drama of love. Man, in his wisdom and you all have wisdom, creates a variety of dramas in order to teach himself. The best way to understand these dramas is to go back into your own life.

Searching your memory of your physical relationships is another technique that you can use to help you learn to understand and to love yourself. In searching the memory within, you will be able to see your lessons with expanded clarity each time that you reach a new level of conscious awareness.

This is an exercise that you repeat many, many times in your life. It is a healing exercise that allows your perception of the event to change with your expanding growth and understanding. As you expand your conscious awareness, you will gain in understanding your relationships of the past, present, and future. This understanding will allow you to heal the energy within you that focuses upon the relationship, and see the energy as an energy of self that is healed.

Go back to the moment that you were born. You chose your parents, your siblings, your birthplace, and the circumstances of your birth. This was the beginning for you in creating within the physical world the life that you had designed within the soul and spirit world of energy.

***It may surprise you to know that when you were born, you came into the world with more insight and more knowledge than you have today.***

When you were born as an infant, you could not use your physical senses, because you had not developed those physical senses. But you were using your soul and spirit senses in a very lively and advanced manner. If you choose to go back into those soul memories, you could indeed remember your birth time and your birth event.

You can, in this identical way, go back into each drama, each event of your physical existence. You can look at that physical existence and the event, and you can very clearly see what your lesson was that you were trying to learn in each and every drama. View these memories totally without judgment of yourself or others.

As your level of consciousness changes, you will be able to understand more of the lesson. So you see, this is not something that you do once in a lifetime and then forget. It is something that you do frequently. As you feel yourself evolving to a different level of conscious awareness, you can look at your lifetime from birth, and you will see the additional lessons that you are working on. As the energy of your consciousness expands, it will attract more of the energy of the event to your conscious understanding.

If you want to open up to the soul and spirit within and learn to love yourself, it will take work. There are no "quick fixes" in learning to understand the complexity within yourself. It is a gradual evolution. You are taking one step at a time. If it is your choice to learn, you must make the commitment to seek out the teachers and to do the work required.

If man makes a choice to work toward a college degree, he makes a commitment to that choice and he works diligently toward eventual fulfillment of that commitment. Your schools within the physical world are patterned after the school of life which is Earth.

This inner work is a very important issue for you to remember and it is something that each and every one of you needs to do. You cannot understand who you are unless you are willing to look at who you are. Do not be afraid. Have no fear. There are no wrongs or rights. You are in reality love, truth, and perfection.

Look without judgment and see without judgment. In seeing you will begin the process of understanding self. You will begin the process of triggering the soul and spirit energies within. You will begin the process of balancing self.

As you go through life you must confront the issue of who you are, what you are, and how you relate to all of those around you. Until you can understand the wisdom, the love, the joy, and peace within yourself, until you can understand the glory that you are as a spirit essence, you will not be able to fully appreciate the human encounters, the human interactions that you have on a daily basis.

*It is when you acknowledge, accept, and respect the value of your physical existence and the value of each and every person that is on this Earth, that you will truly understand and value yourself, the God within you, and each and every neighbor around you.*

We can use some examples, if you like. There are many examples in this world of what you do as you interact. Now, let us say that you encounter a physical person (it may be male or female, as the case is with you) and you suddenly fall deeply in love. This love is so intense that you feel you cannot live, you simply cannot exist, without this person by your side.

Now, this individual may not feel the same way about you. It may be a physical attraction on your part, and no physical attraction on the part of the other individual. It could, indeed, also be an attraction of the soul and spirit within you. If the other person is not at the same level where he or she could recognize soul and spirit energy, then the attraction, again, would not be there.

Let us say that this individual did not respond to the love that you felt. All of a sudden you began to feel rejected; you began to feel unworthy; you began to feel rather ugly, not too smart, and you suddenly found yourself in a total state of despair. You do not feel physically attractive to this individual. So you connect what you perceive as a physical failure with a state of unworthiness within.

This may cause so much trauma for you, that you may decide that you do not want to continue your life. You may decide that you are going to take some pills and do away with yourself.

Now, can you find any wisdom in that drama? Probably not. Because you see, there is not a lot of wisdom that is being activated. There is a lot of physical reacting that is being activated. In THIS instance, the lesson this individual is trying to learn, is the lesson of loving self.

You see, in order to love yourself totally, you have to love yourself regardless of the reaction of other people to you. You must understand that you are going to push buttons for people who are working on the same issues. You are going to be ignored by other people who are working on their own issues. It truly does not matter. You are perfect as you, and you are evolving as you.

The focus toward a love object in your world is a physical focus. It is a focus of physical attraction. It is your belief system that creates the feeling that if the attraction that you feel is not returned you are at fault, you are unworthy. This is when the physical mind, the ego within, becomes desperate.

For you to love yourself, you must get beyond, get totally beyond, the physical attraction. You must love people and in turn love yourself because of the soul and the spirit within. You should not attach yourselves to individuals of intense drama, because this is holding you within the physical world, within the physical concept of physical attraction that is not going to help you in your lesson of unconditional love.

When you choose to stay involved in intense physical drama, you will continue to feel unworthy. If you can walk away from the drama and find the peace to look at the lesson with intensity, you will see that you are trying to learn to love yourself.

You mirror the love that you are searching for to another. You are living a concept of needing this partner to transfer love to you because you are not loving yourself. In turn you react with fear and anger, when you feel the love being withheld.

When you focus on your "concept of need," you allow the physical attraction to expand totally out of proportion to the total person. When relationships focus on interacting only from the physical energy of self, they will be short-lived in your world. When relationships focus upon only physical attraction, there will be insufficient verbal communication, emotional caring, or loving feelings that are displayed in the everyday actions of the relationship.

Receiving love by the transference of the physical contact of another body is not BEING love. BEING love is when you love yourself enough that you can be happy every moment of your life because you understand, you accept, and you acknowledge that you are perfect within.

The love that you have for yourself will relieve you from the responsibility of accepting persecution within relationships, because you will love yourself too much to allow persecution to occur. Indeed, you will have attracted the energy of persecution to attract your attention and to allow you to resurrect yourself.

*Many marriages within your world are a physical re-enactment of the Crucifixion of Christ on a personal level. You create the event of persecution within your life to learn that unconditional love allows you to remove yourself, or resurrect yourself from the circumstances. If you do not learn your lesson you will continue to "hang upon your cross."*

Understand that Christ was acting out the lesson of unconditional love with the Crucifixion. To show us the way of the Resurrection He removed Himself from the circumstances. Man does not have to remove himself by death, as death was the illusion of man.

In life, you will cling to the illusion that death is the only way to remove yourself from your personal creations. This illusion is the manifestation of the physical belief system. As the physical belief system expands, the symbolism of death will expand. You will create the death of your physical self, which is an illusion because the spirit is eternal, to create a new opportunity in a new embodiment.

When these events or dramas occur within your life, it will not be easy for you to look at yourself and the drama and understand. But if you are committed to understanding, it will become very clear. Understanding will allow you to integrate your internal energies with your external energies which then allows healing to occur.

*Understand that you in your wisdom of wanting and searching to learn, will choose the same drama multiple times for the experience, because you are trying to understand your lesson with total clarity.*

The lesson of unconditional love is forever taught to self by you through your interactions with other people. Loving self IS the lesson of unconditional love. Unconditional love IS the lesson of loving yourself. When you love yourself, you can love your neighbor, and the God within you without condition and with total freedom.

*Loving self is the ultimate lesson for man on Earth. This is the lesson that many advanced souls are working on today. It is the lesson of uncondi- tional love that begins within the individual that will, in turn, change the energy of your entire Earth.*

Do you see why it is very important for each of you to work on this lesson?

*Loving self is a lesson that is intense. It is a les- son that begins with the individual at the moment of creation.*

TO LEARN TO LOVE YOURSELF YOU MUST FIRST LEARN NOT TO JUDGE YOURSELF.

To create non-judgment in life you must change many of your belief systems. The belief system is the structure of your daily physical existence.

Do you see the challenge involved?

YOU CANNOT TRULY LOVE ANOTHER PERSON UNTIL YOU CAN LOVE YOURSELF.

I would like to remind you of something, just to show you the challenge that this lesson truly is on a physical level of understanding.

Many of you will develop an allergy to what I am saying. You may create resistance within your body or within your ability to read these words. You may verbally object or silently object. You may catch a cold or develop allergy symptoms. You may deny, resist, reject, and refuse totally to believe that even one of my words could possibly be valid. You may find everything that I have said in total and complete opposition to the way that you presently believe.

Let me assure you that this is perfectly acceptable. There is no problem if you do not immediately understand these words as truth. Each of you must evolve on the physical plane at your own individual level of learning. If you are searching to learn, then continue to read whether or not you believe. Reading can then be accepted as an intellectual challenge. Stay open to the reading.

You do not need to feel guilty, because guilt, again, keeps you from loving yourself. You see, you do not have any guilt or any sin that was given to you by God. God has given you only love, and He wants you to be only love.

YOUR WORLD, AS YOUR LIFE, IS TOTALLY AND FOREVER YOUR OWN CREATION.

*Loving yourself allows you to understand, accept, acknowledge, and value what you have created. In loving yourself you totally accept the responsibility for your creation.*

Never believe that you are here to overcome a sin. You are here to learn. You create the concept of guilt and sin because you do not understand the purpose of the Christ Consciousness. In the identical way that you go to college to learn, you choose to be born as man on Earth to learn. When you do not understand the subject and fail to pass with flying colors the first time, you are going to continue repeating the class until you understand the lesson with total clarity.

When you reach a conscious awareness of wanting to acknowledge, accept, and understand your soul and spirit within, you will begin to understand within yourself who you are.

"Past lives" which you have experienced will begin to appear within your conscious memory. You will begin to meet people who you will immediately recognize as a soul and spirit energy that is familiar to you.

*You may be reading these very words and suddenly realize how accurate my statements are, because the memory of knowing this information is in all of you.*

I would suggest that you think about your life very intensely, and create the opportunity to look within at your own dramas of relationships. It is impossible for the energy of unconditional love to convey itself through the physical ears or the physical eyes into the intellectual mind and escape the judgment of the ego. The lesson of loving self takes thousands of aware lifetimes to complete.

I will be dealing with sharing love throughout this book, and I will be dealing with it in relationship to other people, as well as yourself. But in all instances, love must be within.

Never believe that you can choose a partner to make you happy or to give you love. Because if you demand love, it is seldom given.

*If you are not happy within, you cannot receive happiness externally from someone else. The joy and happiness of relationships is merely an enhancement of what dwells within you. It is a reflection that intensifies your own image.*

Happiness is the action, the physical action, of loving yourself. If you are not happy all the time, then you do not love yourself all the time. Happiness is a barometer that you can look at within yourself. Someday when you fully accept the responsibility for who you are, for your individual choices of life, you will wake up knowing what total happiness means.

You will feel joyous at being alive, and you will know that you do indeed love yourself. At that moment you will also recognize that you are advancing in your soul evolution.

*Loving yourself is the ultimate lesson. When you love yourself with total unconditional love, you will have total unconditional freedom to love others. This does not mean that you can break the laws of man, because at that moment you would find yourself again feeling guilty.*

Loving yourself gives you the freedom to love another person with total commitment.

Loving yourself is a focus that you should maintain for the rest of this lifetime. It is a worthy focus that will benefit each and every one of you.

I would suggest that you do the exercise of looking back into your past, and try to understand with as much clarity as possible what lessons you have designed for yourself to learn. If you look at those you love, your parents, your brothers and sisters, your spouses, or your lovers, you will be able to see a thread of continuity that runs between the lessons. Examine these relationships carefully, in minute detail, without judgment of self or others.

The self-image that you are attached to is especially apparent in your loves of the opposite sex. I say "loves" because you will have many within most physical lifetimes. Each and every relationship, whether it began in high school or whether it ended at the alter, must be understood to understand the lesson and all of its images.

If it is important to you to feel superior, you will choose partners that you can dominate. If it is important to you to feel more intelligent, you will choose partners with less intellect than you. If it is important for you to make all decisions and be in total control, you will choose a child-like partner. If you are only interested in the physical image, you will choose a love that fulfills your belief in a beautiful body. If you feel the need to be taken care of, you will choose a love that will be a parent image in your life.

The important energy to understand in relationships is that each party is attracting the energy that it is searching for at the moment of connection. The divorce rate is very high within your world because there is much growth within your world. As your energy needs change, your physical relationships will change.

Always look at each relationship in terms of your individual energy of self. The lesson of the other actor on your stage had nothing to do with the lesson that you chose to learn. He/she played the role for their own lesson. The agreement to the involvement was made by both parties.

Look at the energy of yourself with total patience and total love. When you can accept and acknowledge a situation in your life, you will take away the energy of the fear of the situation. Understand that each creation within your world was designed by you or agreed to by you. There is no one to blame. In the most dramatic and traumatic of events there is a lesson for you to understand.

*If you do not understand the lesson, you will continue to repeat the event.*

The commitment to understand and love yourself takes work and it takes love. It takes the love within you to look at yourself without blame, guilt, fear, and anger. You are worthy of each and every moment that you spend on yourself.

Spending time alone, away from the frantic activity and noise of the world, will be a beginning. Find a few minutes each day to go within yourself and listen to the silence. Seek out a teacher in your physical world and grow through openness to new information.

*No one else can do your growing for you. The responsibility belongs totally to you.*

Accepting or denying the responsibility for your personal world is another barometer of loving self. As the world has become more technologically advanced, you have accepted less and less responsibility for who you are physically, emotionally, spiritually, and intellectually.

You fail to acknowledge your responsibility in most aspects of daily living. You give the responsibility for your health to medical science. You give the responsibility for your education to the school system. You give the responsibility for your soul to organized religion. You give the responsibility for your daily maintenance to a job. You give the responsibility for your food to the grocery store and food manufacturers. You give the responsibility for your entertainment to others.

For travel you depend upon a car, a bus, a train, a motorcycle, or an airplane. For communication you depend upon the telephones, televisions, newspapers, books, and radios. You prefer sleeping to talking to friends. You are for all intents and purposes self-focused in your world of today. You seek instant self-gratification for your concept of need.

As you deny the responsibility for self, you blame other men, God, the Church, science, the educational system, or whatever you can imagine in your fit of anger for your own inadequacies.

When God gave you the POWER OF CREATION, He gave you total responsibility for what you create. If you choose to deny your responsibility, you will suffer your own created agonies of the body, mind, and spirit of self. Each and every "agony of suffering" will be a lesson in disguise for you.

> ***All that is within your mind will be created by you within your physical body and your physical world.***

The perspective that you create your reality on a moment by moment basis is not easy for you to accept. Acceptance of responsibility is one level in the cycle of development of man. When you accept that you are responsible for your body, your world, and all that is around you, you have gained in your conscious awareness of your creation of your reality.

> ***Your life is controlled by your conscious aware-ness. If you are not aware of a better way to per-ceive yourself, you will continue to accept yourself as you are and not be interested in growth. If you remain self-focused, you will not reach the level of self-realization.***

There is a difference between the self-realization of knowing and understanding self and the self-focus of pampering self with material objects and blaming others for what you feel they should have done for you. Indeed, self-realization and self-focus are the opposites in BEING. Self-realization is loving self with a con-sciously integrated internal focus. Self-focus is living in fear with an external focus.

As you create more advantages within the physical world it becomes more essential that you balance your physical world with the soul and spirit energy from within. Nothing creates a loss of balance more intensely within you than total focus upon the external self. When the only comforts that you acknowledge in life are those of the material world, you will not find happiness within.

You are an integrated being. You are integrated whether or not you accept and acknowledge the integration. You are born with an external focus of the physical self, the ego self, and the intellectual self. You are also born with an internal focus of your rational mind (soul memory), and intuitive mind (spirit energy).

As you live, the inner focus becomes hidden from view by the multiple reactions to the physical senses. You learn to have faith and trust only in what you can hear, see, touch, taste, and smell. You learn to love and to relate in the supreme physical sense which is the integration of all physical senses. The supreme physical sense is the sexual sense.

Throughout time you have allowed the sexual sense to rule your physical world, your personal world, and your intellectual world. Unfortunately the use of the sexual energy within you creates blocks to other energies when the focus is abused. This resistance creates emotional blockage in relationships. The only giving and the only receiving becomes physical. Indeed, the entire relationship may be based upon the physical realities of life with no communication, no emotion, no feeling, and no true love existing.

You are energy and energy by its very nature is in constant movement. Therefore, when you have reached the level within your physical world where you are functioning primarily from your combination of physical senses or the sexual sense, the next movement for the energy of self must be within.

**You have created your own development of your physical world and now the time has come for you to create your own awareness of self as an integrated BEING.**

When you learn to function by all of your physical external senses, the next movement of the self energy is to develop the multiple senses of the internal self. Use of the multiple sensing energies is happening within many advanced souls in the world of today.

Not all of you are functioning at the same level of conscious awareness. There are in the world today many souls who have learned the lesson of unconditional love which is the cycle of integration. Many others are functioning from the cycle of awareness and the cycle of understanding. Other souls are held captive in the cycle of development because of their physical belief system. Within each cycle there are multiple levels of consciousness.

There are no absolutes within the levels of soul evolution. All of you evolve in a unique and individual way, learning lessons from individual dramas, and creating from various levels of consciousness. Indeed, there is no one path that is "correct." In all instances the soul will evolve through the cycles of development, awareness, understanding, and integration in its progress through the path of soul evolution.

*Each consciousness level in each cycle of evolution must reach the physical level of conscious awareness to be understood and learned as a lesson.*

As you begin the development of awareness, understanding, or integration within the physical world, you will be confronted with the fear of the physical ego self. Change is an opportunity for growth for all of man.

Yet the ego self is the self-focused self that wants no part of an integrated state of self-realization. The ego sees your progress in soul evolution as a threat to its survival. The ego seeks control as its means of survival. It is not interested in balancing the energies of the internal self.

*At this moment in your life, you may find yourself longing for attachment to a physical person, material possessions, the intellectual, the physical activity, and the noise of your physical world. Indeed, at this moment your ego will create any and all blocks that it can imagine to resist change.*

The ego does not welcome understanding and it certainly does not welcome integration. You will be entering the cycle of awareness while the ego is strong enough to assert its sense of superiority. As the awareness grows to reach the beginning level of the cycle of understanding, the ego is beginning to feel the force of the energy balance. It can no longer completely control the actions of the mind.

At this moment in your life, soul evolution will escalate if you can begin to allow change within the internal focus of understanding.

The time required in your world for you to move from awareness, to understanding, and to integration is minimal, when viewed in relationship to the time required for man to move through the cycle of development.

Each level becomes easier and less traumatic in terms of resistance and denial. As the mind opens to accept, the energy flow will move more smoothly and rapidly. Suddenly you will find yourself feeling and understanding the energy around you. This is the individual integration of critical mass. The energy has merged together to create an expanded awareness and understanding.

When you reach the level of integration, you are focused upon the lesson of unconditional love. The lesson will create relationships that will allow you to see the multiple images of self with total clarity.

*The lesson of unconditional love can only be learned in terms of relationships. All of the lessons of man are relative to relationships of one form or another.*

The lesson of unconditional love cannot be understood until you have learned to love yourself. It is through the total self-realization of loving self that you are capable of the unconditional love of God, and of your neighbor.

*When you can experience total love of self and total love of your twin soul in a physical lifetime, you will understand the purity, simplicity, humility, and innocence that is found in unconditional love.*

Unconditional love is the perfect image of the love, truth, and perfection within you. It is this perfection of soul and spirit within your physical reality that you will seek to enfinity.

In all of life there are cycles of loving self and others. Each cycle will have a focus. Loving can be purely physical which is the love of self-focus. It can be an accepting love, an understanding love, or it can be an integrated love that consumes the body, heart, soul, and spirit of the individual.

*An integrated love can only be shared and enjoyed when you have reached a level of loving self through total self-realization. This is a love that knows no boundaries in inspiration and sharing. It is totally committed. It is love, truth, and perfection. It is a love that transports self into the creative energy of the soul and spirit which is limitless in its complexity of love and sharing. Indeed, an integrated love is guided by the inspiration and motivation of the God energy within.*

The question of man and his relationship to God, has created confusion within the mind of man. Man is indeed a fragment of the energy of God. As man grows in his energy, God grows in His energy.

Energy expands energy. When your energy is focused upon the God energy, the expansion is more profound within the physical world and within the Universe. Like attracts like. The more complete the energy is in its likeness of self, the more the energy of self is allowed to grow. The more the loving energy of self grows the more the loving energy of God grows.

*Your beliefs control your aware consciousness. What you do not believe in, you will not create. Indeed, you will create the opposite which will be the negative energy of the belief. The loving self creates love. The negative self creates negative dramas.*

Many humans do not acknowledge their inner soul and spirit. They cannot accept even a theory that is outside their current belief system. They do not acknowledge or accept the God energy within themselves.

*Resistance to understanding what is, does not change what is. The denial of man changes only the energy of the external world of man. The spirit and soul live eternally.*

The spirit and soul will continue the activities of the spirit world while you sleep in the physical world. Indeed, there is soul and spirit activity that continues during your waking hours without your conscious awareness.

*Consciousness is an energy of understanding, in each of its states of aware consciousness, subconsciousness, and unconsciousness. Within each state of consciousness there are multiple levels of consciousness energy.*

If you do not believe in the unconscious energy of God within, you will not acknowledge that consciousness understanding in the aware state. That does not mean that the energy does not exist. It means only that it is not an aware consciousness that is acknowledged within the physical world.

Despite denial and lack of acknowledgement, the spirit energy (the Godself), and the soul energy exist at the core level, or inner and higher level of consciousness within you. You can continue to focus all of your conscious energy upon the physical world but you will someday trigger yourself to remember.

Your trigger will usually occur as a crisis of the physical self within your physical world. When the ego and spirit energy are playing their continual tug-of-war, you will subconsciously from soul memory create a crisis of memory energy. This memory energy will be manifested within the physical world as a physical event. If it has been a critical tug-of-war to get your attention, the event will usually occur as a critical or crisis drama or trauma.

*The question is not DO you truly possess a soul and spirit? The question is WHEN will you acknowledge your soul and spirit?*

Acknowledgement is in reality inevitable in all of you because that is your focus of growth to the level of BEING. Indeed, you were created to expand the God energy within the Universal system. This energy of love, truth, and perfection must first be recognized within self before it can expand within the Universe.

*Loving self is your life purpose. Loving God and all of man in the equality of love, truth, and perfection is the soul purpose of each and every man on Earth.*

These purposes will appear as images of lessons in each and every embodiment that you choose. Within the life that you are living, you create your personal path of soul and spirit evolution.

*Nothing in the Universe is an accident. Each man is the genetic energy of God, the spirit of man. To awaken the conscious memory of this spirit energy within, man must begin by loving self.*

*Man always knows on an unconscious level where he wants to go. His choices on a conscious level will determine how he gets there. It is the physical actions of man that reflect the internal understanding of man.*

Personal growth occurs only within the vibrations of the positive energy within you. Growth and negative energy are opposites and as opposite forces they do not create growth, they indeed hold you captive. This is the explanation for the stasis that occurs within you when you intellectualize the soul and spirit within.

In the scientific world of the intellectual man, there is a belief that focuses only upon what can be proven within the physical scientific sense. This is a world of restrictive beliefs that limit the understanding and the utilization of infinite knowledge. Science does not understand infinite knowledge because this is an energy that cannot be measured within itself.

What you can do is acknowledge that the energy of the soul and spirit can be accessed. Accessing this knowledge will give you comfort in utilizing your understanding to increase the electromagnetic life force within. This energy can be used to heal the self, to create a more harmonious world, to balance the Universe, and to create peace, love, and joy within.

Being open to your individual soul and spirit energy will allow an integration of energies to occur in all aspects of your life. This internal integration of energies will then expand to affect the world around you. This is truly an integration of the external intellect, the inner rational mind, and the higher intuitive mind which will result in a global effect of peace and joy.

### *LOVING SELF IS BEING UNCONDITIONAL LOVE.*

Loving self is acknowledging, accepting, respecting, and valuing the three facets of self that create the total you. Loving self is self-realization. It is keeping the energy flow of the mind open to BE all that you can BE.

*Man is relative to Earth*
*Earth protects*
*man destroys.*
*Man is relative to God*
*God protects*
*man destroys.*

# Sharing
# Life

*Man looks*
*but he does not see*
*the relationship of*
*all energy*
*as it surrounds him*
*and protects him.*

*Man listens*
*but he does not hear*
*the vibrations of*
*the Universe*
*that sing about*
*and around him.*

The most expansive and satisfying sharing that you do within your world is the sharing of your life. Life is shared as self, on an individual basis, a group basis, and a Universal basis. You share self with self, family, friends, lovers, marriage partners, ethnic groups, cultures, worlds, and the Universe.

Life is a physical energy that all humans have in common who live upon Earth. Your life on Earth differs in physical energy from life in other parts of the Universe, but in the concept of soul and spirit energy it is the same.

*You are created as a trilocular being of energy. The three facets of self are facets of the Universal energy. On Earth these facets are known as the physical, which is a triad of the physical body, intellectual mind, and the ego; the soul which is the subconscious energy of the rational mind; and the spirit which is the unconscious energy of the intuitive mind.*

These three facets of self are manifested physically within the brain of man. The left brain is the physical, conscious, intellectual mind of man. The right brain is the subconscious, rational mind of soul memory within man. The cerebellum is the center brain which is the unconscious, intuitive mind of spirit memory within man.

*The energies within you are separate, but they are one. They are inherently integrated within you and present the illusion of separation when you deny their existence.*

These energies within you are symbolic of the energies within the Universe. Each energy facet exists within the physical you as 7 relative to 7 or 49 separate levels of consciousness within its own vibrational energy. On an infinite energy spectrum each of these 147 vibrational waves have 7 vibrational waves. Each of these vibrational waves repeat themselves relative to 7 into eternity. Indeed, the energy of you reaches out within the Universe in an enfinite or eternal wave of motion.

As energy vibrates it creates color. The physical energy of man will be seen as red in its entire spectrum of hues. The soul energy of man will be seen as blue in its entire spectrum of hues. The spirit energy of man will be seen as white. As these colors merge in their vibrational energy they form all of the colors known to man.

> *The rainbow is symbolic to man of ALL THAT IS and of all that he is. The rainbow shows the expansiveness of the energy of man and the path of the soul cycle as it moves within the Universe.*

Rainbows are seen within your heavens after the cleansing of rain which washes the film away. As less cleansing is required in your own personal energy you will see rainbows, the complete spectrum of energy, visible without the cleansing spirit of rain.

> *Earth is the planet of healing and cleansing. You are here to cleanse and to heal yourself by learning to understand the full magnitude of your own capabilities. These capabilities that are inherent within you far surpass your limited understanding at this period of your development.*

When you confine yourself to the physical, intellectual, ego energy within, you confine yourself to one-third of the energy that is available for you to freely use within your physical brain. This restrictive belief focuses you on a minute portion of your energy potential. This physical focus limits you to a third, of a third of your energy vibrations.

> *You focus on the first 49 physically focused vibrations of energy within self. This restrictive force manifests constriction within your life force and your creativity. Indeed, restriction prevents the integration of the vibrational energy that is infinite and that would expand the finiteness within your physical world. This constriction of the finite energy is manifested in death of the physical body at an early age.*

There is an organization to the energies of the Universe, of the Earth, and of man. This organization is not a physical organization as you are familiar with on Earth, but rather it is an organization of energy design. It is this design which began within the Universal system of energy that is repeated upon Earth and repeated again within the body and mind of man.

The Universal energy formation is not important for you to understand at this time because it is too expansive for your mind to fully imagine or accept. We can explain it more clearly to you by explaining the energy of your life to you.

*When you can understand yourself by under-standing your mind and body; understanding your consciousness energies that create your life; and understanding the effect of relationships in your world; you will be preparing your mind to go be-yond the self, into the energies of the Earth and the energies of the Universe. Understanding yourself will allow you to understand the total organization of Universal energy.*

Understanding that the purpose of Earth is to give you the opportunity to heal and cleanse yourself should help you understand why it is important to open up your mind to new concepts and new understandings.

Earth has existed for millions and millions of years in your concept of time. You have gone through evolution and devolution in your path of learning. For now most of you continue to be captured within the cycle of development within your world.

*Each time that you have begun to move beyond the cycle of development, your fear has held you firmly attached to the physical world that you "think" you understand. This fear has created de-volution for you and Earth many times over as you attach yourself to your physical reality. Releasing attachment to the physical is a lesson for you within the physical world.*

The cycle of development is the first cycle in soul evolution for you upon Earth. Each time that you leave a physical embodiment and return again to Earth, you begin this cycle of development over again on the physical level. As the soul and spirit evolve, it becomes easier for the physical energies to remain open to their influence on the new physical body as it returns to Earth.

*Those physical beings who can remain open and consciously integrated can access the knowledge of the soul memories and the spirit energy of infi-nite knowledge while on Earth.*

When the soul and spirit comes back to a physical life in a new body, the body becomes captive of the physical world and its belief systems. This captivity creates a challenge to the soul and spirit within to attract the attention of the physical self.

> ***It is the challenge of the lessons that you design for your physical self that creates the dramas and the traumas of your world.***

There is no specific pattern that each and every soul and spirit will follow in its path of learning. Your learning is a cleansing and healing, known in the spirit world as soul and spirit evolution or growth.

> ***Your physical path is designed by your soul and spirit energy. Your path has no absolute design but is created by the challenge of endless opportunities for choices and growth. Always within your design you will create alternate choices which will be physically chosen according to your levels of growth and physical resistance.***

If you can envision your game of monopoly, or chess, or some of your present computer games of alternate choice, you will understand an image of your life design. The choices that you design into your physical embodiment will allow you to reach your destination by choosing your own route.

> ***Life is choice.***

You will make your choices along your path dependent upon what you have remembered, what you have learned as your physical belief system, and how open you are to growth.

If a choice becomes an opportunity within your life that you are not prepared to acknowledge within yourself, you will choose an alternate path. Your choices and your paths are created through the interaction of relationships.

In your energy of growth you will become open and strong within the physical world. If you find yourself in a relationship where a lover or friend is focused upon a poor self-image, your strength and openness will threaten the ego survival of the lover or friend.

Mixing these two energies would compare to mixing oil and water. They will not integrate to form a homogeneous relationship. You would not be creating the fluidity of harmony and balance between you because you are functioning from different levels of soul and spirit energy which affects the physical energy of self.

The physical energy of self is who you are within the physical world. Your physical energy of self represents your beliefs, your restrictions, your openness, your love, your fears, and on and on into infinity. Who you are in your physical energy will determine the energy which you will attract to yourself and take unto yourself.

You will attract to you, that which is within you. If you have a poor self-image, you will only be comfortable with a person whose self-image is equal to or less than your own. If control is an issue with you and it always is an issue if you have a poor self-image, you will seek a partner that you can feel superior to.

This energy attraction will affect your entire life as you will seek lovers, friends, colleagues, business acquaintances, marriage partners, and all relationships dependent upon the energy of self.

*There are no right or wrong choices for you. You are the master of your own destiny. You will choose as you want to choose based upon your individual valuative processes. Valuative processes within you are created from your belief system.*

If you find yourself stuck in your physical world as a soul and spirit, you can choose death which is a valid choice for the soul and spirit energy. Death releases the soul and spirit energy from the physical captivity of the finite body and gives you the freedom to design a new course.

*The lesson of the death will become Karmic in the next embodiment if it was not learned in the transition. Suicide is a refusal to learn a lesson which will always be a Karmic lesson of future embodiments.*

As the spirit evolves it may choose multiple short physical lifespans to attract the attention of the physical world. Short lifespans are designed to cleanse or heal one image of the spirit and soul that is of concern to it. These souls may be highly advanced souls that are tying up loose ends of Karmic energy.

The soul and spirit can also choose to come back to spend time with a friend or a family member to ground a specific energy within the physical world. Indeed, the activity and freedom of the spirit and soul energy is so expansive that we could give millions of reasons for a "quick" or "long" visit within the physical world. The reasons for embodiments may be the same but the path may be different to allow a vision of another image of the lesson.

Visits into a physical embodiment are always choices for the soul and spirit. There is no fear, pressure, stress, or anxiety within the spirit world. These elements remain external to the spirit and soul in the same way that they are external to the spirit and soul in the physical world.

The spirit and soul energy is conscious of the physical energies that it is working with while in the spirit world. This consciousness of the energy creates the pattern of life design for the next physical embodiment. The difference in working with lessons on the spirit level rather than the physical level is the perception of the energy. There is total objectivity with spirit energy rather than the subjective attachment of your physical energy.

*As your physical energy becomes more integrated with the soul and spirit energy within the physical world, you will find yourself losing your physical ego attachment to the physical world. You will have created the energy of freedom within and without. This is the lesson of unconditional love.*

Your physical death is also a choice of the soul and spirit energy. The path of choice in death can be made for as many reasons as there are spirits.

*As you are able to understand the freedom that the soul and spirit has in coming and in leaving Earth, death will become less of a trauma to those who remain.*

Spirits have a responsibility to cleanse and heal Earth and the Universe in the same way that you have a responsibility to cleanse and heal yourself and Earth. This responsibility is respectively accepted by the spirit and soul energy that is the unconscious energy of you. As this energy becomes conscious within you, you will become more focused upon your affect upon the Earth and the Universe.

Many times when a soul and spirit suddenly leaves a physical embodiment, it is to be about their Father's business. Your design of self is also the design of Earth and the design of the Universe. Alternate choices can become a sudden reality for the soul and spirit to create a new direction upon Earth and upon the Universal energy of humanity.

***The spirit work goes on within the Universal organizational system while you are focused within the physical organizational system of Earth.***

How many of you have found yourself working overtime at the office when you had made other plans? When this happens the soul and spirit has the choice in the same way that you had a choice to stay in your office or go home.

The Universal energy is the "office" of the spirit and soul during your physical lifetime. When you sleep you return to the Universal energy of the spirit realm.

In effect, each time you sleep you experience a mini-death in your understanding of death. Your spirit work is then transformed by your intellect and ego into acceptable or known symbols of your physical mind when your awaken. You may or may not remember this energy that you call dreaming.

In terms of the Earth itself, development is created by the repetitious generations of humanity. The Earth also has experienced periods of devolution and evolution as humanity's collective creation. Earth is being developed through the physical life of all humans as the soul and spirit chooses life upon Earth.

***As you think, speak, and act, the Earth becomes.***

Do you see why it is important for you to remember who you truly are and what your purpose is on Earth?

Confusion is a state of physical energy that is accepted in your physical world. It is an energy that you experience as an emotion when your world does not seem to be going in exactly the way that you would like.

***Confusion is the opposite of an acknowledged and understood focus.***

***Understand that in all cases of the energy that is upon this Earth, your reaction to the environment and to the events of your life is determined by your consciousness level.***

If you are conscious of your purpose on Earth, you will move forward with a defined focus. If you do not recognize and acknowledge your purpose, you will be consistently fragmented in your relationships and in your soul evolution.

You will change jobs, change partners, change families, change friends, and on and on as you search for meaning and purpose within your life.

> **Your primary confusion exists because you do not know who you are, or what you want to do with your life.**

Your consciousness level and your reaction to self, other people, the world, and your life are relative to each other. Understand this because when you can see your life circumstances in view of this understanding, it will become easier to look at your life with a new perspective.

> **For you to understand that it is your perception of the world that creates your relationship with the world, allows you to see the continual opportunity for you to change.**

It is when you reach the point where you do not love yourself anymore that you create the opportunity to change. The opportunity to change can be created in the form of physical dis-ease, physical disease, mental illness, accidents, and death.

> **Anger, depression, a poor self-image, and fear will be the emotions of your world that will be prevalent in your feelings when you find yourself dissatisfied with life.**

Anger is an element of fear. There are basically only two emotions that exist within your emotional energy. They are love and fear. All other feelings and emotions are elements of these two.

When you are in the energy of fear, anger, hatred, and hostility of others, you have created for yourself an energy of desperation. This energy of desperation is in reality an energy of confusion, because if you understood why you are here on Earth you would not be feeling desperate or fearful.

> **You are here to cleanse and heal the Earth and yourself, not to create confusion and desperation.**

*When you become "stuck" in any activity, you experience frustration and depression.*

This confusion, frustration, and depression that you experience in other aspects of your life, is symbolic of the confusion, frustration, and depression that is going on within you as your ego and spirit experience their tug-of-war.

On an internal basis you are clearly aware that you are "stuck" within the physical focus of the cycle of development on Earth. On an external basis you find yourself stuck in the dramas of your life.

At the present time you do not understand how to remove yourself from this captive position. Your belief system does not allow you to envision your options other than those created by your intellect. If you recognize that you have options or alternative choices, you will be challenged to choose between your options and your visions of the physical world.

*Your belief system creates the valuative process as judgment, the good or bad, right or wrong perspective. The lesson for you is balance. You DO NOT give up your physical world. You integrate all facets of self within your physical world.*

It is consistent with your belief system that each decision is an either/or choice. Your life is based on the judgment of right or wrong, good or bad, and on and on. You believe that the spirit and soul are trying to destroy or control the physical body, the intellect, and the ego. Indeed, the soul and spirit want only to help you balance and celebrate life. They are seeking balance in which they will be free to evolve and grow while in the physical energy of your body.

*The soul and spirit can only evolve and grow through the experiential learning of a physical embodiment. As humans you have chosen physical life as your path of learning.*

If you perceive yourself as a victim of circumstances, as being buffeted about in the world by whatever comes along in your life, you will indeed fear what is happening around you and to you. You will be threatened by any hint of change, any unknown concept, or any feelings that make you doubt your personal belief system. This physical ego focus is your security, your stability, and your survival within your physical world.

This is the focus of your ego to keep you from understanding more about yourself. If you understood that you could indeed be celebrating life with every breath that you breathe, you would give up the concept that the world is only physical. When you give up your belief that the world is only physical, you give up your fear of survival which is the life force of the ego.

If you can see yourself as creating your life, you can see that you have the opportunity to change your life to the creation that you choose. When you understand that you are responsible for your consciousness level, you understand that you can indeed create your world by the perception that you choose to view the world.

When we speak of creating your life, we must speak of accepting responsibility for who you are, where you are, how you think, and how you act. Responsibility is accepting the love, truth, and perfection that is inherent within you.

Accepting the responsibility for being love, means that you must be and act with love in all interactions of your life.

Accepting the responsibility for truth, means that you must BE truth by creating consistency of all your thoughts, words, and actions within your life.

Accepting the responsibility for perfection, means that you accept that you are perfect as you are and that you are capable of being all that you are. Accepting the responsibility of perfection is acknowledging the energy of faith within you.

In your culture it is your belief system that you can give away your responsibility. You believe that you can make the medical profession responsible for your health, the schools responsible for your education, the church responsible for your soul. This shifting of responsibility creates your belief within you that someone else is always responsible for you. You have been taught this belief system from the beginning of your life.

Many of you live your entire life and continue to blame your parents for who you are. You perceive them as responsible for your world because you fear accepting the responsibility within yourself.

You will blame the medical profession when they cannot restore your health because you cannot accept the responsibility for the disease that you have created within your physical body. You have a responsibility to restore and maintain your cellular function. If you fail in this responsibility, you create blame toward another rather than accepting personal responsibility.

*Many of the teachings within your world are beliefs of the past that do not serve you anymore. Your physical focus upon the intellect has allowed the intellect to create your future from your perception of the past.*

Your perception of the past was determined by your consciousness level at that moment in your time. As you expand, your perception will expand. You consistently restrict your understandings by your belief system. These belief restrictions make it more productive for you to create from the openness of your soul and spirit energy.

In the spirit world your concept of your past is viewed as an opposing belief system. Why would you choose to create your future from your past instead of creating your past from your future? Do you find your past so perfect that you feel it is worthy of repetition?

*Repetition is the highest order of learning on Earth.*

Belief systems are learned by repetition of past understandings. Belief systems serve only to restrict you in your growth because they prevent you from being open to the opportunity to change.

The creativity of the past is gone, and building upon the obsolete creates a circumstance for you of never being able to get beyond the past. Each and every thing that you create is obsolete because the natural movement of energy is moving faster than your intellect.

This basic intellectual focus of your world reveals an understanding of your world that limits your mind. When you focus upon the past to create your future, you define your concept of time as a limiting factor. You see your life as having a beginning, a middle, and an end. You view your world with the same intellectual understanding.

Because of this intellectual perspective of time, you study the end of other men's lives, which is the past, to predict your future. This perspective of repetition has been shared and taught throughout the history of Earth. There is wisdom in choosing only positive energy for repetition.

To help you with your understanding of the sharing of life we will give you the spiritual definition of time. All of time is happening now. NOW IS. All that you have ever been or will ever be you are at this very moment. If you focus upon the past, you become stuck in the energy of that moment.

*You base your intellectual concept of time on the finiteness of life.*

Time was created by man, for man, to give him an organized structure and discipline to live within. It gives him an intellectual measure or understanding of life. This understanding of the structure of life added purpose to the mind of man, since he could not understand death. Indeed, man accepted the concept of birth much more gracefully than he accepted the concept of death.

*Man has been taught that he is born, he lives for a period of time, and then he dies. Death becomes the end of life and the end of man. If man believes in the Book of God, he should understand that life is eternal. If life is eternal then there is no time. The spiritual definition of life is eternal energy. Being born is not the beginning of life, nor is death the end of life.*

There are millions of people in your world today that cannot accept the perspective of multiple lives as man. Those same people will tell you they believe in eternal life. Their conscious perception of life is that they really are sent into a physical life by God as punishment and when they are forgiven for the sin that precipitated the punishment, God will accept them back into "Heaven."

*Heaven and hell are physical concepts that you create within each lifetime by the way that you live your life.*

Now these people do not perceive life as a cheerful interlude if they see it as punishment, do they? In addition, this perspective of life gives the responsibility back to God to "make them perfect." Do they perceive Earth as being populated by sinners and outcasts?

Each and every soul and spirit within this Universal energy of Earth is responsible for self and the energy that exists within your world. You have the power of creation. This energy of the eternal spirit of you is love, truth, and perfection. This power of creation and this love, truth, and perfection that is you is your inherent birthright from your Creator.

> **Your creator has given you the energy, the wisdom, the power of creation, the love, the truth, and the perfection to be all that you can be. What you create with these blessed gifts is your responsibility.**

In the same way that you create children and they inherit traits from you, you have inherited traits from your Creator. In the physical sense, when you have children, they look like you, they have hair like you, they have eyes like you, and perhaps they have a body build like you. Internally they will have inherited a genetic system that is halfway like you and halfway like your partner in the creation.

Everything that is above within the Universe is repeated below upon the Earth and within man. All that is upon the Earth and all that is within man is the design of the Creator that is being duplicated.

> **God is eternal, man is eternal. God is spirit energy, man is spirit energy. There is no time within the Universe, there is no time on Earth. There is no judgment by God, there is no judgment by man. God has the power of creation, man has the power of creation. God is love, truth, and perfection; man is love, truth, and perfection. God is unconditional love, man is unconditional love.**

If you read these statements carefully you can see the differences that man has created between himself and God. If you recognize behavior within man that is different from the above statements, you can identify the lessons that man is here to learn. Learning these lessons is the healing and cleansing that man comes to Earth to accomplish.

If you find that you do not live in the image of God in all of the energies listed above, do not despair. You are not sinful, guilty, immoral, or being punished for not being all that you can be at this moment. You are here to cleanse and heal through the conscious learning of lessons.

> **You are all that you can be, but you do not now have a conscious acknowledgment, acceptance, or understanding of yourself. You do not respect and**

*value the wisdom and beauty within yourself. Your*
*focus is upon the physical you, physical posses-*
*sions, and physical relationships of your world.*

When you were created as a spirit you were given the power of creation. You were given the inherent emotion of love, the inherent understanding of truth, and you were created perfect. Do you see yourself as perfect? Do you see yourself with love?

*If you do not love yourself, then you do not have*
*an aware consciousness of the love, truth, and per-*
*fection that is within you.*

You do not perceive yourself as the perfection that you are. When you do not perceive yourself with this conscious understanding of perfection you will live in the emotion of fear. The spirit of you that God created in his image, is the love, truth, and perfection of you. These are inherited traits and do not need to be learned. They only need to be remembered.

How do you release your feelings of fear, your feelings of unworthiness?

You release your feelings of the external physical world by understanding who you are internally. By understanding who you are externally and who you are internally you will create an image of self that is integrated of body, mind, and spirit.

You perceive yourself in relationship to the external part of you which is the physical body, the intellect, and the ego. You see this external physical body as dependent upon the circumstances of the physical world around you.

It is true that the physical body is dependent upon the physical world for its physical support from nature. This "needed" support is limited to air, water, and fresh natural foods. This natural support provides the electromagnetic energy units that your physical body requires to restore and maintain normal cellular function. All other physical "needs" are created for comfort of lifestyle.

You tend to forget that you are more than just an external physical being. The soul of you is infinite, and the spirit of you is enfinite. When you acknowledge that there is more to you than just a physical body that functions externally within the physical world, you will be balancing yourself. You will be creating a new life for yourself on Earth.

You will be saying, "I am physical, but I am also a creation of the experiential learning of the soul within me. I have been through this Universal system for thousands and thousands of lifetimes and I have taken unto myself multiple lessons and images of lessons. I have learned through experiencing that I have all of the knowledge that is available within the Universe. I have within my soul unlimited knowledge. I am also a spirit energy that was created by God. In that spirit energy I am love, truth, and perfection. I have the power of creation that has been given to me as an inherent birthright."

When you repeat these truths to yourself or out loud you will be speaking spiritual truth and it will add to the spiritual energy of the Universe.

When you can perceive yourself as more than a finite physical body, you will begin to understand the value that is within you. You will lose your sense of unworthiness. You will create relationships that are worthy of you. You will begin to look at those relationships in terms of lessons of learning experiences. You will not feel depressed and unworthy if you do not have a physical relationship to support you.

> *In reality, everything that you are, you are within. When you understand yourself, you will understand the Universe. When you love yourself, you will love your neighbor as yourself, and you will love your Creator because within the Creator is the image of you.*

This is an important message for you because you see yourself as a victim of relationships, as a victim of events, as a victim of circumstances. None of this is true. If you wish to read more on the victim consciousness it can be found in our text entitled, Bridges of Consciousness: Self Discovery in the New Age.

You have created your life in the exact design that will allow you to learn the lessons that you have come here to learn. It is your design and you should love it. You first need to understand that you are more than you can see on the surface. You are not blown back and forth by the winds of events. You are an integrated being. You are body, mind, and spirit.

> *If you cannot accept the understanding of the inner you intellectually, you will continue to be integrated. Denial does not change what IS. Denial*

*only restricts your using your full capabilities
within your physical life.*

When we speak of the "mind" we are speaking of the rational mind, the subconscious, the unlimited knowledge of the soul within. When we speak of the "body" we speak of the physical self, the intellect, and the ego. When we speak of the "spirit" we are speaking of the intuitive self, the unconscious self.

It is your spirit self that is the perfect image of the Creator. Your spirit energy is your power of creation that dwells eternally within you as the love, truth, and perfection of you.

*It is by virtue of the spirit energy, the Godself,
the inherited traits of God, that all of man is created equal.*

All of man, because of his love, truth, and perfection, has the power of creation. God is not responsible for saving your soul. You are responsible for what happens to you. You have designed this power of responsibility into your life.

The schools in your world are there to facilitate education but you are responsible for what you learn from the opportunity for education.

The medical world is not responsible for your health and your body. You are responsible. You cannot abuse your body and expect someone else to make it as good as new by "fixing" it. You have the responsibility and the opportunity to maintain it yourself.

To change yourself and to change the events of your life, you need to be consciously aware of how you are perceiving and creating those events. As you raise your awareness you will be able to see the opportunities that you create for change.

*When you get sick, when you give yourself dis-
ease, you are trying to capture your attention. How
else would you capture your attention except by
creating events in your life in which you are un-
comfortable. You force yourself to stop, to look,
and to listen. Once the disease is created, you have
the opportunity to heal yourself.*

You can heal yourself by changing your lifestyle and healing the disease or you can choose the healing of death. For the spirit within, physical death is a healing. Death frees the spirit to design a new life plan. Death, when chosen, is always the choice of the spirit. Death is not an accident although it may be created as an accident within your physical world.

> *It is at the crisis moments of your life that you suddenly remember that you do indeed have a soul and a spirit. You create events that cause discomfort so that you will open up your mind to alternatives. When you see who you truly are, you can perceive that all of life is choice.*

When you were given the power of creation by your Creator, you were also given free choice, free will, and free intention. This is the definition of the power of creation. Each and every circumstance of your life has been created by you, but this creation was not always a conscious creation. The major part of creation occurs for you within the physical world on an unconscious and subconscious level.

> *You have created your world from a soul and spirit level of creation. When you can raise your aware consciousness within the physical world and understand this awareness on an intellectual level, you have created the opportunity to change.*

Do you see the cyclic energy within your life? This energy of life is the energy that you share with all of life that is around you. It is a challenge for you to understand that each and every instant of your life you have created. In addition, each and every energy within your life impacts on the energy of multiple other souls and spirits.

If you wake up in the morning mad at yourself, your energy will be transmitted to every other individual that you come in contact with for that entire day. Even the postman will feel your energy subconsciously when he comes to your home. Do you see how you share your life even when you are unconscious that you are sharing?

Your active creations are limited to your personal energy field except for the passive influence that you create within other energies. If an event occurs to someone else in your life, you did not create the event. The other soul and spirit created the event although on a soul and spirit level you were aware of the creation and agreed to support that spirit in its choice.

You are responsible for making yourself sad, sick, fearful, depressed, angry, mean, and on and on. You create your energy secondary to your perception of yourself. Your negative or positive energy does influence the choice of other spirit energies around you.

If you are consistently a poor marriage partner, the energy of you may convince your spouse to live elsewhere rather than continue to expose his/herself to you. You did not create his/her action of leaving, but you had an influence on the choice that was made.

The soul and spirit of you will actively create disease within your body to capture your attention. It is the soul and spirit within you that is out there promoting itself to create an internal balance. It will attract your attention to encourage you to acknowledge the soul and spirit with equal time.

You do know how the politicians always ask for equal time to be heard? If you focus only upon the physical part of you, the soul and spirit within you will be capable of being a politician.

When you become too attached to the physical world, too comfortable in your intellectual endeavors, and your ego beliefs, dramas will suddenly happen. This creates an opportunity for you to share your life on a different basis. It changes your perspective of life and it changes your consciousness level.

You turn on your television and you will be told that you are to follow certain instructions in life. Your body is to be a certain shape; your house is to be in a certain neighborhood; your car is supposed to be a certain make; you are to eat specific foods; even what you watch on the television is suggested.

This is the creation of multiple belief systems that are focused within the external world. These beliefs are accepted by you as absolute truths because of the primary belief in the concept of television.

The repetitious exposures of television and radio become the beliefs of your physical life that you focus upon. Your television, radio, and paper media have a profound impact of learning on your culture that carries with it an expansive responsibility to help change the focus of humanity from negative energy to positive energy.

The soul and spirit within you is going to rise up and demand equal time to capture your attention. It wants you to acknowledge this love, truth, and perfection as well as this infinite knowledge of the Universe and the Earth that dwells within you. The inner and higher you is being ignored. It wants you to balance yourself as an energy. You cannot be balanced if you are focused exclusively upon one aspect of the self.

Do you think that an airplane would land safely on a runway if it had only one tire inflated? When you focus only upon your physical self you have released the energy from the soul and spirit. You have deflated two tires on your airplane.

When you try to come in for a landing, when you try to understand on a conscious level who you are, you will see yourself only in terms of the physical you. When you are aware of only the physical you, you may not like who you are. This creates the image of unworthiness within you.

> ***Your sense of unworthiness creates the energy of your life that you share with other people.***

It is during these moments in your life that you will begin to feel the ego/spirit tug-of-war. You will know that something does not feel right, but you will be challenged to identify what it is. You will be conscious of a restlessness, anxiety, and perhaps an overwhelming fear and depression.

You may consider suicide. You may create the belief that you are unworthy. You may believe that you are not as important as someone else. You may feel unworthy, hopeless, despondent, and unfulfilled in life. You may become obsessive in your behavior, and/or develop a dependence on alcohol, drugs, sex, relationships, and unworthy thoughts. You are indulging in self-focused negative energy to structure your life.

These negative energies of depression, anger, fear, or hostility are your life energy that you are sending to all of your friends. Subconsciously and unconsciously your friends will understand these energies and many of them will not want to be with you.

There is an energy path that connects you with the spirits and souls within this world that are here to support you. Friends that do call you during these times are your primary support system. Their energy is strong enough not to be affected by yours. The energy that you send out over your own energy waves is created by you within your mind.

> ***When you create a negative energy force field around you, that energy reaches out to other***

*people and to the Universe. The energy which you create impacts the entire world around you.*

Indeed, it can also affect physical objects around you. This energy effect is responsible for the physical problems that you may have on the highways with your car, accidents, problems within your home, and physical problems with your body.

Several years ago when my conduit became aware of how she affected physical objects she found that when she focused her energy she could reverse the damage. To do this your energy has to be strongly focused. When she is super-charged with energy, she also finds that her light bulbs will burn out.

Recently when she was saddened by a family event, she got in her car and found that none of the gauges worked. She drove for 30 minutes to her destination and the car drove perfectly. When she arrived she asked a friend to examine her car. The car did not malfunction for the friend. He took the car to a mechanic and nothing was found. When my conduit got back in the car 24 hours later everything worked perfectly.

The personal event within her life had drained her energy supply so expansively that she pulled energy from the car to be able to drive. The car transferred the energy it didn't need to operate perfectly and sent the energy into my conduit's body. In life you develop strong energy fields with physical objects and with nature that will help you in the identical way that you help them. This is the energy exchange and support that exists within your Universe.

Have you ever had an experience of depression in your life and found that if you went out into your yard and worked with the plants and trees, you suddenly felt joyful and totally restored? These energy connections that you love and care for, care for you in return.

Air, water, and fresh foods all have an electromagnetic energy that is duplicated in the frequency of your cells. These elements are needed by man to continually restore the cells within the body. This energy connection is consistent and will affect the lifespan of your body.

If you deprive your electrical appliances of their energy source they will not function. If you deprive your body of its energy source, it will cease to function.

The effect of your energy upon you, your friends, and your surroundings is how you create your life. It is your life. As you develop an understanding of your life and your relationship to the Universe you will be able to grasp the expansive influence that you have upon the world.

You create fear by the perception of being only physical. You feel you are unimportant to the Universe because you do not understand the intricate web of energy that connects you with the Universe. On a conscious basis you may never fully understand this web of energy. This is the force of the soul and spirit and it cannot be understood intellectually because you do not have the basis of understanding at this time.

Indeed, the magnitude of the energy forces within you and within the world are incomprehensible by the intellect. You share these energy forces in the physical body in the same way that you share them in the soul and spirit sense. Being unconscious of the sharing of your life, does not mean that you are not constantly sharing it.

If you believe only in the facts of the intellect, you are severely limiting your own creativity. Your life will continue to focus on a restructuring of your understood facts of the "past." Because you have an intellectual understanding that the physical body is finite, the intellect itself will be confused by the purpose of such a magnificent structure as the body in your limited understanding of physical life.

Your intellect is designed as the functional intelligence for the soul and spirit energy. The soul and spirit energy does not create physical action in your terms. They must have a physical connection of energy that will be able to take their information and activate it in the physical world. The spirit energy is the inspiration within the life of man. The soul energy is the motivation to place the idea into action. The intellect creates the action within the physical world.

Inspiring ideas are sent to all of you by the millions. If you ignore the motivation of the soul energy which has the knowledge to carry out the inspiration, the intellect will not develop the idea in physical form. Developing the idea within the physical world requires accepting the energy of the soul and spirit, and then devoting many hours of consistent physical intellect and physical work to make it a reality of your world.

When you think of soul and spirit energy, you think in terms of miracles. You will never be able to turn water into wine until you understand all that you are. The first step in this understanding is to understand you, your life, and your relationship to the Earth and the Universe. The second step is to accept and acknowledge the responsibility that you have for that creation.

***There is no quick fix or instant gratification that can be given to you as a miracle. The miracle is for you to "want" to understand.***

When you see the miracle of self as having a beginning, and an end, you limit your enthusiasm for accomplishment within the physical world. An idea "pops" into your head and you think about it for a few days. You measure it against all of your other activities. Suddenly it no longer seems important. This idea may have been excellent. But you made the choice not to integrate the inspiration with motivation and creation.

Twenty years later you find your idea being discussed on the television. You listen in total amazement and say, "That is my idea. I could have done that!" The difference is that you did not follow through with your inspiration. The way that energy works is by an interweaving, intermingling, and crisscrossing of inseparable forces. When the inspiration occurred to you, you had an opportunity to develop it because you were in the energy vortex that supported that creation. You did not commit your physical time and intellect to the development of the idea.

Thousands of people will have the same opportunity to access specific energy at one time. The inspiration and the motivation are available. Where you lose the opportunity is in the commitment of physical time, physical intellect, and soul motivation to your own growth. You do not accept your followthrough because you do not understand how your life works. You do not use the integration of your energies to complete the project.

The understanding that your life is going to end, that your biological clock is ticking, strikes fear within you and affects your entire life by the effect upon your body and mind. It creates within your understanding, limits of capability.

You set different priorities of the physical world based upon the limits that are real for you. You have a list of physical activities that are important to you and you focus upon these to the exclusion of the internal inspiration and motivation. Your understanding of "time" creates your limitations.

Indeed, you think your "imagination" is out of control. Your imagination is a spirit and soul "image" of what you can do. You see a reflection of the creation within the soul and spirit energy.

***You must have faith that you can do whatever you want to do, if you want to do it badly enough.***

Your intellect/ego energy may clearly tell you that your idea is impossible. Remember the ego has its own agenda for your life and its control.

When you chose the physical body, you slowed down your energy to create physical matter. When you decide to leave the physical world, you will speed up your internal energy and the body will be discarded. You will at this point or some point soon thereafter enter into another physical body and continue with your learning.

***Death does not create perfection. You create perfection as you live within the physical world.***
***When you become perfect you will be unable to stay within the Earth plane for long periods of time.***

The more perfect you become the faster you may choose to learn your lessons and return to the spirit world. When you reach the point of ultimate perfection and enlightenment, you can choose to join your Creator in spirit energy. You can also choose to continue working within the realm of Earth.

***Death of the physical body does not mean that you are joining your Creator. It means that you have made a choice of the soul and spirit within to leave that body, to design a new life and to start again.***

The challenge that you create in changing your present lifespan is that you must once again start in the cycle of development and repeat the process all over again. You can repeat thousands of lifetimes before you gain a consciousness level that will allow you to maintain your soul and spirit memory in physical life. It is only when you change your conscious awareness that your soul evolves.

If all of your work is done on a subconscious and an unconscious basis, you do not create balance. If all of your work is done on a physical and intellectual basis, you do not create balance. Balance for you is to use all facets of self in an integrated and inseparable energy.

**The lesson for man is to balance himself within the physical realm with his soul, spirit, and physical energy.**

In this balanced state you can mirror the image of unconditional love. In addition you will be living with total awareness within your physical world. You will be aware of yourself in the physical state, the state of soul memory, the state of unlimited knowledge, and in the state of love, truth, and perfection. You will fully understand on a conscious physical level your power of creation.

There will be no doubts within your mind and there will be no desperation or confusion. When you understand life on this consciousness level, you accept your creation of reality. You accept on faith what escapes you intellectually.

You understand free choice. You understand change. You accept your lessons without blaming other people. You evaluate your lesson and understand what the event means for you. You accept, acknowledge, and appreciate what you have learned. You have no judgment, no fear, and no defenses. You are open to learn and to BE within your physical world.

How do you reach the state of valuing who you are as an integrated Being?

You learn to understand by working with that intention. In the same way that you enroll in a college and take numerous courses to learn a specific subject, you must be committed to working on yourself to open up the conscious memory, and the conscious understanding of the soul and spirit within.

This decision requires a commitment to openness and searching. You must not fear looking within and without at yourself. You must look at yourself with total love, total openness, total joy, and total peace. You must accept who you are at this moment, and accept the opportunity to change.

It is your belief system that keeps you from seeing yourself. Therefore, you must look carefully at your belief system. Know that you have free choice to change it. When you believe that you "have to have," that you "need," your "concept of need" is a belief.

Your desire is a craving of the ego. These are illusions within your physical world. They are illusions that control and structure your world and your individual life by the energy they create within you. Desire is always focused upon a physical "concept of need." Fulfillment of your desires may enhance your life or they may hinder your well-being but they always feed the ego within.

Have you ever heard a small child say "I desire a new doll?" or "I need a new doll?" A child does not relate from the ego. Because of this lack of ego function a child will say, "I want a new doll." For a child "want" is understood as play, enjoyment, and fun. It is not misconstrued within the mind as need.

In reality, you need nothing except the air, water, and the proper foods to restore your cellular function of the physical body. All else is secondary gain in life, it is secondary to functioning as a human being. If you destroy your body, you interfere with the creation of your physical life.

You need only to maintain your physical body. After that you need understanding, acknowledgment, and acceptance of who YOU are. You do not need to sleep eight hours a day, to eat three meals a day, to have a lover constantly in your life, and you do not need to believe most of your beliefs.

Beliefs, when they are not satisfied to your understanding, create your "concept of need." Unsatisfied beliefs give you the feeling of losing control over your world. Loss of control takes away your sense of worthiness, your sense of power, and your feeling of accomplishment within your life and your world. You are perfect as spirit energy.

You can have aspirations and inspirations. You can want accomplishments or comforts. That is choice and you have free choice. It is by your choice that you create the world around you. You create working, you create loving, you create education, and you create your spirituality. It is by your thoughts, your words, your actions, and your intentions that you create.

If there is consistency between your thoughts, words, and actions, you create truth. If there is no consistency between what you say and what you do, you are creating chaos and confusion within your life. You are sending a message to yourself that you do not know what you want.

*The energy of inconsistency creates massive energy changes within you and within the world*

**around you. It will "short circuit" you in life and in your relationships.**

How do you look at your belief system realistically and acknowledge what you want and not what you think you need? You do this by looking within. You open up the energies of your soul and spirit. You begin your creation of integration.

With integration of your soul, spirit, intellect, and physical energies, your perception of self, of life, and of the world changes. You see with a new clarity and a new focus. You release attachments. You develop faith. You expand who you are into a glorious Being.

**Everything that you are, you are within.**

This is manifested within your physical world by the reality that you take nothing with you when you leave, not even the physical body. How many people do you know who have taken along their bank account when they die? Money is an illusion in the spiritual world. Money is a tool within the physical world.

Your culture is built around money which creates a physical "need" for man to work. But if you perceive your work with joy rather than a need to make money, it will reap you greater rewards. The need to work creates the interaction with people which supports and inspires your energy forces.

Providing yourself with physical comforts gives you a peaceful environment in which you can honor self and celebrate self. It allows you to share energies and enjoy the strength from those energies. Working is a way of giving and receiving in life.

Interaction with all people is a way of giving and receiving in life. Without the interaction of relationships, you limit your energy field and your energy gain. When you limit your energy exchange, you limit yourself.

If you find no joy in your work, change your work. You have created for yourself the opportunity of crisis if you "hate" what you do. Life is your creation. When you accept the joy and capabilities within, you will have no fear of change.

You must look within and listen to the silence to give the soul and spirit an opportunity to balance the anxieties of your physical world.

**The lesson of balance is a lesson of extreme importance within your world because it is an**

*acknowledgement that you are more than you
perceive as physical. The lesson of balance is an
acknowledgment of your own eternality.*

There is hope, joy, and peace in knowing that you are eternal.
When you can view your life as only a single image of the total
design, you will have no fear of death. You will be joyful with
the perspective of starting something new. You will see each day
as an opportunity to be all that you can be in love, truth, and
perfection. You will BE love.

*This positive energy of love will become your
life and it will have a direct influence upon your
world and the world of those around you. Indeed,
your love will then join with the Universal energy
of love to create an expanded Universe.*

As you begin looking within yourself at the soul and spirit
energy, you will give it the opportunity to be. You will find
yourself consciously perceiving the world differently. As you
perceive the world differently your words will change, your
actions will change, your intentions will change, your understandings will change, and your emotions will change from
confusion to a quiet peace and joy.

Inner work can be approached by looking at each situation
in your life and its effect upon you. View these events with love,
not with blame. Allow your vision to search for what you learned.
When you find the lesson accept it with joy. Always within the
event you will find the message.

You will find the lessons of patience, love, balance, truth,
perfection, faith, support, eternal life, and on and on. These
lessons will be shown to you in multiple images. When you have
experienced all of these images and learned, you will begin to
see with total clarity who you really are in the sense of an
integrated Being.

*When man comes to Earth with lessons designed
into this Earth activity, he does not consciously understand his lessons when they first appear.*

Lessons appear in the everyday events of life and will be
shown to you in how you perceive your life. All of life is
determined by the consciousness level within. You perceive life
relative to the beliefs, the understandings, and the experiences
that you have. All of your experiential energies merge into one

and they become an energy of conscious awareness within your intellectual mind.

*This energy of conscious awareness allows you to perceive from your understanding of self, other people, and the world around you. As your level of consciousness changes, your level of understanding and perceiving life changes.*

IT IS THE BELIEF SYSTEM OF MAN THAT ACTS AS AN OBSTRUCTIVE FORCE TO NEW THOUGHTS, NEW IDEAS, AND NEW UNDERSTANDINGS.

*Because you have these external obstructive forces to the soul and spirit energy, you will manifest them within the physical world as denial.*

If you can open your mind and your heart to the energies around you, you will be able to raise your level of consciousness. Each and every experience, each and every contact, each and every thought, and each and every action that passes through the intellect affects the consciousness level within you. Within your world you have multiple consciousness levels.

*Your interactions in life and your relationships in life are the energy forces of experience that allow you to move from one consciousness level to the other.*

Consciousness levels are created by those individuals that focus upon that particular level of awareness. This consciousness level then becomes a Universal energy force that is available to all of man.

*When a consciousness level is understood by a majority of man, the energy force will reach a point of critical mass and will be accepted by all of man as a Universal understanding.*

As you change your level of consciousness and change your individual life, you will change the picture of Earth. You will change the energy that controls Earth. You will make an impact on yourself, on your surroundings, in your individual world, in your community, in your state, and in your country. Indeed, as your consciousness level becomes positive the energy of the Universal stream will become more expansive.

As your energy changes, the energy of the world will be changing by accumulating the energy that each and every individual is radiating. This is the way that you create your life, and your consciousness levels.

Do you understand that you are responsible for what you create? Do you understand the expansive impact that you have as an individual upon your world? If the effect that you have upon your world is not conscious within you, the effect continues on a subconscious and unconscious basis. The effect is then created without your conscious control.

*If you ever begin to feel unimportant within your world, remember the impact that you have by living. Then consciously control the energy of your life. You are sharing your energy with the Universe.*

Life is full of dramas, traumas, daily learning experiences, events, activities, work, love, and play. All of these experiences and events are necessary and they are all there to create the energy of your awareness.

We can use an example of a man being born upon a mountain top where he is totally isolated from the world. This man has a consciousness level of the Earth that far surpasses the man who lives in the city. He does not have a consciousness level of traffic problems, of scientific development, or of men walking on the moon. His consciousness level is limited to his understanding, his perception of his life and his world.

If you perceive your world to be only work and you cannot find the time to integrate that work with a little play and celebration with your friends, you limit your perspective, your understanding, and your consciousness level of life.

*You grow by the triggering of internal energy forces through external energy forces. The triggering of energy forces creates memory within your intellectual mind of your soul and spirit energy.*

In life, you have been taught that the intellect is supreme. This focus was developed during the millions of years that man was developing his body, his culture, his cities, his world, and his intellect.

Man focused upon the intellect to help him with his physical creations. His intellect was perceived as self. It was his second acknowledged tool for advancement. His first acknowledged tool was his physical body.

In the beginning man acknowledged his physical body as his one tool for advancement. But as he grew and expanded he realized that his logical mind could save him many hours of physical labor. Because of his change in consciousness he began to focus upon the intellect as his supreme tool in development.

With time man developed the computer from the intellect of his mind. His mind took facts that were understood about electrical energy and integrated that energy concept with traits of the mind such as memory. With his new consciousness level he created a machine that can work faster than he can work.

> *In developing a machine that can create faster than the human mind, man acknowledged that the intellect is not supreme AS IT IS USED.*

The machine was developed from an accumulation of past fact understood by the intellect. The inspiration and the motivation to develop the machine came from the spirit and soul within man.

Man has developed spaceships to travel to other planets within the Universe. Now he can study those planets with the use of the computers and other machines which he has developed. Within the intellectual ability to create these machines has been intellect, inspiration, and motivation.

> *Each time that man raises his consciousness level of how the Universe is organized and how it functions, he is looking beyond his own perspective.*

The time has come to focus not only upon the intellect but to allow expansion, to allow growth, and to allow the soul and spirit within to be heard. For those of you who are searching for this energy within yourself, you are reaching out, you are seeking, you are opening up, and you are inviting in this energy of you, of who you are.

When you can understand who you are, you will understand the Universe. When man focuses intellectually upon understanding the world before he understands himself, he will create dramas and traumas secondary to his intellectual focus.

*Physical life is the way that man has chosen to learn. Life is the stages of development being actualized. The Earth is your spaceship of physical creation. Earth will support you only when you support it physically, intellectually, and spiritually.*

My purpose in being here with you is always to help you to understand yourself. Understanding yourself is not closing the mind to all but the intellect, physical self, soul, or spirit and choosing to be one or the other. It is being all that you can be. It is being all inclusive. It is being integrated.

Why would you want to integrate yourself? What is your goal?

When you can understand all of the energy that you have lived within, all of the experiences, and all of the lessons that you have designed into your soul evolution, you will see your own power of creation.

When you understand yourself and understand your power of creation you will be all that you can be. This understanding will give you the opportunity to create joy and happiness within your life. You will give yourself the opportunity to live in the "Heaven on Earth." You will Be all that you can be. This is the goal of the soul and spirit when you seek integration.

When you focus internally into the energy of the soul, you will begin to find people, begin to find circumstances, and begin to find experiences that are suddenly very familiar to you. Because you see, all that you have ever been or will ever be, you are now.

Understanding the energy of who you have been, will help you to understand the energy of who you are now. The energy that you are at this moment is the energy that you have been from the moment of creation.

*The energy of you is part of the energy of all of man, part of the energy of Earth, part of the energy of God, and part of the energy of the Universe. In the sense of energy you are integrated. Integrating your physical understanding of your own energy will create for you a new consciousness level of self. YOUR CONSCIOUSNESS LEVEL IS YOUR RELATIONSHIP TO YOUR PHYSICAL LIFE.*

When you look at these energies of self, it is not important who you were in the concept of physical identity. It is only important to look at what you learned. To find yourself rich and famous has no bearing on who you are today except in the energy of the experience of learning. It is this experiential learning that allows the soul to move forward, to grow, and to expand.

Focusing on identity within your past would capture you within the same identity consciousness that you focus upon within your world today. The identity consciousness is an ego consciousness.

**All ego energy will hold you captive within the physical consciousness level of energy.**

When you begin to expand into your soul and spirit energy, you will meet other people that you suddenly feel a kinship with. Their energy will be recognized by you. You will feel love. You will feel comfortable. You will feel as though you have come in contact with a family member.

You may go to another country and walk down a street and feel that you have been there before. In your world this is called deja vu.

In soul and spirit energy this is called remembering. You are remembering, you are recognizing, and you are awakening to the energy of self. As this energy of self merges into the physical energy that you are today, you expand. You reach a different consciousness level in your physical life. You are bigger than you were yesterday because you have accepted and acknowledged an energy within.

When you can access the spirit energy within, you will access the inherited energy of God. You will BE love, truth, and perfection. You will merge this love, truth, and perfection into your soul energy and into your physical energy of self.

**The resistance to the God energy in your physical world is found in the ego judgment of man.**

When you can integrate your spirit energy, you can heal yourself. You can at this moment change your level of awareness. You can change your level of consciousness. You can become more than you have previously viewed yourself to be.

You will change because your consciousness level has changed. You will lose your attachment to the physical focus of your energies such as dis-ease and disease. These are conditions of the physical world that hold you captive within the physical consciousness of self.

You expand, you grow, and you become balanced with the integration of your soul and spirit energy. You develop a conscious physical awareness of all that you are internally and externally. This removes only the negative energy from the physical self and replaces that negative energy with love, truth, and perfection. You live your life from a different consciousness perspective and you interact in all of your relationships with a new understanding and love.

Why would you want to focus on love, truth, and perfection as a human value in your world?

It has become apparent in your world that you need to access the spirit and soul within in order to bring some control into your physical dramas and traumas. These events occur within your individual lives, your communities, your world, and upon the Earth, secondary to the physical energy that you radiate.

There will always be human dramas and traumas within your world until you expand beyond your need for this energy. When your focus can be shifted to support the energies of your physical body, instead of fragmenting the energies of your physical body, you will learn an image of the lesson of balance within the preservation of life.

> *The lesson of balance allows you to take the energy of your power of creation, that was given to you when you were created as a spirit, and use it effectively within yourself in the physical world.*

The effective use of your positive electromagnetic spirit energy within the physical world teaches you the practical application of these words. You use your perspective of energy in other aspects of your life. Your internal energy can also be used to preserve and heal your life.

The interference of your version of electricity will affect the electromagnetic energy force fields of the body. These force fields function from a different Universal principle that makes your electrical energy negative in relationship to your spirit and soul energy. But your intellect accepts what it can understand in physical action more quickly than it accepts new concepts, and new ideas that do not support your physical perspectives.

***You can heal your physical body of all disease
and traumas that you create. Your world of science
focuses upon healing from the intellectual perspective of past facts as they are JUDGED.***

Changing the perspective of the scientific world toward the
preservation of life will need to be the motivation and the
inspiration of the spirit world. Your inspiration and motivation
will integrate with the physical and intellectual ability of your
world to create ways of preservation.

Because of the physical potential in your world for massive
burns from your nuclear components, this should be the focus
for life preservation for you at this time. In the understanding of
allowing new tissue to grow, removing the possibility of infec-
tion, and eliminating pain as you balance the energies of the body,
you will learn to treat multiple traumas.

***You can be more than you are scientifically and
humanistically in your world. Indeed, this new intellectual understanding will bring to your life an
expanded awareness in balancing your physical
energies. It will be a balance that will sustain you
and will protect you. It will create for your world
of science a new perspective of healing that will
revolutionize medicine.***

The fear of the unknown should not be a resistance in
changing healing perspectives. The facts of your scientific world
do not support advancement in the cures of disease and trauma
as much as they support maintenance of physical life.

Maintenance of life is viewed as a necessary perspective by
your world. Death should be viewed as the choice and opportunity of the spirit and soul. When the spirit and soul choose death,
nothing will interfere with this choice on a physical level.

Healing and support of the physical body are ways of
learning the lessons of balance within the physical world. You
must learn to balance yourself within the physical world before
you can be balanced as an integrated Being.

If you focus solely upon the intellectual, you will find
yourself judging the entire world through your intellectual perspective. Your life will be dependent upon the facts that you have
gathered and the beliefs that you hold as truth. These beliefs are
the beliefs that focus you into your ego energy.

*Beliefs originate as judged concepts or perspectives of intellectual facts which will be based upon what has been observed in the past, not what is.*

When you attach yourself to what you believe is fact, it becomes an ego belief. Once something IS it remains as energy but changes within physical reality because energy by its very nature changes. Because of this Universal Law, a fact is, but it is not. It is separate as an energy, but it becomes one with energy. As energy, it is changing.

*The ego of man will hold the energy of his ego belief as a captive fact, not open to change.*

When you live your life with an intellectual focus and refuse integration, you limit your experience and your level of conscious awareness. You erect your own barriers, your own walls that you must overcome to change and to grow.

When you can stay totally open, you can gather to yourself all understandings. From these images you can make a choice of free will. Choice and free will are elements of the power of creation.

*In the energy of personal creation is the free will and intention of man. Free will gives man free choice. This is an energy that was given to man by his Creator.*

Are you able to see the integration, the interweaving, the intermingling of all of these energies that are around you? Can you see within yourself how you move within this intricate web of energy? Do you see how you choose those energies that will help you? Do you see how you walk away from the energies that will restrict you? Or do you find yourself attached to beliefs and people whether or not you are happy, inspired, motivated, and creative within your environment?

*It is your choice to be where you are and you will make your conscious choice in relationship to your own energy.*

Free choice is your path in determining your life. When you understand that you create your life from free choice, you will create with more love, more truth, and more perfection within your physical world. You are at that moment consciously using the energy of the spirit self.

For you to understand the difference between intellect, intelligence, the rational mind, and the intuitive mind, you must understand that you are more than physical. You must be willing to welcome the soul and spirit energy into your life as equally balanced participants. When you create this balance in life, your life will be beautiful, peaceful, and creative.

*Always in life man will be faced with the dramas and the traumas of everyday existence. Each and every drama of life is the choice of the spirit within. It is part of the life design.*

There are no accidents within the Universe. Events may appear to you to be accidents, but they are not. They are part of a design that you have chosen. The vibrations of the energy will be relative to the choice as they flow out into the Universe.

*If you want to affect people who are far removed from you, you are going to choose within your life a drama that will seize your attention and the attention of other people.*

You can compare a life event to taking a pebble and dropping it into the water. If you drop a small pebble into a still pond you will produce vibrations and these vibrations will move peacefully and gently out into the water.

If you take a big rock and you drop it into the pond you can see those vibrations change. The force of the rock will create waves that swell up and die down only to swell again with more force as they create their own energy.

You will choose your dramas in life according to how many people you want to affect. You will get your own attention by the weight of the drama. The expansiveness of the drama that you choose will create your relationship to your life.

Dramas are always collective choices. The energy of the individuals will be as both passive and active participants. If you are the one who is dropping the rock you are the active participant. If you are struck by the rock as the water is, you are an active participant. If you are the one that is affected by the waves you are the passive participant.

You have chosen to be a participant because by your involvement, you have the opportunity to change your consciousness level in life by the precipitating energy of the active participants.

All of life is created by the interaction of relationships. Therefore, there can be multiple active participants and multiple passive participants, depending upon the nature of the event.

If there is an airplane accident and 286 people are instantly killed, you will have 286 active participants. If there are people that are killed in the crash on the ground, they are active participants. The passive participants will include all of the people that are related to those that are killed. They will experience the strongest vibration and, therefore, are in varying levels of active and passive participation.

The levels of vibrations will then spread out to all passive participants who felt an effect from the energy of the event and the deaths. This will include those who read of the incident, saw it on television, listened to an account being reported on the radio, or heard the story through a friend. Others may not know of the event and will have no effect at all from the energy created.

Do you see the effect and how the energy vibrations will change from a dramatic swelling to a smooth surface?

Dramas are always opportunities to change from one level of conscious awareness to another. You change from one level of consciousness to another by an increased awareness of events and people, an openness to emotion and feeling, and by the exposure to new experiences.

As the waves rise and fall from the event, challenges to change will be created for many people. The change will be relative to the force of the vibration and the openness of the individual to the energy vibration. If you are exposed to an energy vibration and you refuse to respond to the energy because of your belief system, you will be denying the opportunity to change and grow.

When resistance and denial occurs, you will create the opportunity to be involved in more expansive events until you capture your attention. Have you ever heard someone relate a sequence of dramatic events that occurred within his life in a string effect? This person is trying to get his attention to raise his level of consciousness.

Spirits will choose to enter into the physical realm with the express purpose of creating change. Change must be created in numerous ways for the intention to be fully understood within the physical world. In your physical perspective the spirit activity may be viewed as dramatic or traumatic.

It is only the intensity of the vibrations that you are feeling that will create the desired effect. Seizing the attention of the physical world creates drama that is not understood in your world. The physical reason for the drama will not be understood by the consciousness of man. On a spirit level you will understand.

In life the physical body is finite. It has a beginning and it has an end. When you are born you are moving towards physical death. When you die, it will be your free choice. Your choice will be designed into your relationship to your life. In the physical perspective death will not be accepted as choice until you are open to the spirit understanding within.

Your choice of lessons can be viewed in how you treat your body, the activities that you choose to be involved in, and your concept of life and living.

*You will always BE, live, speak, and act relative to your belief system which is your consciousness level within the physical world.*

If you are gentle and loving; if you eat the right foods; if you take as much stress off your body as possible; if you avoid addictions; and seek peace and calm, you are being nice to the physical you. How you treat yourself will be relative to how you treat other people. You are the outside image of the inside energy of you. The energy within creates the energy without.

Taking care of the physical body is the same as taking care of your house. If your roof begins to leak you buy new shingles. If your plumbing breaks, you must have it fixed. The body is your physical house in this life.

You design the physical body as finite because you know as a spirit there will come a time when you need to leave the physical body to go on to your next lesson. When you decide to end your physical embodiment you may create disease, you may simply make a choice to sit down and die, or you may choose to be in an accident. The choice is yours.

*Physical life is the assimilation of the physical world that is used by you as a spirit to evolve.*

*In life you are responsible for what you create. Life is the design of the physical energy of you, the use of integrated energy by you, and the vibrations*

*from you that reach out into all levels of conscious-*
*ness.*

The energy of the soul and the energy of the spirit are eternal. What you are today in physical form you will change to soul energy in spirit form when you leave this life. All of the experiential learning will merge into the love, truth, and perfection of the spirit energy of you.

*All energy of your soul and spirit will be*
*cleansed and healed by your Earth experience.*

You are constantly in the process of evolving your soul and your spirit energy with the purpose of reaching a state of perfection. What is perfection for the spirit? The spirit is focused toward the energy of unconditional love. This was the energy of Jesus of Nazareth at His Crucifixion. You are following in the path of the Christ Consciousness.

*The energy of unconditional love is the opposite*
*of judgment within the physical world. When you*
*judge, you do not love. When you judge others, you*
*are in reality judging yourself. You are bringing*
*your own belief system to the surface of your con-*
*sciousness which will give you the opportunity to*
*change it.*

The energy of your judgment does not affect the other participant. Its effect remains within your mind for you to examine and perceive. When you love others unconditionally you accept, acknowledge, respect, and value them for who they are. Judgment is denial of who they are because they do not fit the criteria of your beliefs. This is your challenge to change your beliefs.

*Judgment is the physical manifestation of deny-*
*ing self reflected in the energy of denying another.*

When you learn to integrate the soul and spirit energy into your physical life, you will begin to balance the ego self which removes the "ego need" to judge. As you learn not to judge yourself and others, you will free yourself of the "ego response" of fear, guilt, sin, anger, and hate. You will become love. As you remove fear and all elements of fear, you will remove denial, resistance, and restrictiveness from your life.

As you live love, you will be reaching a state of perfection in Being unconditional love. You will become consciously aware of how the energy of life develops in circle after circle of vibrational energy that is interwoven, intermingled, and inseparable from each other. You will find yourself at peace with all of the other circles of energy that are also spirits within the world.

You will accept your connections to all energy and you will see with clarity the lesson the energy is teaching you. This is life as created by the Creator and you create life by duplicating the energy of the Creator.

*When God gave man the power of creation, He gave man the physical manifestation of creation by allowing him to create within his world, within his body, and within his mind.*

Your creation is all that you are, and you are all that you create. It is your creation that makes your life what it is today and everyday that you live. In your life you create the interaction of events with other people. Your world is totally your creative design of life and living.

When you understand this act of creation with a conscious awareness of the fact that you are the one that is doing the creating, you will raise your level of consciousness. Understanding will raise your level of consciousness and you will be in constant celebration of the energy of you. This will allow you happiness, peace, and joy at all times.

Understanding these lessons is the reason for you to continue working on multiple images in multiple embodiments. When you understand one lesson, you will move forward to the next lesson. The physical manifestation of this concept is duplicated within your school system.

If you need to learn physics in order to obtain a degree, do not expect the school to give you the degree if you fail the exam. You will be allowed and encouraged to take the course over and over and over again until you pass and are prepared to receive your degree. If you do not choose to repeat the course you can give up without learning the lesson.

When you give up without learning your lesson on the spiritual level, you will create disease within your physical body and you will create the opportunity to change your perspective of the lesson. In each and every instance you are the creator. If you continue to resist the lessons of life and learning, you may choose death.

*Not all death is chosen to resist lessons. It may be chosen to learn a lesson, to teach a lesson, or for a multitude of reasons.*

Death is not chosen consciously but it is chosen subconsciously by the soul within and unconsciously by the spirit within as a learning experience. Suicide is death by the physical consciousness which is an indication of the ego's struggle with the internal soul and spirit. Willing natural death with intention is an indication of the balance of the physical, intellectual, soul, and spirit self.

In life you work with the subconscious and the unconscious energies of the soul and spirit self and you tug away at the energy of the ego. The ego physical self believes life has to be one way. Your soul and spirit will refuse to give up and you should never think of giving up any part of self. You are seeking balance.

You are committed to expanding self. Being committed to working with the soul and spirit does not mean that you should "give up" the physical world either. Removing yourself from physical activity, physical responsibility, and physical interaction is an avoidance of the physical you.

It is considered necessary by some when they begin the spiritual path, to concentrate upon their spirit self and deny the physical world. This will create imbalance in the other direction, not balance. You are seeking an integrated balance of self which requires that you function as a spiritual person from the physical perspective.

If you are in an airplane coming in for a landing, it really does not matter which tire has been blown out. Any tire that is not fully inflated and capable of handling the physical balance of the plane will create disaster in the landing.

This balance for which you are searching will give you joy and peace. Joy and peace will change your perspective of your world and it will change how you interact within your world. You will begin to love the very concept of life because you will see the value of that life as you are living it. You will see the value of your soul evolving with each new experience.

This quiet place within is seeking "equal" attention with the physical world of self. To reach your inner and higher self you will need to balance your physical world with the inner world by focusing upon the inner self for a period of time each day. Removing yourself temporarily from the activities of the physical world will allow you to find a new world within yourself. You will want to focus internally on this world once or twice a day to be in total peace.

As you make the choice to consciously evolve your soul by reading, by listening to lectures, by thinking, by meditating, and by acting with a new sense of consciousness; you will strengthen that peaceful place within.

You will indeed notice the difference, if you allow yourself to slide back into a strictly physical focus. You will find yourself suffering from fatigue, anxiety, confusion, depression, anger, fear, and/or hostility.

> *As you move as a yoyo back and forth between the physical and the inner self, you will experience confusion of purpose. Denying first one facet of self and then the other facets of self is symbolic of the ego/spirit tug-of-war.*

You will become very conscious of the difference that integration makes. When you are moving forward in your soul evolution, it is perfectly normal to slide back a little at certain times in your life. You are creating for yourself an opportunity to see the difference.

You learn in life by experiencing, by viewing the opposites and if you never view the opposite, you will see from only one perspective. You will never develop a consciousness of the relativity that exists between balance and imbalance. This is experiencing the relationship of self to life.

> *Nothing that you experience is judged wrong in the spirit world. It is only your choice of lesson. It is your creation of Being. There is only the IS of the NOW.*

You choose your life experience. Your soul and spirit growth is relative to the relationship that you have with your life.

Right and wrong are judgments of the physical world. You will have to answer for your actions within the physical world if you break the laws of the physical world. Breaking laws within the physical world creates lessons to be learned within all facets of self.

***Breaking physical laws is the creation of new dramas and new experiences that are designed to grab your attention and raise your level of conscious awareness.***

We have given you a brief overview of the spiritual perspective of your relationship to your physical life. It is not complete as it has no end. Life is eternal.

The energy of you creates new events too quickly for you to comprehend. We have focused upon only one dimension of your Being.

It is our wish that this will help you better understand the relationships that you have with yourself and with other people within your physical world.

# Immediate Family
## Relationships

The immediate family of man is an integration of soul and spirit relationships that each of you choose as part of your learning experience within your world.

*The immediate family is the lesson of unconditional love that begins at physical birth and continues throughout your life.*

The soul and spirit lessons of immediate family relationships are designed to exclude the confusion of physical attraction. When sexual interaction occurs between immediate family members, it is symbolic of the ego denial of the soul and spirit energy. This expansive denial focuses the ego attention on exploitation of the physical body.

*Sexual interaction between family members is an experience of soul and spirit devolution. Devolution is a regression of the consciousness level. This regression will create its own manifestation of physical action within the physical, emotional, and spiritual world of each individual.*

The dominant aggressor will be subjected to the physical laws within your world if the interaction becomes known. The "victim" within your world is involved in a personal lesson of Karmic intensity.

The lessons will be a choice for those involved because of the Earth lessons they have designed and the collective agreement of the souls and spirits involved to be supportive. In the soul and spirit energy of this interaction will be the unconditional love of the family relationship. As you evolve as spirits on Earth, this level of consciousness will cease to be an issue.

Understand that all physical manifestation on Earth is created by you, dependent upon your individual level of physical consciousness. As you develop, the interaction of sexual intimacy is created at different consciousness levels. When you are integrated, sexual intimacy is a celebration of the soul and spirit interaction. If you are in the primary stages of development, sexual intimacy is focused strictly upon physical gratification without consideration of the soul and spirit influence.

*Spirit families are created among developing spirits by the focus of intention and the level of soul evolution. When you create the confusion of physical need as an active energy within a family relationship, you are denying the evolution of your spirit. In this instance, the denial of evolution creates devolution.*

In your world, there are many, many influences of other souls and spirits. You will have friends, colleagues, casual acquaintances, and intimate acquaintances that come in and out of your life from different countries, cultures, ethnic groups, and world events. Each relationship will have its own influence.

*You will have a variety of people within your individual world that help you create your world by their agreement to be an actor upon your stage.*

The influence of the immediate family and the relationship of the immediate family is unique in the world of spirit energy. When you decide to come to Earth to live a physical life, you design for yourself a life plan focused upon multiple or single purposes. This life plan is necessary in the same way that if you are going to build a house you must first design and plan the house. The design you create within your spirit world becomes the path of your life in the physical world.

When you create your life design, it will be created during your sleep period with other soul and spirit energy. You will communicate with the souls and spirits that are going to play a role in your life process, and you will write the script.

*As you create your life design, you will contact many known friends of the spirit world. Some of these friends will be in physical form, and some will be in spirit form. All will be known and loved by you. All will agree to be an actor upon your stage.*

When you choose your family members in your life design, you will be choosing them because they have made a commitment to you as a soul and spirit. They are committed to traveling with you in the physical world until they complete their role in your life design.

*The family that you choose will always be there for you in their soul and spirit energy. They are committed to being your spiritual safety net when you need them. How you relate to them in the physical world will depend upon the lessons that you have chosen to learn in this lifetime.*

ALL PHYSICAL RELATIONSHIPS ARE CHOSEN RELA-
TIONSHIPS.

You were not born of your father and mother by accident.
They agreed to play this role in your life. You chose them because
of their willingness to play the role out of their love for you.

You also chose them because when you design your life,
you design a life purpose. The role design of all family members
is directed toward the intention of your life purpose.

*The life purpose is a variety of lessons that are*
*focused toward the evolution of your soul. This va-*
*riety of lessons will create for you the lesson of un-*
*conditional love.*

The images of lessons that you will be working with in any
one lifetime will be in preparation for the understanding of
unconditional love. When you understand unconditional love
with total clarity and can integrate it into your physical world,
you will have reached the level of enlightenment.

*Integration of a lesson requires that you intellec-*
*tually understand and verbalize the lesson, that*
*you live your life by using the lesson in your daily*
*activities, and that you BE the lesson in your atti-*
*tude and perspective of life.*

When you choose your parents, they agree to play a specific
role in your life purpose by being part of your life design. For
example, if you have had a great deal of resistance to understanding the God within you; the good within you; the spirit of you;
you will choose parents who agree to live a very religious life.
They will agree to be your daily reminder of God. Their role as
a memory trigger will be manifested within the physical world
through their devout belief in religion.

The focus of your parents or parent upon religion is their
commitment to remind you that there is a God. Living with a
daily reference to religion will support your intention to remember that there is an energy that is greater than you, that created
you. The manifestation of God as the Creator is found in the
physical manifestation of man as a creator. This is your silent
message, "He is your Creator, I am your creator."

As you live in this religious environment, you will be
hearing words and seeing actions that have been seeded from
this belief in the God energy. This belief will not allow you to

forget the possibility of the God presence, even though you may at some time in your life find yourself in a state of denial.

***You are being taught a belief and you must first believe before you can deny.***

In believing, you have the freedom to choose your own path of learning. As you live, your life may take many paths. Living the opposite energy does not release the belief, it enhances the belief. Your choices will not change the belief that you were taught. It will always be there, even in your state of denial.

***Denial is a state of growth. The energy of being creates the denial of acceptance. Denial creates the opposite of an issue to capture your attention.***

You cannot deny an energy that you do not feel as a personal issue. If you are apathetic about a subject, it is not an issue of opposites. You have either completed the lesson of that energy or you have not yet confronted the lesson. It has not been chosen as a lesson of importance in this lifetime.

A parental commitment to you will reinforce a lesson of their own life design. Learning is always a giving and receiving with spirit energy. The giving and receiving may not be apparent on the physical level but a lesson exists for each and every spirit on a different level of consciousness.

At some point in your life, you may find that you feel repulsed by your mother's religious fervor. She is simply playing her role. As your denial becomes more intense, her reminders will become more intense in your perception. You chose her as your mother because of her commitment to play this role for you with intensity.

You choose parents to help you with other roles that cover the entire realm of physical reality. Life for you is a design that is created through the cooperation of other souls and spirits who agree to be family members. Your soul and spirit support begins with their agreement to help you enter into physical form.

Family members can create more irritation and punch more buttons within your life than anyone else will ever be able to do, with the exception of your twin soul energy.

This twin soul energy is the closest spiritual member of your family and will have a profound effect within your life, despite the role that has been chosen. The twin soul can play any role within the physical world of family.

*If the twin soul energies choose not to be part of
the physical family at birth, this decision is made
jointly to allow for a different and more intimate
union of the spirit souls.*

Remember that any button that is punched within you is a
lesson that you have chosen to learn. If it were not a lesson, it
would not have triggered a response within you. If it is not an
issue, you will not focus upon the energy.

Issues that suddenly appear within your life are the issues
you need to see with total clarity. They are triggered within your
soul memory and the physical response then follows.

It is very common to feel that you receive no love from your
parents. If you feel that you do not receive love, you have created
this issue to remind yourself to give love. This reminder to give
love is a reminder for your entire life that is manifested within
the safety net of the parental love.

*By viewing the opposites in life, you learn what
you do not want to do and what you do want to do.
You have chosen to learn by experiencing the opposites because of your own sense of unworthiness.*

ALL OF LIFE IS CHOICE.

When you choose to learn your lessons from the perspective
of the positive influence, you will do that. Living in positive
energy will allow you to see the inspiration, motivation, and
intellectual wisdom of self with perfect clarity. You will find
yourself living within a total sense of peace, joy, happiness, and
love. You will BE love, truth, and perfection in your energy of
self, life, and all other relationships.

If your choice is one of negative energy, you will create
opportunities of challenge in your physical life. Until you accept
yourself as worthy, you will choose to perceive your lessons from
the opposite, negative experiences of life. Therefore, all choices
of life will support the unworthiness that you feel within. You
will repetitiously validate your unworthiness with fear, anger,
depression, loneliness, and isolation.

*As your soul evolves it learns to focus upon the
perspective of what it wants to learn and to see
what it wants to learn with the joy and happiness
of understanding choice.*

From the perspective of conscious choice, you can see life with total clarity. Clarity will come only when you understand with the awareness of your conscious physical reality. Your conscious awareness always exists from the level of understanding that you have acknowledged and accepted.

Conscious awareness is acknowledging, accepting, respecting, and valuing that which you understand. Understanding with conscious awareness is far more advanced than intellectualizing. Intellectualizing is the repetitious regurgitation of accepted fact without emotion, feeling, respect, or value.

*It is essential to love self and all of man unconditionally. As you learn to love self, you will find yourself loving others without judgment. Loving without judgment is unconditional love. Unconditional love is the ultimate lesson for man.*

You are learning to love yourself and the energy from which you were created, the God from which you were created, and your neighbor as yourself.

*Each lesson in life is truly a lesson of love.*

You focus upon the image of loving by the dramas that you create within your physical world. Each lesson will appear in multiple dramas, traumas, and interactions. Each will be offered for your understanding of the same lesson in many different images. The message is always the same. It will not appear to be the same to you, but still it is the same.

*You must first learn to love yourself before you can love others.*

The family creates a bonding of the soul and spirit energy that has committed itself to being there to love you as you pass through the lessons of physical life. Your family is the spirit energy of unconditional love.

*The family energy of unconditional love may not be understood by you on a physical basis, but that does not mean that it does not exist. Spirit energy is the energy of the unconscious or intuitive mind. Soul energy is the energy of the subconscious or rational mind.*

The family energy of unconditional love is focused within the soul and spirit of self despite the physical focus of self.

Therefore, you may find it a challenge to recognize the love of family members in your present level of conscious awareness.

***Recognition of all love becomes more challenging if you are attached to the cycle of development.***

If you have a relative to whom you do not communicate, one that punches your buttons, you may be learning how important it is to communicate within your world. Understand that this is an image that is allowing you to see what you do not want to do again in another physical lifetime.

As an example, if you were abandoned by your parents at birth, it will be an issue for you not to abandon your children. How clearly you learn your lesson within the physical reality of your world will be seen in the physical action that you take to avoid abandonment of your children.

Indeed, you may choose to avoid having children because of a subconscious fear that you would abandon them. The lesson of your abandonment is triggered by the perspective of being a parent. If you simply say or feel that you do not want to abandon your children but do not take concrete action to be a good, loving, and available parent to your children, you have not learned the lesson within the physical sense.

The lesson of abandonment is learned by being the opposite. Many parents who were abandoned children create the strongest family circle. Their intention of being a loving, supportive parent is their reality of life.

My scribe's mother was abandoned by her father after the death of the mother. Abandonment occurred at the age of four years in the form of death by the mother and physical abandonment by the father. Both forms of abandonment are seen as one in the physical world of the child.

Living the life of an abandoned child taught her what she did not like in life. This sense of aloneness and unworthiness created a challenge for change, a true opportunity to change her later life.

She focused her adult life on creating a close and loving family of children. She chose to create and live the opposite to her earlier years of experience. She shared this life of parenting with her twin soul energy which supported the closeness of the family relationship.

Abandonment can be a lack of communication rather than a lack of physical presence. When a parent stays within the home environment but does not accept the role of parenting, an image of abandonment is being created. Indeed, a parent may not be in the immediate physical presence of the child but may contribute through physical activities and communication more than an available parent.

Do you see the active role that is the basis of support and communication in your physical world?

Lessons allow you to accept, acknowledge, appreciate, respect, and value the opposite of what you are experiencing. You are given a clear vision of what you do not want to duplicate or to repeat with other people.

The role of your life is the role that was chosen by you. To see the lesson of that role you need to look at what you have learned and not become captured in the energy of blaming another for your role in life.

*Blaming a family member or anyone else for your life drama is transferring the energy to another person which multiplies the negativity within you. Family members have chosen to support you in the role that you designed. Their lessons are different from yours.*

As you learn the lesson of love, your love will be apparent within the physical world from your actions.

Unconditional love continues for the soul and spirit energy. It is only within the physical world that physical resistance is created as negative energy. You see, energy, whether it is positive or whether it is negative, will be manifested within the physical world in its like form.

If you are negative in your everyday world, you will manifest negative creations of negative events within your daily life. If you are positive and you believe that everything in your life is beautiful, you will transmit that energy to other people in your life and to your family members. They will feel the physical effect of your positive energy, and you will have that positive energy returned to you.

Many times in a family situation there will be what we call in the spirit world "walk-ins." What is a walk-in? In the spirit realm there are families of spirits. These families are committed to growing together in the spirit world and in the physical world. These are the spirits that are your physical family and friends.

*Sometimes a spirit from another family chooses to join a spirit family other than their own to learn a specific image of a lesson. In the spirit perspective these spirits who crossover family lines are known as walk-ins.*

Have you ever looked at your family and said, "Jenny doesn't fit the mold of the rest of the family. She is different. She doesn't understand us. She doesn't do the things we do. She doesn't like the things that we like?"

Jenny may not communicate with you in a way that you can understand. Perhaps in a conversation you may feel that you are discussing two subjects independently instead of discussing the same topic together. This perspective can create confusion within your mind because you felt sure that the intent was focused upon a specific topic of conversation. You will feel unsure about what diverted the conversation.

The different perspective occurs because of the opposite focuses of energy toward the event. If you see an event in one energy and someone else sees the event in another energy, you are focusing upon different perspectives or images of the same energy. Perspectives create different images because the focus is coming from a different level of conscious awareness.

An example of this in your world can be found in business, science, or any specialty that exists. If you become ill, enter a hospital and have never in your life spoken or been to a doctor before, you will feel as though he is speaking to you in a "foreign language."

If you have not yet discovered typewriters and you try to speak to a computer specialist, you will think they speak a "foreign language."

If an accident occurs within your world, ask ten observers of the accident to relate their observations to you. From these ten different focuses of energy, you will receive ten separate versions of the accident. Each observer is coming from a different energy focus.

In each of these examples the perspective of knowledge and understanding of their communication created a different focus from that of the listener, because it was coming from a different level of conscious awareness. This diverseness of consciousness levels is becoming more apparent because the importance of the consciousness level is being illustrated physically within your world.

Jenny is a walk-in with a different spiritual consciousness level from the physical, spirit family she has chosen to join. You have a soul and spirit from another family of souls and spirits that has asked permission to join you. You have made the choice to allow this person to interact in your family for a lifetime in order to learn a specific image of a lesson.

This is the true definition of a walk-in. That does not mean that the energy of that soul and spirit is not committed to you, to your life purpose, and to your self-realization of that life purpose. It simply means that the culture, the belief system in her lifetimes has been focused differently.

The level of evolution for that spirit may be different than yours. The ultimate purpose of the spirit energy will always be the same. The choice to join another spirit family is equivalent to changing physical schools in an effort to learn a specific subject with more intensity.

Spirits and souls are created by the influence of their physical lives. If you do not know how to be a good person in the physical world, you will not change when you leave your physical body. Death does not bestow perfection upon physical man or the spirit and soul of that physical man.

You will come back, you will choose another life, and you will start working on your lesson again. If you find yourself living thousands of lives to learn one lesson, you may choose to see life from a different perspective. You may seek to be part of a family from a different spirit culture that is working from a different perspective of understanding.

*The primary difference in spirits upon Earth is not found in the purpose of being on Earth or in the spirit family to which they belong. The primary difference among spirits is found in their level of conscious awareness while in physical form.*

In all of life these consciousness levels are exhibited as seven relative to seven. If you look at man in the physical sense at birth, you will see an infant that has no ability to move. That infant is entering the beginning of the cycle of development. It will learn to roll, to sit, to crawl, to pull up, to hold on to furniture and walk, to stand alone, and to walk alone.

These beginning activities are stages of your early physical development that you re-create in each and every instance of birth and learning. With each stage of learning you develop a different level of conscious awareness.

As a baby begins his development, he will become aware first that he has the ability to move his limbs. He will pull his legs and feet forward and examine them, he will flail his arms about his head. He will examine his fingers intensely as he tries to remember why they are there. He will jump, jerk, stretch, and in time he will roll over.

When the baby can roll over, he immediately develops a different level of conscious awareness. He finds that he has the power of creating movement. He has the power to see with an expanded perspective. He has an expanded consciousness of other physical realities.

In the life of the family you learn development. You learn to protect each other, to love each other, to care for each other, to share, to feel, to give, and to receive. You learn to roll over, to sit up, to crawl, to walk with help, to stand alone, and to walk alone physically, mentally, and spiritually.

With each and every movement you develop a different and expanded level of conscious awareness of your physical self, your physical capabilities, and your physical world.

As you develop through the Law of Sevens, your consciousness changes, your awareness changes, your understanding changes, your perception changes, and your acceptance and acknowledgement of self changes.

*Each and every experience of life which is interwoven with the interaction of family and friends, creates a change in your level of conscious awareness.*

It is in this way that you create the energy within you, around you, within the Earth, and within the Universe.

*If your focus is upon the negative perspective of life, your experiences will be negative. If your focus is upon the positive perspective of life, your experiences will be positive.*

You can easily see that it behooves each and every soul and spirit to try to be as good as possible while on Earth. That is the way your soul and spirit evolve. It is the way you grow.

The family members that have joined you in this life have done so by mutual agreement. They are learning their lessons while you are learning yours. You function as an integrated support system with all family members in your spirit energy.

Would it surprise you to know that the image of the lessons are totally different, but the ultimate lesson is the same?

The final goal of all lessons IS unconditional love, but the way we learn our lessons has millions of varieties. Those varieties will occur through mutual agreement or collective choice. The nature of energy is movement and change, therefore, life will constantly change as the lessons change.

The actors on the stage will choose their roles and will play their roles from the perspective of their own lesson. The lesson will determine the size of the role and the expansiveness of the drama. You will choose to be an active participant or a passive participant. Your role will be focused toward the perception of your lesson at the same time that it supports the lesson of all other actors.

In this example I am speaking to you using the analogy of life as a stage, the drama, the actors, and the role. In this analogy please understand that the role does not create separation within the spirit energy.

*All spirit energy is equal and the roles are equal, but the acting is created for the purpose of supporting the drama. The drama contains the hidden lesson. The drama is created in the physical energy. It cannot be seen with your physical eyes or heard with your physical ears. The lesson will be found in the internal energy of the inner and higher self. It can only be understood as an energy of conscious awareness.*

In spirit energy there are no roles, there is only interaction. From the perspective of your physical understanding the analogy of the role is helpful.

*All lessons are learned through the interaction of relationships.*

If your life appears to be one big drama for you, then you need to understand that you are working very hard to learn your lessons. You are trying to see certain images with total clarity. You will play the role until you can understand the truth of the acting.

*In your sleep periods, it is the members of your soul and spirit family and your chosen physical family that help you on the soul and spirit level.*

Most of man is under the impression that he sleeps all night. Sometimes he will have an awareness of dreaming, and he will remember those dreams in very physical form. He will see himself interacting with other people, with perhaps animals, with perhaps nature, with friends or family members. The intellectual mind of man transforms the sleep experience into a form of physical memory that is acceptable to the intellect of man.

What you do in your sleep period is interact on a soul and spirit level to learn, to grow, and to expand your spirit and soul energy. You will be doing this work with not only your immediate family members, but with thousands and thousands of family members that exist within the soul and spirit family.

It IS this soul and spirit family that normally seeks physical embodiment together. The time of entry within your physical reality will not be the same, but that does not mean that the relationships are not valuable. As you live a life with your physical family members, your spirit family members are also living a life with the family of your soul and spirit energy.

If you do not find yourself getting along well on the physical level with some family members, give yourself permission during your sleeping period to settle your physical differences. This spirit interaction will allow you to understand the lesson.

Understanding the lesson is settling the difference which removes the issue. It is understanding on a soul and spirit energy basis exactly what image you are trying to clarify while in physical form.

*Conscious awareness on a physical level must come from the depths of the internal self. It cannot be intellectually created externally in the physical world and attached to the spirit energy.*

The immediate family is a soul and spirit energy that offers you a physical safety net. It also offers you a soul and spirit safety net. You may not have a conscious understanding of this supporting energy but that does not mean that it does not exist.

*You function from your conscious awareness, but you also function from the subconscious or soul awareness, and the unconscious or spirit awareness. Your soul and spirit focus is to integrate yourself internally so that you can function with a balanced conscious awareness of these three facets within your physical life.*

Integration of the total self is essential for you if you want to understand yourself. As man, you have an "ego need" to intellectualize your world. The intellect and the ego are the physical divulgence of the mind. It is very comforting to you to intellectualize what is happening to you.

It will be more productive for you if you can replace your "ego need" to intellectualize with an inspiration and a motivation to understand yourself. If you create a wish, a want to understand, to feel, to be integrated, and to use more than the physical presentation of the ego/intellect, you will.

It is this intellectualization of your physical world that creates distress within physical families. Intellectualization is the world of love and fear, right and wrong, good and bad, and righteousness and sin. Intellectualization is the physical world of judgment for you.

*Because of your ego need to judge, it is important for you to understand that your family exists for you on the consciousness level of the soul and spirit energy.*

You cannot intellectualize soul and spirit energy. When you intellectualize, you are external to self. You are focused upon the physical, the perception of the ego, the judgment of the intellect, and the material concept of being. When you integrate the soul and spirit, you are functioning with feeling, with heart, with understanding, with acceptance, with a knowing, and you are functioning with love.

*Any attempt to intellectualize your soul and spirit energy from the ego self, attaches you to physical energy and resists all integration of soul and spirit energy.*

If you focus on intellectualizing your relationships with your family, you are not focused upon loving your family. The family is the most significant lesson of unconditional love that you create within each and every physical life.

*It is the family that you first challenge yourself to love unconditionally.*

What IS unconditional love?

Unconditional love is loving a person without judgment. If there is no judgment, there is no restriction, there is no resistance, there is no constraint, there is no if. You love them simply because they are who they are.

If they are your mother, father, brother, sister, aunt, uncle, grandmother, or grandfather, you love them without judgment. You do not create within your belief system an image that they must duplicate before you can love them. You do not create restrictions for their looks, their actions, their intellect, or their beliefs before you can love them.

So how do you love them?

You love them by accepting that they have a perfect right to be who they are. You accept, acknowledge, respect, and value what they have taught you simply by the energy of being who they are. It does not matter if you do not understand who they are intellectually, you simply love them within the faith of unconditional love.

*In loving another human being, you are committed to support and honor that love by the truth and perfection of your actions within the relationship.*

If you cannot act the commitment of love, you are intellectualizing love and creating "love" as a physical attachment, not as a spiritual understanding.

*Love is the energy of unconditional acceptance, acknowledgement, respect, and value that is created by the supportive action of loving commitment within the physical world.*

How a family relates will be a perfect example of the level of conscious awareness within the members. The interaction of the relationship should clearly define for each and every family member the love that is within. The internal love and integration of the spirit self is what reflects the unconditional love within you to the physical world.

If you have family relationships that do not reflect love, they are captured by the judgment of the physical world. This interaction reflects the ego need of the individual rather than the loving energy of the soul and spirit within. For family members this is a lesson in learning unconditional love.

If you have a sister or a brother, or a mother or father who is a walk-in, the important lesson is that they have chosen (just as YOU have chosen them) to play a role in your life. Your spirit love for them is reflected in the act of acceptance of the role they are playing within your life.

Your lesson will be to love them unconditionally, and to not judge their differences within the physical world. Acceptance of them as they are will be a reflection of your unconditional love.

You see, they are perfect just as they are. When you judge, you are trying to change that individual to live by your ego/intellectual belief system. Their belief system is unique to them and does not reflect your standards of behavior.

***When you have a sense of unworthiness within, it becomes important to your ego as a validation of self, to judge all other people by your belief system.***

You expect others to validate your worth by duplicating your beliefs, your lifestyle, and your standards. You want to remove them from their freedom of choice to be who they are, and force them by your ego will to be like you. You say in effect, "Tell me that I am perfect by being as I am." For man, this is his ego playing "The God" role.

When it is your belief that you can only love somebody if they are a mirror image of your external ego self, then how are you ever going to learn to fulfill the first two commandments in the Book of God? How are you going to learn to love unconditionally, first God, then yourself, and then your neighbor, if you are focused upon judging others as wrong?

In the physical world you will find multiple physical differences of the body, and the mind. If you have a list of criteria that you feel each and every person that you love must adhere to, then you are going to be very lonely.

The criteria that you will focus upon will be that part of yourself that your ego finds it enjoys the most. Therefore, when you find this duplicate of your intellectual or physical energy within another person, the ego itself will become threatened.

In this instance, the ego will be threatened by the person as well as the relationship. It will not matter what the relationship is within your life. It may be a close family member or it may be a lover, or a spouse.

Do you see how hard it is to please the ego within your life?

**The very criteria that the ego judges others against, will threaten the ego the most if it is exposed to the same valuative process.**

Placing restrictions on your family and on the people that you love will hold the relationship captive within your judgment energy. Have you ever heard anyone say, "I would love her IF she did this, IF she did that, IF she didn't talk so much, IF she had black hair, IF she were taller, IF she were fatter, IF she were skinny..?"

Have you ever heard this? "I would love my mother, if she didn't nag me. I would love my father, if he hugged me once in a while."

In these multiple perspectives you will find the images of many lessons. Some important lessons in this scenario would be the lesson of non-judgment, the lesson of communication, the lesson of giving and receiving, the lesson of patience, the lesson of balance, and the lesson of unconditional love.

You see, you are judging. Judgment is an ego action. Judgments can only be made when you have the belief in right and wrong. If you believe that your mother cannot tell you anything or offer you advice, you would perceive her advice as nagging. If you gave her permission to offer you advice, you would acknowledge your love for her, and you might find some value in the advice. If you did not believe in the advice, you could simply go your own way, or you could gently communicate your feelings in a two-way conversation that might be advantageous to both of you. You would both be speaking from the perspective of your individual belief systems, and in giving and receiving together both perspectives have the opportunity to change.

Many of you will create judgment criteria for your family to adhere to. The beliefs that served you yesterday may not serve you tomorrow. As you change and grow, your beliefs will change.

As your culture, your world, your society, and your family grows, your beliefs will change.

Each and every experience of life will create a change in the physical level of your conscious awareness. As your awareness expands, you will find that your belief system will be altered. Therefore, it is better for you and your family if you do not create rigid belief systems for yourself or for them to follow. Belief systems become restrictive forces that are hard to go beyond or to change in your life.

It is important for each of you, especially with children, to learn to listen and to learn to love. Because, you see, listening is love. When you listen to a family member, you have validated their value. You have validated your ability to allow them to be who they are. You have validated their intrinsic self-worth.

You have shown your appreciation for them as an individual more significantly than if you had bought them a new car. You see, to have someone show you respect and appreciation, to show you the value that they find in you and in the relationship, is validating your individual existence. This is true of you, and it is true of other people and your relationships with other people.

*When you can freely give and freely receive acceptance, acknowledgement, respect, and value from another, you are validating the spirit energy within both self and the relationship.*

Now, think for a moment about yourself. It is nice when someone listens to you, when someone appreciates, respects, and values what you have to say. It is enlightening to feel the energy of love. You begin to feel good about yourself. You begin to love them at that precise moment. You see, your love energy expands you and your world.

It is very simple and easy to feel the joy and love of appreciation. You are communicating the lesson of "do unto others as you would have them do unto you." When you show love to your family, it will be returned a hundredfold. You should not seek the return of love in the material sense, because it can never be as expansive or as beautiful as the love from the heart.

The more love you give, the more love you get. This is the way Universal electromagnetic energy works. It attracts like to like. If you are angry, hostile, withdrawn, dishonest, fearful, judgmental, and a number of other negative emotions, you will find yourself being ignored by family members and by friends.

If you are critical of your family, you will get negative behavior. This is especially true with children. It is also true with spouses, mothers, fathers, sisters, brothers, and other family members.

The actions of anger, anxiety, hostility, rejection, resistance, and denial are all negative energy. These energies are created by you when the ego/intellect refuses to integrate the soul and spirit into your physical consciousness because the ego fears change.

*All experiences in life have the opportunity to become either positive energy or negative energy, depending upon the energy of the individual and how the energy is magnetized.*

Negative energy creates a strong destructive force that will quickly magnetize other negative energy into its force field. This negative force field will build and build and build, until your whole life will be a drama of unbelievable events occurring one after the other.

This energy escalation can start in families among parents and children where one event provides energy for the next event. Attachment to negative energy can lead to much heartache within your physical world.

To change the magnetic force field is to learn the lesson that precipitated the drama. Once the lesson is accepted, acknowledged, respected, and valued, the energy will become positive for you.

Change that is created through the action of positive energy is powerful and exciting. Positive energy action is the way to dramatically change your world on a personal level, family level, and Universal level.

You have the power to control your actions and the actions of those around you BY THE ENERGY OF YOURSELF. Believe me when I tell you this is true. If you are a positive person, and you walk up to someone with a positive approach, you will generally get a positive response. If the other party is captured in negative energy, accept the challenge to help him change his energy with your own interaction.

If you have children, and you are constantly telling them everything that you judge is wrong with them, your children will not want to be in your presence. Their anger toward you will accumulate and it will be transferred to other areas of their lives.

They may take their anger out on other family members, in the classroom, or on their bodies in disease. They might choose to be with their friends or with other people that may be positive or negative.

*The problems that exist in your world begin within the immediate family circle and with the ability of the immediate family to be loving, supportive, and good role models for the children.*

Material possessions do not affect the intrinsical value of relationships. When parents or family members attempt to buy the love of children, they are sending them a silent message. This focus on material possessions begets generation after generation of humanity that has no concept of the value of love and responsibility.

*Families love each other by their approach to each other, and their ability to allow each individual to be themselves without judgment. This is living the lesson of unconditional love.*

Family relationships have become a challenge in your world of today. In the last 20 to 30 years serious behaviors that began as individual challenges have reached Universal magnitude. When the energy of the family escalates, it attracts energies of other families to it. If this is a negative energy force field, this energy force will continue to spread until it covers your world, and your Universe.

*The focus upon negative energy can change the family relationship. This change may appear in physical reality as destruction of the family unit.*

In your world, you have created impressive challenges within your families with drugs and alcohol. Challenges with drugs and alcohol begin in the home with an acceptance of the "concept of need" for medicines as drugs, and the "concept of need" for drinking alcoholic beverages.

Children do not have the ability to differentiate between drugs given through the medical profession and drugs obtained through other sources. To the child the action of taking drugs is learned as an acceptable behavior. Drinking is learned as an acceptable behavior because the message is silently witnessed in the parental behavior.

It is the action of taking drugs and alcohol that becomes the silent message within a family unit. Silent messages become subconscious messages for children. In the belief system there is little, if any, allowance for quantity or quality.

Street drugs will become a natural expansion of prescription drugs as the child seeks a noticeable physical effect. This physical effect will be consciously sought in a subconscious effort to understand the reason for drug usage. The physical response is coveted for validation of the reason for common usage, especially parental usage.

Why would anyone want to harm themselves? Because they do not love themselves. If a child receives a silent message with drugs, alcohol, sex, stealing, lying, and a multitude of other behaviors, they will judge their own sense of worthiness by their ability to reproduce the same effect that they learned.

If you assume the parent enjoyed these behaviors and you find yourself not enjoying the same behavior, you will judge yourself as unworthy and abnormal. If you are living in an environment where you can talk and the parents will listen without judgment, these issues can be clarified. If you can demonstrate your love for your children, they will feel your love of them, and it will create love within them.

In families, belief systems are developed within the home and outside the home by the influence of contemporaries. Issues that are not discussed and understood within the family unit will be explored elsewhere. Avoiding the issues of drugs, sex, alcohol, and other problems within the family unit will necessitate an alternate source of learning for the children.

*Children will constantly have multiple expo-*
*sures outside the home that will require love and*
*communication within the home to be understood*
*appropriately.*

So you see, in reality, your entire world is a system of energies. You are energy. Your body is energy. Your world is energy. The kind of energy that you choose to create within your immediate family becomes the energy that is created in the community, in the state, in the country, in the world, and in the Universe, because energy is magnetic. Like energy is attracted to like energy.

Children are the miracles, the shining stars of the cosmos. They come to you in purity of spirit energy, and you pollute them as you pollute the Earth around you. It is a challenge for a child to grow to adult life and not learn to deny the soul and spirit energy that is within. An advanced spirit may choose a short life to teach family members in the love of sharing.

All changes that you want to make within your world must first begin by making changes within yourself. The influence that you have will begin to change your family and the energy of your family begins to change the energy of your community. As these energy vibrations expand, the energy of the community begins to change the energy of your state. The energy of the state begins to change the energy of your world. This becomes the action of dropping a stone into the water and watching the waves as they expand outward. These waves of vibrational energy affect all that is touched.

This is a magnetic energy response. It is the energy of your creation that happens, whether or not you understand, accept, and acknowledge the origination. Within this family of yours, your immediate family that has been created by the soul and spirit energy, is the supportive and loving energy of you on a soul and spirit level.

It is your responsibility to integrate your loving spirit energy into your physical world. If you can acknowledge that you have a loving spirit energy within, it becomes easier for you to accept, respect, and value the same energy within another human being.

*In your world the opposite of love is fear. It is through fear that you learn to judge, to resist, to reject, and to deny. If you fear learning about yourself, you will not want to learn about other people. Indeed, you will focus exclusively upon self-gratification in your efforts to reward yourself. This will be your subconscious desire to validate your own worthiness.*

As your "need" energy expands the vibrations become more intense, because the "need" becomes more intense. On a subconscious level, you strive first to love yourself. Subconsciously you understand that when you love yourself, other people will love you. Loving self means accepting self. Loving other people means accepting other people. Fearing any element within self, or within other people creates judgment, not love.

*You fear expanding your consciousness level to accept the responsibility for yourself and your love. Loving self and loving others is a responsibility of non-judgment.*

Fear is the opposite of love and in this creation of judgment you magnetize the fear which will expand with the expanding efforts. The more your fear expands, the more unworthy of love you feel. Your fear and unworthiness is then transferred as blame to others for not understanding and loving you.

**The secret to changing your energy pattern is to accept love and to BE love.**

When your need is expanding and your effort to change is expanding, your fear is expanding. You will fear the expansion itself. Your cycle of expansion will create a captive energy of the essence that you are producing.

This cyclic energy can be seen in many relationships of the opposite sex as well as in family relationships. Indeed, in your world this is known and understood as "trying too hard." You will create work in your energy of fear.

Each of you have the ability to create a "Heaven on Earth" for yourself and your family. When you can wake up each morning and feel blissfully happy and content within your world, you are beginning to learn what love means. You are beginning to love yourself. You are beginning to love being. Being is the action, the physical presence of the love within.

As you respond to the love of self and family, the energy of contentment, happiness, and joy begins to create new vibrations within your life. Your relationship to the world begins to show daily changes as you magnetize positive energy to positive energy. As this expansion occurs, you will be able to look at your family, your spouse, your children, your brothers, and your sisters. You will look at them with a smile on your face. You will be happy and joyful, and you will be very capable of sharing your love.

**Sharing love is love in action within the physical world.**

The focus of the family members is to help you learn within your own soul and spirit what unconditional love is. To learn, you must not fear a commitment to love. You will learn best by doing. You will want to experience. Many of you will deny the interaction of love because you fear being hurt, rejected, denied, controlled, or threatened.

*Fear is your perception of relationships. Fear
will occur only if you create the energy of unworthiness within you.*

It is within the relationship of family members that you can
see yourself. Look at your family and how you are showing your
unconditional love to your family. You can begin your new
relationship by appreciating that you are in each other's lives by
choice.

*Know that you have chosen to live in this life to-
gether, to learn and grow together, and that the lesson, the ultimate lesson of creation is
unconditional love.*

It is never too early or too late to love by sharing interaction
within your family. It is never too late to love through interaction
with friends and lovers.

Do you understand that you have the capability as a soul
and spirit to go back within your soul energy and change the
energy of any lifetime?

You can indeed turn each and every lifetime that you have
lived into a life of love. When you love yourself, you can perceive
all relationships with love. Perceiving relationships with love,
removes all judgment of right or wrong from the energy of the
relationship.

*Releasing judgment creates the positive energy
of love that will heal your mind and body.*

Your immediate family is there to be your safety net, because
on a soul and spirit basis, you have been around with them
thousands and thousands of times before. Your relationships
have not always been what they are today. Indeed, you have been
all things to each other. Because of your "past" relationships, the
energy between you and your family members is binding of soul
and spirit energy.

If you can develop a conscious awareness of the beauty in
your relationships, the physical relationships within your family, you will begin to see the soul and spirit relationships.

The influence of "past" relationships became very apparent
to my conduit several years ago, because she had a child who
"mothered" her all the time. From the time the child was born,
she was always mothering her mother. This became somewhat

of a curiosity to my conduit and at the same time it felt very natural and comforting.

As this child grew, the mothering expanded. She would take care of my conduit, doing nice things for her, talking to her, explaining her perception of life and showing her love in multiple ways as all mothers are inclined to do. She would shop for her, cook for her, clean for her, and she was there whenever she was needed.

Throughout the years both my conduit and her daughter have become aware of many lifetimes which they have spent together in close family relationships. In the relationship of mother, daughter my conduit was her daughter's daughter many times.

In some of these lifetimes they both became aware of an early separation which interfered with the completion of the relationship in that life. This energy of mothering was then re-created in this lifetime to heal itself. In this physical life they have found themselves mothering each other which has become a joy in both their lives and has strengthened the relationship.

For my conduit this relationship has been especially rewarding since the death of her mother, because it provides an energy that was suddenly absent from her physical world. Healing the energies of past relationships is the joy of unconditional love at its finest.

> *To perceive life as a healing and cleansing*
> *while on Earth, is being in touch with the purpose*
> *of Earth life. It is through the healing and cleans-*
> *ing of the soul in the physical realm that the spirit*
> *of man evolves.*

You can look within your family, and you can observe the relationships. You can see, perhaps, that maybe YOU were the mother, or maybe YOU were the father, or maybe YOU were a brother or sister. This will strengthen the love that you feel on a physical basis, and it will awaken you to the understanding that you have, indeed, spent many lives with this spirit and soul.

This consciousness allows you to understand the expansiveness of your love for this spirit and soul energy that you are choosing to be with in this lifetime.

Soul and spirit relationships will be apparent in spouses. "Past" marriage relationships can be found in behavioral patterns, and in the lessons being worked upon. Spirits who have Karmic energy to experience will frequently choose to be in a spouse relationship.

The marriage relationship is chosen because of the intimacy that is involved, which awakens the spirit within more quickly. Intimacy in an integrated marriage will exist from all facets of self. It is the perfect energy from which to heal and cleanse your soul experience.

When the spouses are twin souls, the marriage will be one of total commitment and unconditional love. The relationship of twin souls in marriage, as a physical consciousness, can only happen when both of the spirit energies involved are advanced to the level of integration.

Indeed, both spirits must be evolved to the level of integration or one soul will deny the spirit energy of the other soul out of fear. Marriage between twin souls occurs frequently, without a conscious physical knowledge, as the spirit within seeks evolution in a safe and comfortable energy.

Your immediate family is a group of souls and spirits that has committed themselves to being there for you on a physical level, on a soul level, and on a spirit level. They are present in your life to love you and to help you learn. Their commitment of love is very profound. When you can understand this energy of spirit love and return that love, you will not judge them but you will allow them the freedom to be themselves.

*Always BE open to listening, and IN that listening, you will hear the energy vibrations of your soul memories. This will help you and it will strengthen you.*

You are physical and you live within the physical world. But to understand yourself, your family, and all other relationships, you must acknowledge, accept, respect, and value the soul and spirit within. You must live within the physical world with a consciousness of integrating all that you are externally and internally.

Your physical body, your ego, and your intellect are the total of the external you. Your soul and spirit are the energy of the internal, eternal you. This soul and spirit within can work for you in the physical world, or if you deny it you can create mountains of pain in your physical life.

Let me show you how painful it can be if you try to resist, or deny, or ignore any part of yourself. Any time that you have an arm that is severed or a leg that is severed or any part of your physical body that is severed, you will forever as long as you are physical, suffer pain within the severed limb. You will feel that part of your body as though it existed.

You will feel pain within your toes if you have lost your leg. If you lose an arm, you will feel pain in the arm that is gone. The pain can occur at any point in the lost limb. It will be real and it will be painful. This pain occurs because of cellular memory.

**In your world the ability of the cellular memory is denied which creates the pain of memory.**

If you choose to focus only upon your physical self and sever the soul and spirit of yourself, you WILL suffer the pain of denial. Within the intellect and the ego is knowledge of the total self. Whether it is accepted or rejected, the cellular memory of self is still there.

If the total self is not acknowledged, you will suffer the pain of the unseen, of the unaccepted, of the unacknowledged part of your mind. This pain of denial occurs in the same cellular memory that will create pain in a lost limb.

Cellular memory is a reality of your physical being. Think about yourself and what it means to you to be part of the human race. See your relationships as gifts of love to yourself. See your family as shining spiritual gifts that you have chosen to have with you in this physical world.

*Cherish your family. Honor them. Respect them. Love them. See yourself as love as you relate to them. Understand that the love within you is yours to give and in giving, you receive. The truth of love is found in the physical action of love. The physical action of love is caring and sharing all that is in your life with another.*

# Ego Resistance In Relationships

It will frequently happen in life when your soul is evolving that you will come upon an energy that is acting as a resistance to growth.

Indeed, this could be viewed as just a little truck on the stairs. You are a spiritual child who is capable of leaving obstacles in your path of play. Do not let obstacles confuse you, see them as challenges to overcome in your movement forward.

The resistance of the ego is a powerful energy, a profound and very expansive energy that you must deal with. Indeed, learning to balance the ego is a major lesson of your physical world.

When the intellect and the ego find themselves threatened in their perception, they become fearful. They will create a blockage within your world to keep you from wanting to go forward. The same type of blockage will be manifested within the physical world as a physical problem.

This physical blockage is indeed the struggle between the spirit and the ego. **Your ego shuts out the light that allows you clarity of vision into your soul activities and your inner thoughts.** Your ego resistance can be quite expansive but it is not something for you to be concerned about. It is a normal response for you to resist change.

When you understand that you create the opportunity for change within your world by the events of your physical world, you will be able to define the ego spirit tug-of-war.

*Change is a two-way street. It is created by giving and receiving.*

You realize that blocking your own growth or resisting your own growth shuts out the light. And you realize that you have a block developing the resistance. Resistance will occur within the physical world as something that is not pleasant to you.

Resistance will be perceived as denial of the relationship. This will be only a temporary energy that will leave as it came. Resistance is a normal action for the intellect and the ego, when they feel that the spirit and the soul are awakening.

*Your ego, intellectual fear will create a physical event of resistance.*

You have created the opportunity to change. The positive spirit energy is there, you simply cannot see it. The drama of the event is your resistance to accepting. Yet as you work with the ego and the spirit you will find that your balance returns.

Resistance will be a challenge that you can overcome if you are willing to face it truthfully and work to balance the energy of the ego. If you deny the existence of the spirit energy within you,

you will continue to create negative events in your determination to get your attention.

*In all family relationships of the physical world you will find resistance occurring as the individual works to grow within. This resistance will differ from family member to family member and will occur on occasions throughout life. This is the way of seeing beliefs mirrored in another person that offers the protection of unconditional love.*

Resistance may occur within the physical family relationship and within the soul family relationship as old issues are worked out within each energy pattern.

*Family members will forgive each other more willingly than they will forgive strangers because of the physical ties they consciously honor and the internal soul and spirit energy that exists unconsciously.*

Your family is your greatest source of learning. You are daily faced with the interaction of others that will please and displease you. You will find yourself working out your understanding of dominance, power, control, submissiveness, judgment, fear, and all of the myriad of emotions that are negative.

In addition, you will be exposed to the positive emotions of love, support, joy, peace, happiness, and sharing that provide you with the opposite energies. These positive energies are your emotional safety net.

Through the interaction and experience of these opposite energies you are allowed to see the immediate problems that you have chosen to work with in this lifetime. These energies will then be worked out in an active or passive manner. If you choose to be directly involved in an interaction, it will be active interaction. If you choose to observe the interaction in other family members, it will be passive interaction.

The silent messages of passive interaction within a family can become profound lessons for later experiences in the same way that an active interaction will teach. Indeed, there are times in life when the passive interaction is more profound than the active interaction because it is less clouded by the emotion of active participation.

There can be instances within family relationships where anger becomes the dominant emotion. This emotion will then create a separation between family members. This separation can take the form of non-communication, or bitter interchanges.

*The lesson in this dual role is one of forgiveness. In learning to forgive other people, you learn to forgive yourself. When there is a lesson that has been chosen as the focus for a lifetime, it will continue to occur in different circumstances throughout life.*

Let me use an example that will show you how your beliefs integrate into your lesson and affect all interaction. Let us suppose that at birth you are female. During your early years you began to believe that your father wished that you were male.

This belief then creates guilt within yourself for being who you are. From that time on you will find yourself struggling in life for male approval. Male approval is symbolic for you of paternal approval.

You will seek to control because you will believe that if someone allows you to control them they are validating your worth. They are giving their approval to you for being who you are. This need for acceptance, acknowledgement, respect, and love is so profound within, that you seek a life with the illusion of power over another.

Control to you becomes symbolic of acknowledgement, acceptance, respect, and love. In your need to prove your own self-worth to the ego-self you will create a life of control, dominance, and jealousy which will create non-communication with anyone who threatens your control.

You will see yourself as invincible. You will believe that you are always right. You will not forgive anyone who does not follow your rules of life. You need to image self in another to validate self.

When you find another that does indeed image you, you will not be able to tolerate their presence because you do not like the self that you see in them. Within this unacceptable image of self, you will not recognize yourself. You will recognize that this individual has traits that you cannot forgive.

*Searching for who you believe that you should be, will attract to you the opposites in energy one day and the same energy the next day. This will*

*happen because you do not know who you are.*
*Your internal energy is creating the ego/spirit tug-*
*of-war within.*

Your attractions will be determined by where you are at the moment. This is your way of experiencing the opposites and learning to discover self. This is a frequent occurrence for both males and females within your world.

*You judge yourself as you believe that you are*
*being judged by your parents.*

This is a belief that will be worked through in various levels within the family. If you have children, you will want your children under your control. You will expect them to be who you choose for them to be. Your parents will also be expected to validate you by believing that everything you say or do is perfect. Your brothers and sisters will be expected to follow your control. If they choose not to follow you, you will exorcise them from you in complete unforgiveness.

Any family member who dares to disagree with you will be insulting the value of you, and the intellect of you. You hold within you a profound "need" to be perfect, because you feel imperfect. This is of course your own illusion that holds you captive.

Your friends will need to play your game your way or you will never forgive them. You will create many marriages or none dependent upon your fear of being alone. You will need the constant reinforcement of relationships of the opposite sex. You will many times have several lovers at once, because it would not support your "worth" if you did not have many suitors waiting for your presence. In addition, being alone is a constant fear that can be avoided if you have many opportunities for love.

Validation of self-worth in physical, sexual relationships allows you to forgive yourself for being other than what you feel you should be. This pseudo-validation, in turn, becomes its own belief, because the validation by another will not create forgiveness of self.

*When the relationship ends, you will not see the*
*image of self that you are reflecting. You will find*
*imperfection within the other party to blame.*

All negative emotions within your world begin because you do not love and value yourself. Discovering the belief that supports this lack of self-love will begin the discovery of self. Once the belief is discovered, you can gently lay it aside and set about healing the wounds that you have created within yourself. As you heal your wounds, you will heal all family relationships and all relationships with your friends.

Your need for control and dominance is created because you do not love yourself. If you love yourself, you can allow your family, your friends, your colleagues, and all people to be who they are. You accept that they are in the growing process and that they must grow at their own level of energy vibration. Your love will allow you to always be supportive in your interaction with family and friends.

In a family where the focus is on the intellect only or on the physical body only, the choice may be made to accept the interaction of a handicapped child. This choice will be the choice of the spirit who is choosing a life of intellectual or physical suppression or perhaps both, by a family that is living a life of emotional suppression. This balance will be sought externally to trigger the emotions within.

> *Life is a choice. In the spiritual agreement that is reached between the infant, the parents, and other family members there will be a lesson focus for everyone.*

If the focus of the lesson is denied and not learned it will be repeated either in daily life, or in repeated embodiments of the spirit. Resistances are your blockages or attachments to the physical world. They are the lessons that you work through in your relationships.

When you sleep you leave your body and work within the multi-dimensions of the spirit world. On awakening you have chosen to resume your physical life. Death is a choice of re-embodiment and can be chosen by the spirit at will for multiple reasons.

> *When you focus upon the physical facet of self, which is the physical body, the intellect, and the ego, to the exclusion of the soul and spirit, you will at some point choose to suppress the physical body and the intellect to focus upon the soul and spirit energy.*

*The soul and spirit energy is manifested within the physical world through the emotions and feelings of the heart. This can be a choice of the lesson of balance and each soul and spirit can make this choice as an active or passive participant.*

The soul and spirit energy, which is manifested in the emotions and feelings of the heart, should never be confused with sexual attraction. This is the purpose of the family relationship which excludes sexual attraction in highly developed souls and spirits.

*By learning the lesson within the family relationship, you can more clearly understand the true revelation of integrated love in a commitment of the opposite sex. You will understand the equality that allows for partnership bonding.*

The family is the first lesson in equality for you. If you do not perceive your family with equality, you will not perceive your life with equality. This resistance to equality will create all relationships within your life from unequal energy.

Equality is defined with a physical focus within your world. True equality does not mean that you must all have equal physical attributes or physical possessions.

*True equality is the freedom to BE self. If you allow your family the freedom to BE self, you will allow yourself the freedom to BE self. This equality of freedom will then become your focus and will be seen in all of your relationships.*

If you perceive self as superior, more intelligent, better educated, with more status, wealthier, better looking, and on and on, you are creating inequality in the relationship.

*Equality is love. Love is non-judgment. Freedom is the opposite of control. These are some of the lessons of family relationships. Learning these lessons within the family unit, creates a more balanced and happier you for the rest of your life.*

# Physical Denial and Acceptance

The family relationship is a spiritual design. This design is focused upon images of the multiple lessons that each individual has chosen to learn.

The events of the family are designed as alternate choices into the relationship but are surrounded by free will, free intention, and free choice. Free will, free intention, and free choice gives each member of the family total equality.

*As lessons are accepted or denied, alternative events are chosen to support the choice of development. In all instances there exists spiritual agreement and support.*

When the support is apparent on a physical basis, the intention has been acknowledged to remain open to acceptance. If the support is absent within the physical energy, the lesson is being denied.

A balance and harmony of energy will exist between family members that will support the spirit energy despite the physical participation or the physical focus of energy.

Physical denial is an exercise of free will, free intention, and free choice. On a physical basis the energy is not properly balanced for open and active participation. The lesson will be learned at another time.

*When denial occurs there is a resistance of conscious awareness to the event that may block the experience from conscious memory for years to come in your time, and perhaps for many lifetimes of physical embodiments.*

Physical denial can be identified by failure to acknowledge, accept, respect, value, and participate in the energy of the event. This denial will be frequently found in the death of a loved family member. If as an adult you refuse to attend the funeral of a loved family member, this is denial of your own physical immortality. If you fear facing your own death, you will be unable to face the death of someone that you know and love.

Sharing in the transition of the spirit and soul energy is an opportunity to trigger the emotional energy within you. It is an acknowledgment of the physical energy that has served the soul and spirit in this embodiment. This event creates within you the opportunity to balance the energy of the internal with the external. In this respect, grieving and the communication of the emotion is a lesson in balance for you.

It is a belief of your world that the male should be strong and therefore not show emotion. This is a belief that family relationships challenge. If the male fails to show emotion, he denies his soul and spirit energy. If the female fails to show emotion, she denies her soul and spirit energy.

Family relationships offer the male an opportunity to be in touch with the soul and spirit energy of emotion. If the male denies the family relationship, he is denying the challenge of emotion. He is creating resistance to his soul and spirit energy within.

This is also true of the female but the male is used as an example because of the belief system in your culture that creates a learned resistance.

> *Some individuals who fear emotion will also fear family relationships, friends, and all other interaction with people. These people become the criminals of your world because they act without emotion. They live without emotion. They deny the soul and spirit energy within and they react only as physical beings. They do not love themselves and therefore they have no love for other people.*

These are lessons that are confronted within family relationships. If the denial remains as the controlling force within the physical life, the physical life will be focused upon fear of interaction secondary to the fear of emotion. These individuals will easily indulge in physical crimes against the physical body.

> *The total absence of feelings and emotions of the heart allow physical atrocities as lessons.*

In the spirit sense this is a choice of both participants, although this perspective is a challenge for you to understand. If you observe the murders within your world, you will find many of them occur between family members or friends.

> *The spirit energy of unconditional love agrees to the lesson which will trigger the emotion within. Indeed, the event may be chosen as a Karmic lesson for both participants. Understanding the lesson*

*will balance the emotion within for all passive participants.*

This safety net of unconditional love is much stronger than your imagination is capable of understanding. Atrocities are not acceptable within the physical world. Allowing them to exist does not allow acceptance of the lesson. Other lessons will be learned by the physical laws that will become effective when they are broken.

The relationships of the mother and father within a family is the relationship of the primary teacher. These relationships will be chosen by mutual consent and will be focused upon a multitude of lessons that will remain as reminders or triggers forever within your world.

The image of the lesson may appear singular or non-existent in the perception of the child or in the perception of the adult child. This does not mean that the lesson does not exist. It means that you are not consciously aware of the lesson within your physical reality.

As a child you will absorb the energy of the lesson. You may resist or deny the lesson, you may choose an opposite energy, or you may live the image without a conscious awareness. Your perception of the energy does not neutralize the true energy.

The lesson will be found in the actions of the parents as well as the verbal communication. You chose your parents and they chose you. Your agreement will focus the actions on what you need to learn as well as on their own lessons.

The love that exists between you is equal and the interactions will be a giving and receiving. You will judge these interactions by your physical belief system which will allow you a very limited physical symbology of the spiritual lesson.

As you grow toward your own self-discovery, you will become aware of the lessons of childhood with a greater intensity and a different perspective if you allow that to happen. If you remain forever captured in this lifetime by the intellect and ego, you will create a Karmic lesson in the spirit sense.

As you grow and balance your own energies, you will see the interaction of your mother and father from a different perspective and with greater clarity. Indeed, you will stop blaming them for who you are and begin appreciating who you are. They did not create the growth within you. They cooperated in your choice of lessons to allow you to grow. How you perceived their cooperation is your responsibility and part of your lesson of acceptance.

As you grow into adulthood, it is extremely valuable to go back into the energy of childhood memories and look at what you learned. Look with total clarity and no concept of blame. Do not focus on what you feel that you did not learn but focus entirely upon what you did learn. Release your attachment to the negative and dwell only on the positive.

In the beginning you may feel resistance at this exercise. Continue to work with the memories. Remember the fun and the joy of your life. All memory will not return instantly.

Continue to review the experiences from birth to the present over and over again. As your perception of yourself consciously changes, your past memories will change. You will begin to see them with a totally different perspective. You will begin to feel good about yourself and what you have learned.

This exercise requires a commitment to growth and to discovering yourself with love. It is not a "quick fix" that you can think about for five minutes and feel satisfied. It requires years of discernment of self. This in turn requires courage, commitment, and love of yourself.

As you work with these memories of childhood and your mother and father, you will find other memories that interact. These memories will include other memories of your family beginning with sisters and brothers, cousins, aunts, uncles, grandparents, best friends, and on and on.

In the spirit world these family members and close friends are all soul and spirit family members. The interaction that you remember was the acting upon the stage of your life. You were involved in the drama of growing, learning, and soul evolution. You wrote your script and you played the lead. You are now what you have created by the drama.

As an adult, you now have the opportunity to repeat the drama as a parent of children. You become the primary teacher. You will choose to be or not to be a parent. The choice will be made according to the lesson that you have chosen. You will have alternate plans available to you. In being a parent you will act out the lessons that you have learned thus far in life.

The lessons that you have accepted with understanding will be captured within your unconscious memory and you will focus upon that memory as easily as you will focus upon your conscious memory. If you purposefully return in memory to the positive energies of your life, you will allow yourself to discover your purpose for life.

*The purpose of your life will be directed by the lessons that you have been working with from childhood. Each and every event will have its purpose and its message.*

Children themselves are a message in sharing and interaction. You show your commitment to sharing the lessons of life and soul evolution. These lessons can be shown by sharing in other ways but parenting is a common choice for man.

Children also create for you a safety net of unconditional love in spirit energy. If this love is also shown in physical energy, it has a special quality of support and comfort within your world.

Being a mother or father is also accepting a responsibility for life that is finite and infinite. It is accepting the dichotomy of life. It is a commitment to being integrated with others within the physical sense, as well as the spiritual sense while you continue to be self.

*Parenting is not the only way to show through your physical actions the desire for integration. Integration of self is truly an integration of life purpose into life activity.*

Discovering your life purpose will amaze and astound you. Do not let that deter you. Be with the energy of the purpose until it finds its own perfect balance within. It is the physical world that believes in the concept of time and space. In the spirit world neither are a reality.

When you acknowledge your soul and spirit relationships as an intrinsic part of self, your ego creates resistance to sharing self. It becomes a challenge to acknowledge that you are on the path of evolution.

Always and forever the path of soul and spirit evolution is an integration of all that you are internally and externally within the physical world. Integration is balancing the total self.

*Balancing self creates acknowledgement of the physical, the intellectual, the soul, and the spirit energy as one energy. This balanced energy is inspired as one. It is BEING ONE.*

Despite the resistance of the ego, your spirit is anxious to continue to evolve self into an integrated unit. This is the way to understand your total self and your consciousness levels.

In physical life when resistances and denials are prevalent, other family members may choose to play a role in events that will awaken you. These roles within the family will create a series of events that will seize your attention. The events themselves will be determined by the lessons that are being learned.

The family is with you in the spirit energy of your sleep as well as your wakeful periods. This is a soul and spirit energy that continues to interact, whether or not you have a good relationship, or whether or not you see your family frequently. The spirit and soul energy of the family is the safety net of physical life. This togetherness of spirit energy is a soul design transcended into your physical life.

There are no geographic boundaries within the spirit world. In the physical world man is a nomad and may lose contact with family members because of geographical distances. In the spirit world there is no time and there is no physical geography to be considered.

Indeed, the culture of man at this time creates separation from family members as a necessary part of growth. This belief system of man creates the loss of wisdom and love that was at one time handed down from the old to the young.

*When you lost respect for age, you lost respect for those who have aged. When a culture loses respect for age it sets in motion a disrespectful energy that becomes the energy of self, as you age. If you do not respect age, you will not respect yourself as you age. This is a part of your culture that will change.*

Your intense focus upon the physical body creates the loss of respect for age. This loss of respect for age is symbolic of the change within your physical body with age. In this instance, the focus upon the physical body creates a conflict with the focus upon the intellect. The belief attachment to the body has served to create a separation of the old from the young, or the physical from the intellectual.

Reversal of beliefs is also a part of the history within your culture. As it says within the Book of God, "For all things there is a season." Physical life is the season of development for the body and intellect of man. It is also the season of awareness, understanding, and integration for all of man.

Your beliefs restrict and deny your ability to develop beyond the physically accepted understanding of life and living. This is your "need" to separate self into a limited physical being.

*It is this separation of the physical presence that is balanced by the movement of the soul and spirit. When families can be together physically they provide an additional balance that strengthens the soul and spirit bond.*

Events will occur where the soul and spirit of a family member may choose to leave the physical plane. It is important for all of man to understand that the choice of the soul and spirit to leave was totally understood by each family member when the soul and spirit entered the family on a physical basis.

This choice can occur when a spirit wants to help other family members with decisions on a spirit level; when the spirit may want a short period of time to communicate with other family members on the physical level; to awaken the soul memory within other family members and on and on because, indeed, the lessons are endless.

When the spirit leaves in infancy it should be understood that the spirit is an advanced spirit that can only help with lessons for a short period of Earth time. As the soul and spirit becomes advanced, it is limited to short periods of time in the Earth's atmosphere. It will many times choose a dramatic death to emphasize the message that it came to awaken.

The more advanced a spirit becomes, the more difficult it is for that spirit to stay grounded within the physical world. Unless there is a specific purpose of being a long-term messenger to Earth, advanced souls will choose infant death. When an advanced spirit chooses to become a long-term messenger to Earth, it may face many physical challenges within the Earth's atmosphere and may choose death quickly once the message has been completed. Death should be accepted on Earth as the choice of the soul and spirit within.

Indeed, it may take many births and many infant deaths for the advanced spirit to gain the physical balance to stay within the Earth energy for the required amount of time. In the spirit world there is no time. When I speak of time I am referring to your understanding of time.

It is normal to feel a fear of your own desire to move forward in your soul and spirit evolution. As you grow, you will need to accept your challenges and to understand yourself. This will give you permission not to be fearful, not to worry, but to be open to expansion and growth.

*Soul evolution is the process of integration that occurs when you raise your level of conscious awareness within your physical world despite your resistance and fear.*

Your level of conscious awareness is an indication of your integration on a soul and spirit level. Your conscious awareness can be more easily understood than any other physical manifestation. When you live the balance of that integration in your family relationships, your intimate relationships, and in your relationships with friends and colleagues, you are a living example of the spirit within.

You are focused upon fear and physical resistance to that integration more frequently than you are focused upon integration and love. Each soul and spirit must move along its path of evolution in its own "time" to be what it will someday be. Your fear reflects upon your ability to integrate and to balance, and therefore, it creates your resistance to evolution.

*Integration is essential to your individual growth process. Keep that foremost in your mind, and look at yourself in total love with total positive energy. It is your love of yourself, your belief in yourself, and the positive energy that you will create from that love, that will help you to integrate, to balance, and to evolve without fear.*

Understand that fear and resistance are physical reactions within your physical world. You are physical and that is the energy that grounds you to the physical world. Each time that you climb up that spiral staircase by one step, you will find resistance showing up for you in some physical form.

Know that your resistance is there and perceive it as a challenge to overcome. Thank it for its concern and for creating a new level of awareness within you. Then gently ask it to leave you. You see, it is only if you attach yourself to negative energy that you should become concerned with it. If you give it its freedom, it will indeed leave you.

When you see resistance within the physical realm on an 'intellectual' basis, you still continue to see yourself moving forward in a very structured space. But in that space, you have created your own blocks from your individual belief system. Belief systems of the individual become the belief systems of the family, the community, the state, the world, and the Universe.

*Beliefs allow that tiny seed that is you to go without the nourishment that would allow you to become a rose.*

The rose is symbolic of the life and growth within man. If you lovingly care for your roses, you can plant a little twig in the ground and it will grow, and it will bloom. As it blooms, the rose opens wider and wider and wider, to burst forth in pure beauty and joy.

The rose is symbolic of your life. It is indeed like a life that blooms in full to become a family. The love that shines in one bloom will continue to shine in all of the roses that follow.

In the creation of a family, love can shine and reflect upon the entire Universe. It is by the support and love of your family that you find the spirit within to grow and to shine as a symbol for mankind.

*The safety net of unconditional love holds each and every spirit in the hand of God.*

*The ego*
*is the master of I.*
*The soul*
*knows self from experience.*
*The Spirit*
*loves me as all.*
*The intellect is a slave*
*to the master of I.*

# Lovers in
## Relationship

*The ego*
*dictates.*
*The Soul*
*motivates and teaches.*
*The Spirit*
*inspires and rejoices.*
*The intellect*
*accepts.*

*Relationships teach*
*from the wisdom of the soul*
*if the master will allow*
*learning in its slave.*
*You think you are open to accept*
*but the master resists being taught.*

*Man with his free will*
*can choose for himself.*

My explanations within this text should be considered spiritual overviews of the male and female. The explanations are by no means complete within themselves as this would be a book within itself.

Each individual exists within his own unique web of energy. These are simple observational explanations that will give you a healthy start on the valuative process of how you can successfully share your time with another person.

All relationships that are shared by you add to the experiential learning of you. In the role of lover, the soul will face the multiple dramas of life and learning. There are many roles for lovers within your Universal system.

***The role of lover in your world is the role of intimate friend.***

You choose your lovers based upon the beliefs within you that you wish to validate. These beliefs are beliefs of your physical reality based upon what you have learned and judged by your ego "concept of need."

It is from this system of beliefs that you create your individual world and the world around you. Included in this system of beliefs are specific beliefs relating to those individuals that you wish to love. In the spirit sense these are beliefs that you have chosen to understand in this lifetime.

Choosing a lover that reminds you of the beliefs that you wish to validate will keep the spirit memory consciously active to help you understand the belief.

***Beliefs are energy forces of the mind that direct man.***

As your understanding changes, the energy of some beliefs will be perceived differently and focused differently. Other beliefs will be released because as you move into a different level of conscious awareness they will not serve you anymore.

If you are strong, you will seek a lover who is strong. If you are repressed, you will seek a lover that is repressed. If you are afraid of emotion, you will seek a lover that is afraid of emotion. If you see yourself as unworthy, you will seek a lover that you see as unworthy. If you live in fear, you will seek a lover who lives in fear.

This list could go on and on indefinitely as there is a specific identity to each and every individual. The energy that you reflect from self, you will attract to self.

As energy changes within you, it will attract like energy to you. People are energy. If you have been attracting a certain type of person to you and you change, the type of person that you attract will change. As you grow, your friends will change. You will find yourself being surrounded with people that are in the same rhythm and harmony that you have discovered.

Have you ever noticed within yourself or a friend how you always have the same type of friends? Your energy of beliefs will attract you to the identical body type, personality, intellect, and beliefs of another person.

You may marry and divorce, take lovers, marry again, and each and every person will appear to come from the same mold physically and intellectually. The energy within you has not changed. You are captured within a certain framework of belief system that attracts a certain type of lover and friend.

***You attract what you can accept. What you cannot accept within yourself, you will resist in a lover.***

An open and non-judgmental person will have a garden variety of friends. Each and every friend will be loved equally because of their image of soul and spirit energy. This individual will not be threatened by any personality because he/she will be totally comfortable with self.

Being comfortable with self is an indication that you recognize that you are more than a physical body. You acknowledge the soul and spirit energy and will allow it to be equal in your daily life. You will seek balance and openness and you will be balanced and open.

You will find pleasure in playing, dancing, swimming, and all other activities that express joy and rhythm. You will use and enjoy your physical body as enthusiastically as you communicate with your soul and spirit.

The balance that is required for dancing is a physical indication of the balance within. People who love to dance have a good chance of being physically and mentally healthy as well-balanced individuals.

There is a difference between loving to dance and dancing to be polite. Dancing is a form of play that allows an intimate sharing of energy. It is a creative form of interaction for lovers that allows you to begin to understand each other on an enjoyable and safe basis. Hours can be spent dancing which will develop an energy integration and understanding that sex may never create.

Children love to freeform dance and if left alone will be very creative. Children know only love if they are properly cared for, and are good examples for adult lovers. They are creative with their play and this allows expansive insights into each other. Children have an innocence and purity that they project with total humility and love. Play and shared time can be a productive way for lovers to learn to accept and to know each other.

Many males feel self-conscious if they are expected to dance. Dancing is an expression of emotion. If a male is afraid to dance, you can expect him to be afraid of expressing other emotions as well. See if you can interest him in a fun day of play. If he is afraid to play, beware. In choosing your lovers look to these simple expressions of sharing and emotion. If a male is afraid of sharing in dance, in play, and in any seemingly child-like fun, he is afraid of emotion.

The male energy is focused upon the physical world around him. This energy is the energy of the ego and the intellect. It is the energy of material possessions. The male energy looks at life from a factual, disassociated, unemotional, and analytical approach. With many males a woman will feel that it is impossible to touch their hearts.

The spirit and soul has chosen to be male with the intention of learning integration of emotion and feeling which is the energy of the female. His attachment is to the physical body, intellect, and ego, therefore, he will experience overwhelming internal fear at the very concept of emotion.

The male has chosen the masculine gender to learn the lessons of emotion and feeling, which are the opposite to what he is comfortable with. He does not view his life as a learning process beyond his intellectual capability. He has been taught to be strong, macho, a fighter, powerful, controlling, and the protector.

**Nothing in the culture of your western world has prepared the male for his spiritual lessons.**

The need to deal with emotion, especially his internal emotion, "his feminine feelings," frightens him. From the understanding of his intellect, emotion is inappropriate for the male. His fear of his own emotions and feelings will be so overwhelming that he will frequently disassociate himself with the event that may precipitate any emotion.

*Emotions and feelings create an instant tug-of-war with the ego. Emotions and feelings are directly opposed to the male belief system, to his intellect, to his ego, and to the role of the self as he believes it to be.*

If the male finds himself in love with a woman who triggers the emotion and feeling energy within himself, he will frequently end the relationship before he will confront his own feelings. Indeed, men search for women that make them feel "comfortable" in the physical sense, not women who will trigger the energies of emotion and feeling within them. Males will seek females of like energy.

When the male is captured in emotion and feeling spontaneously, he will frequently vent this emotion and feeling in the form of physical destruction of property, fighting, killing, or maiming because he does not understand how to deal with what he considers "female feelings." Indeed, males fear any and all expression of emotion that might make them appear weak in the eyes of the world.

**The ego has never been known for its humility.**

Abusive husbands are abusive because they do not understand or know how to control the emotions and feelings within them. They may not realize there are emotions and feelings they need to confront because these feelings will be transcended into anger, fear, hostility, and destructive behavior.

Abusive wives are also a problem within your world today. These are the male energies within the female that are focused upon power and control. This female is at a level of awareness that is only slightly beyond the male gender focus. Indeed, her focus is so close to the level of pure physical development that it creates confusion within the physical manifestation of emotion and feeling.

When you are afraid of emotion, you are afraid of losing control. Whether you are male or female is irrelevant. A relationship with an individual as a lover who is afraid of emotion will create extensive dramas within your world.

No one aspect of a person's personality should be singled out as a complete valuative factor. All of you have many integrated energies. Many relationships will result in the express "need" to integrate. You are here to help each other with the challenge of lessons. Understanding the lesson will allow the relationship to be more successful.

In the female that is here to learn the lessons of physical intellect, you will find a strong need for control. This control will be obtrusive for the most part with a concentrated focus upon the intellect and the business world.

This need for control will be focused on all aspects of living, working, loving, and playing. The ego will be struggling to be the best. You will find in this female more of the male characteristics that are focused toward the ego/intellect with a strong avoidance to true emotion and feeling.

Emotion and feeling will be approached by a very organized, analytical, and intellectual process. This process of intellectualizing emotion and feeling will be found as the basis of all relationships from childhood, lover, marriage, and motherhood. Indeed, it will be a challenge to discover the loving, caring, emotional, and feeling female within.

In this female the truth can only be found in the consistency between her words and actions. She may say, "I love you" and her actions will then become expansively judgmental. Judgment is the opposite of unconditional love. This will allow you to see her love as an intellectual concept, not a true emotion and feeling.

Your intellect and ego are overwhelming forces. This is the focus of the physical world. Since the physical world is the primary focus for man, many of the emotions and feelings within man are understood from this limited ego/intellectual perspective.

*In all instances, each individual is different. In the multiple levels of consciousness that are available to you, you will find integration occurring that will allow each person to have some emotion and feeling focus, and some intellect and ego focus. But until integration is more common in all of you, you will be able to identify the roles that you attach yourself to.*

Intellectually all of you understand the concept of emotions and feelings. Your perspective of your action within the understanding is the challenge. Looking at your emotions and feelings within the self and integrating them into your daily life as your guiding action becomes the challenge.

Accepting these understandings on a faith basis will help you see the resistances within yourself. In seeing your own resistance and denial of these energies, you can develop a conscious awareness of them which will help you become more integrated. Awareness will create a more harmonious and balanced relationship with your lover.

Neither male nor female will accept an intimate relationship if they cannot look at the image within self that is reflected. This would create fear and panic for the ego. The ego would be presented daily with multiple challenges to change, to be better, to learn from the buttons that would be pushed. The ego would feel threatened to the point of survival.

*An intimate relationship of this energy voltage would be inspired, motivated, and creative but it would require strong, open, courageous, and committed lovers who were anxious and willing to grow.*

# The Master/Slave Relationship of Lovers

The male will frequently be threatened by any indication of strength in a female. A female will frequently be threatened by any indication of weakness within a male.

*The threat is created within the ego because those traits in a lover would be viewed as threatening the status or role of the ego self.*

For this reason, strong men need strong women and strong women need strong men. The weak will gravitate toward each other as their energies attract each other. If these relationships end as master and slave, that is their "concept of need" and they are perfect for each other.

The master/slave energies are the same energies from different images. If the energy is balanced and accepted by both parties, the relationship could be successful.

In your world the criminal carries a weapon and the policeman carries a weapon. The energies of both are coming from a sense of power and only the intention is different. The master and the slave are both coming from a sense of power. The master is controlling and the slave is controlled. The sameness of these energies is not recognized by the individuals. This allows them both to be captive to their emotions of hate and fear.

*The role of the policeman and the role of the criminal both create the perfect climate to transfer the emotions and feelings of the heart into the physical actions of control and power.*

You can look at various relationships in the work places of your world and you can see the roles of power and control. Doctors and nurses are another example. The physician has been given the "power of God" by your society in predicting life or death. The nurse is legally controlled by this power within the medical institutions but has always been focused upon emotion and feeling. With emotion and feeling the nurse many times has more control over the health of the patient than the physician. The sameness of these energies is not recognized by the individuals.

The pimp and the prostitute is another example of the master and slave role within your world. Here again, you have the power of the pimp and the controlled prostitute. There is a covert control with the prostitute who influences the wealth of the pimp if he/she chooses not to work. Once again the choice of not working for the prostitute would result in a show of power and mastery until the slave was again under control.

The example of the pimp and the prostitute is an exaggerated energy of the relationships that are created by dominance and submissiveness. Dominance and submissiveness are the actions of the master and slave relationship.

In many instances the energy would not be exaggerated for some relationships. The role of dominance and submissiveness within the male and female relationship is the predominantly accepted role within your world.

*It is this sense of power that attracts many lovers to each other in the opposite images. It is only when the male and female are both integrated individuals that they can handle an equal and healthy relationship as lovers.*

The master/slave relationship is the primary relationship that exists within your world today. It is a relationship of imbalance where the fear of the individual is acted out in opposite roles upon the stage of life.

*Equality in relationship requires an internal strength, courage, humility, unconditional love, and integration that permits each person to be beautiful and complete as human beings. This integration may only become evident to both parties as the interaction of the relationship creates events that trigger the courage, strength, emotions, and feelings within.*

The belief system of man focuses upon the gender role and any deviation from that role will not be acceptable to man, if he is focused within the external self. Focusing upon physical attraction focuses only upon the external self. The external self is hiding an inner and higher self that is reminding the intellect and ego of its presence on a daily basis.

*Intellectual and ego denial of the soul and spirit does not make it go away. It is integrated within all of you. The challenge for you is to consciously want to increase the degree of integration.*

Choosing lovers from the external focus will create unfaithful, unstable, violent, angry, jealous, fearful, and resistant relationships. These are the external emotions of fear. Fear will frequently exist in these relationships because there is change. When you are not comfortable with self and who you are, you will fear change.

*Change threatens the survival of the ego that is living in fear.*

Personalities that focus totally upon the physical world, the intellect, and the ego will resist and deny change. They prefer their structure to be disciplined and unchangeable. They do not have the spontaneity to gracefully handle change. Their role is their role and they cannot and will not see beyond it.

Nothing but the physical world truly exists for the individual with a hardcore physical focus. They have not yet developed the vision to see beyond their accepted ego belief system. Indeed, the very inference of something other than what conforms to their belief system will threaten their sense of self. They will be loud and verbally abusive in supporting their way as the ONLY way.

These are not self-assured individuals who can be open to new understandings. Internally there is an unconscious and subconscious war going on that they do not acknowledge or accept as a reality within their world. They are transferring their internal fears to the physical world by the only action they understand when they ostentatiously support their belief system.

*A person who firmly believes in the "master and slave" relationship role would not be able to consider equality and partnership bonding as an alternate relationship.*

Change is a threat to ego survival. Change is a threat to the accepted structure of beliefs. Earth, as the physical world of man, grows and changes by an act of nature. Man, too, has this inherited ability to change as an act of nature if he does not create obstructions, resistances, and denial to the process. In the same way that man interferes with the growth within the Earth's nature, he interferes with the growth within his human nature of self.

*When the acknowledged role of the ego is threatened, the ego feels powerless to be what it believes it must be by the nature of its accepted role. This powerlessness then erupts into physical outbursts of anger or destructive behavior because the ego is unable to understand its own emotion of fear. The ego does not invite change and will not tolerate change gracefully.*

Attracting a lover from the beauty of the physical body will require the lover to accept change within you. Attracting a lover from the soul and spirit within creates an understanding and acceptance of physical change.

In an equal relationship there will be great satisfaction in the beauty found in growth. Change will occur in all aspects of the physical reality of you. If your power is focused upon controlling the physical to avoid change, you are setting yourself up for an emotional upheaval.

*If you are open to the soul and spirit within, change will occur with the inspiration of the spirit and the motivation of the soul. When the soul and spirit energy is integrated with the physical energy and the intellectual energy, man creates growth, understanding, joy, happiness, and peace in a relationship.*

You may find yourself repeatedly in a situation that is unacceptable to you. It is not your lover's responsibility to fulfill your needs. He is who he is. You are responsible for attracting the energy within him to yourself. Look at the image that you are sending out. Understanding yourself will help change the image.

You will attract a lover relative to your own conscious beliefs. If you attract a lover from the energy of your soul and spirit self before you are ready to acknowledge and accept the soul and spirit within, you will not acknowledge and accept the lover on a physical basis.

*When you deny the soul and spirit energy within yourself internally, you deny the lover's energy externally.*

You choose your lovers based upon the physical attraction that you feel. Physical attraction is created by the ego belief system. If you are focused within your ego self you will attract energy of your lover from the ego self. You will mirror from self what you can accept within your physical reality. What you mirror in yourself today will not be what you mirror with internal growth.

*If you are focusing upon the awakening of your soul and spirit self, you will attract the energy of the soul and spirit within. If you begin to deny the soul and spirit energy within yourself, you will deny the attraction to your lover. If you acknowledge the energy within self that attracts you, you will acknowledge and accept the lover.*

Have you ever found yourself attracting the same type of lover into your life over and over and over again? This lover may be abusive, controlling, angry, judgmental, dominant, or submissive. Have you found your life with this lover totally unacceptable to your happiness?

*The energy of the external physical self will attract multiple negative energies when your beliefs create negative energy.*

When the belief system is focused upon the dominance and submissive roles of the male and female, your physical attractions will be determined by this energy. As long as the belief is present, the ego will be threatened if the roles are not maintained.

Attracting an energy that removes your power of self will be manifested many times in dis-ease or disease, depression, fatigue, and an overall inability to function at your usual energy level. This depressed energy can lead to suicide ideation.

> *Your feelings of unworthiness will become over-whelming when you find yourself as a master or slave when you are attempting to grow internally. The internal will refuse to accept the "needs" of the ego self.*

Focusing upon the physical is self-gratification of the physical. Internally the ego/spirit tug-of-war will continue. As your balance changes from ego to spirit, and from spirit to ego your attachments to negative and positive energy will change. As you balance your energy, you will be attracting a more balanced energy within your lovers.

> *Giving up the roles of dominance and submissiveness will require significant inner growth.*

You will choose your lovers based upon where you are at the time of the relationship. If you are focused upon validating the physical "concept of need" within you, you will choose a lover to participate and to mirror your own sense of ego need.

> *Relationships based on dominance and submissiveness are usually intellectual opposites. The need to dominate will include intellectual domination as well as ego domination of the physical body.*

If you are focused upon growth within the spiritual sense, you will choose a lover who will mirror that specific energy within you. It will be your choice to be open and loving in your relationship.

You create for yourself an ego/spirit tug-of-war. Being in this ego/spirit tug-of-war allows for growth. If both parties are growing and have a commitment to the relationship, the loving and caring will also grow. If one party is more willing to be open than the other party, the relationship will be a challenge to endure. Your choice will reflect your lesson of the moment.

Your beliefs will influence all of your choices. If you are male and you believe in male dominance, you will choose a subservient female that you can dominate. This will validate within you your need for dominance.

Dominance is a fear of loss of ego self-control. Loss of ego self-control will be feared with any triggering of emotion. In this instance the female who is subservient also feels the need to be dominated. Her need to be dominated is then validated by her choice of male.

In the physical world dominance is translated as protecting, and submissiveness is translated as being protected. These dual perceptions of self-gratification then create acceptance of the relationship and a fulfillment of ego needs by the lovers. This too, is a master/slave relationship.

Indeed, the pimp and the prostitute have the same identical perceptions of self-gratification that create the validity of their relationship to each other.

Submissiveness in the physical world will create submissiveness in the inner world of the physical body. This becomes the act of creating dis-ease or disease within. In your need to be dominated physically, you will allow internal domination by allowing the parasitic organisms that live within you to become dominant.

**When you see yourself as powerless, the body becomes powerless.**

This need for dominance and submissiveness is in reality an ego fear of integration with the internal self. The internal self is seen as an emotional and feeling self that would be unable to provide adequate control. Therefore, you create the power of control to maintain control, or you give away your power of control to another that you feel certain has the power to keep you in control.

If a lover is focused on an intellectual dominance as well as a physical dominance, he will choose a lover who has not developed the intellect and is physically submissive. In your culture this creates recognized roles such as the "baby" or "dumb blonde."

If a lover is fearful of growing old, he will choose a lover to validate his youthfulness. Many times the male will unconsciously focus upon an age where he felt the most masculine in an ego attempt to recapture that period of his life.

In your culture the perception of physical perfection, age, dominance, control, power, and intellect has become a male role judgment that is frequently used by the male to support and validate his own concept of self-worth. He will seek the opposite image of his energy to love him which validates that he is what he believes himself to be.

For example a 60-year-old male may marry a 20-year-old homecoming queen because he wants to return to the years of his college days when he dated the homecoming queen. This supports the ego image that he is still as attractive and masculine today as he was then. His "concept of need" creates an illusion within his mind. This is an active resistance to being who he truly is.

When this happens the intention that created the relationship is at fault and the relationship may survive or fail for many reasons. But the love that should exist within the relationship is usually not an issue with either party. They are each acting out their individual ego needs, and when the drama is over another one will take its place. This is the physical exhibition of "show and tell" in relationships within your world.

The negative energy of needing to control and dominate attracts the negative energy of submissiveness. These negative energies will attract each other because they are both images of the lesson of understanding self and your power of creation. This energy will then reflect back to the image of self with a sense of unworthiness and defensiveness in the conscious choices that were made.

There are multiple reasons why relationships that are based on the dominance-submissive concept of power and control, are not happy, creative, motivated, and inspired relationships.

Master/slave relationships will frequently survive in your physical world, because what fear brings together it will habitually keep together, because the need for self-gratification is allowed to incubate.

Dominance and submissiveness are beliefs that have been created by the male since the days of Adam and Eve when the males themselves "interpreted" the roles based upon their "concept of need."

*The role of the male is the energy of the cycle of development. The role of the female is the energy of the cycle of awareness. The male energy is focused upon the physical body, the intellect, and the ego. The female energy is focused upon the emotions and feelings within which is an integration of the soul and spirit energies. Each is seeking what it does not acknowledge in this embodiment.*

The male has been focused upon the development of his body, his ego, and his intellect from the beginning of Earth time. Woman has been focused upon an awareness of the emotions and feelings that are inherent within all humans.

*As the spirit evolves through multiple embodiments, it chooses the gender role of choice dependent upon the lessons to be learned.*

Each gender is focused upon learning the opposite of what it is in this physical embodiment. The male is focused upon becoming aware of the female energies internally and the female is focused upon becoming aware of the male energies externally. The external energies are opposite to the internal energies which creates the ego/spirit tug-of-war.

*Without learning and accepting balance of the internal and external energies, man can and does truly create havoc within his world.*

Learning and accepting are slow for man because without a conscious awareness of the beauty of integration, resistance is created secondary to a fear of the unknown. As awareness develops within all humans the perception of self and the perception of need changes.

Awareness creates an understanding that "you are all." As this understanding occurs, you will choose to develop relationships of "equal partnership" because you are indeed equal in all but the physical gender that you have chosen to display in this lifetime.

*The gender of man is the external balance of the internal energies. The sexual organs are the physical symbols of your energy focus. The male sex organs symbolize his external focus. The female sex organs symbolize her internal focus.*

You have chosen your gender to compliment and celebrate your life. You write the role, produce, direct, and act on the stage of your world.

Equal partners will be an acknowledgment of equality and value, an acceptance of each other without judgment, and with total respect and appreciation for each other. Equal partners will be able to celebrate each other and their life physically, intellectually, and spiritually.

Indeed, the celebration of the supreme physical sense will create joy in the choice of gender. The balance of the physical will add to the creation of balance within the soul and spirit.

Lovers who are attracted by the soul and spirit energy within will inspire and motivate from that energy. It is this soul and spirit energy that inspires and motivates change and growth internally and externally to man in his physical world.

*If man is focused upon a lover only because of physical attraction, he will become bored with his choice in time because the inspiration and motivation for growth is missing.*

Without the inspiration and motivation of the spirit and soul energy, the creativeness of man is limited. Without soul and spirit support, the creativeness of man must depend only upon the intellect of man.

This singular intellectual focus produces an energy of reliving old beliefs that is not inspiring because it relies upon belaboring old issues rather than creating from the freedom and love of the soul and spirit energy. The intellect takes past experience and builds upon the events from the ego perception of relativity. The ego perception of the relationship between lovers will be focused upon the "I" concept of need.

The creative spirit builds from the energy of multiple images that has no basis of proof within your physical world. The intellectual approach is the story of science and education within your world. The scientific approach has no emotion and no feeling. It is designed upon past fact. This will give you a sense of your failure to accept creativeness in a relationship that maintains a physical focus.

When you truly love another person from the soul and spirit self, you are totally committed to growth within your lover and within yourself. Growth will not be a conscious issue but it will flow naturally from the spirit and soul energy of inspiration and motivation. The soul and spirit energy will then integrate with the intellect and new creations will occur.

*Your focus in preferring an equal partner will create within your world a new and different energy. The energy of dominance and submissive-*

ness has created expansive judgment and beliefs
of the "roles" of man on Earth. As a culture
evolves through the cycles of awareness and understanding this energy of roles will disappear.

The roles of dominance and submissiveness create judgment
of right and wrong which in turn creates the concept of guilt and
sin. The belief in punishment for guilt and sin then creates fear.
The true basis of fear is the fear of separation from God.

*Through the ages of your time you have been
taught that if you commit sin God will not love you.
You believe that He will no longer walk by your
side. These beliefs are false illusions of man but
the belief effects the personality, attitudes, and actions of man.*

If you choose a role in life that is judged wrong by your
culture, you will live in fear because it is your belief that your
sin will separate you from the love of God.

If you believe that as a man you must be dominant and as a
woman you must be submissive, you will feel guilty if you find
that you cannot in truthfulness to self "act" that role in your life.

*The fear of being something other than what
your culture dictates creates the attachment to the
roles which you play. The role becomes your "identity" within the physical world. An actor who frequently plays one role on the stage will be
identified with the role. A man who plays one role
in life identifies himself with the role and will consider himself judged by the role.*

The belief in the roles of dominance and submission in the
role of lovers is firmly attached within the mind of man because
he has been taught that God has dictated the role. This is an
illusion within the intellectual/ego mind of man.

*God created man and woman to be His equal
partners in the creation of the Universe. He created man and woman to be equal partners on
Earth. Truth is found in the actions of man that are
consistent with the words of man.*

It is interesting to understand that your world itself has been
dominated since the beginning of time by the male. Your laws,

your science, your education, your rights as human beings, your government regulations, and your religions have all been interpreted, formulated, and designed by the male who is focused upon the intellect and ego.

*This physical focus of the male interpretation throughout time has created a critical mass attachment to physical energy as the only energy. The physical energy of man is the negative energy of man. The soul and spirit energy of man is the positive energy of man. The male is focused upon the negative, physical energy. The female is focused upon the positive, soul and spirit energy.*

Indeed, you have allowed your world to be created the hard way without benefit of the creativeness of the soul and spirit energy of the female. This has required that every facet of your world and your life evolve through all of the levels of the cycle of development one by one. As man experiences the slightest threat to his ego, he has created devolution to maintain his role of dominance.

Does it surprise you that relationships have followed the same pattern of development with an identical design?

When you attach yourself to a belief it affects the world, the culture, the Universe, and all of reality for thousands and thousands of years. The belief will continue to affect your world until you can develop a conscious awareness that the belief is being perceived, interpreted, and judged by man and not by God.

*As man believes, man creates.*

When you believe in fear you create fear from fear. If you believe in dominance and submissiveness you create the role and you create fear in your ability to play the role. The energy of dominance and submissiveness that begins in the belief system of the individual expands to the family, the community, the state, the country, and the world. All energy has the ability to magnetize energy of like vibration.

*The energy of dominance and submissiveness that first comes to fruition for man in the role of lover has a direct effect upon the energy of the world. As the individual believes, so the world becomes. You create your individual reality and the reality of your world through the energy of your belief system.*

In choosing the opposite image of an energy to love, you allow yourself to judge what you believe you are not. You present yourself with the opportunity to learn the lessons of judgment, balance, and unconditional love. If one person in the relationship changes and grows faster than the other person, the relationship will not endure unless it is captured in the fear of change.

*Relationships between lovers that are based on dominance and submissiveness are focused on the acknowledged inequality of the relationship.*

Inequality creates unworthiness, judgment, physical affliction, desperation, distrust, jealously, anger, and fear within the relationship. These are emotions of negative energy that will not support a loving and productive relationship between lovers. They are the exact emotions the role is created to control.

# Homosexual Relationships

In addition to the role of the heterosexual lover there is the role of the homosexual lover as it is known within your world. Within the context of the homosexual lover there are multiple roles.

I will not focus upon the drama of the roles because they are identical to the multiple heterosexual relationships of lovers. I will focus upon the soul and spirit energies that create the roles within your world.

The homosexual lover is creating another image of the lesson of balance by experiencing the role of dominance and submissiveness. Homosexual lovers are more integrated into their female energies, or male energies as the case may be. They are not comfortable sharing their emotions and feelings and/or their aggressiveness with the opposite sex. Their attachment to the physical self is extreme.

Therefore, sharing their like emotions with the same sex is more acceptable. In the experience of both male and female, they feel they are better understood by those experiencing the same emotions and feelings.

This belief of man in the ability to understand feelings, emotions, behaviors, and actions only if you have experienced them is not unique with the homosexual. In science alcoholics are treated by former alcoholics, drug addicts are treated by former drug addicts, abused people are counseled by formerly abused people. Do you see the energy connection?

*The world approach to male dominance from the beginning of your history has created homosexuality. It has been judged by man harshly because man understands that sexual confusion is latent within all animal species including man. Because the ego belief of man has created the roles of dominance and submissiveness, it has encouraged the interaction of the same sex within relationships.*

If a male becomes consciously aware of his female energies within, and he chooses to approach life from the perspective of his emotions and feelings, he will be judged by man as feminine. One recourse for a relationship at this point is to find another man who understands and is willing to have a relationship. The same is true in female relationships.

The dominance and submissiveness of the homosexual world is the same as in the heterosexual world. Despite the developing integration of the male and female energies in the homosexual, both the male and female communities of homosexuals continue to function from the perspective of your male dominated society.

The structure of their community life and their individual relationship mirrors the image of the heterosexual relationship. This is their attachment to the physical, intellectual/ego controlled world which they are striving to release by integration of their male and female energies.

The focus of the homosexual in choosing the same sex for a relationship is another indication of their continued attachment to the physical belief system. The physical belief system is the system of the male-linkage where the cycle of development is predominant.

Once this attachment to the physical energy is released, these individuals will find very gratifying relationships with the opposite sex who appreciate, respect, and value the integrated energies within them.

*Because the world of man fears judgment by man, he does not understand that all of man must*

*integrate the male and female energies to evolve*
*as a soul and spirit.*

The judgment that exists and "identifies" this integration as wrong, creates the energy of homosexuality. This judgment is a judgment of man that is focused upon maintaining the physical world as an intellectual/ego world.

The belief in dominance and submissiveness is an illusion of the belief in power. It is as destructive in the homosexual community as it is in the heterosexual community. This intellectual attachment to dominance and submissiveness creates the sexual aberrations in the homosexual community in the same way it does within the heterosexual community. Indeed, man is attached to his role of power and control with all of its varying degrees of peculiarity.

*The challenge for man is to understand that integration of the male and female energies is normal and indeed encouraged as another step in soul evolution. When this understanding is accepted, there will be no guilt, sin, confusion, or anger involved in who man is or the way in which he lives his life.*

It is society's judgment that the males and females who are entering into the first level of sexual awareness in the spirit sense, are "wrong" in the physical sense.

*This is not the judgment of the spirit world because we do not judge. We ourselves have integrated male and female energies which we have balanced through our individual Earth lives. There is only unconditional love within the spirit world which is the exact opposite of the judgment within your physical world.*

If the individuals involved in this sexual merging understood and accepted themselves and the changes which they feel, they could live normal lives without the threat of disease.

*Your male dominated society that cherishes its role of dominance is the source of judgment, which is the source of the creation of homosexuality as a major issue within your world.*

Any behavior that is labeled "wrong" by the judgment of your society has the ability to become popular for self-gratification rather than self-realization. This has become a reality within the homosexual community that has allowed many individuals to attach themselves to the community because they have a need to be judged "wrong" by society.

These are not souls and spirits that are balancing out the integration of their male and female energies. These souls are firmly attached to the cycle of development and have entered into the homosexual community because of their sense of un-worthiness. This sense of unworthiness creates the need to associate with people that they also identify as unworthy. For them homosexuality is practiced for self-gratifying, self-protec-tive reasons.

Each man who feels the strength of his dominance also feels the tug of his female energy or he would not seek a submissive mate. This fear is then transferred to those souls who have openly admitted their "differences" as hostility, anger, fear, and judg-ment.

*If there were no fear of the internal female ener-gies by the individual and by society, there would be less homosexuality today than has existed in previous Earth time. These energies would be ac-cepted, cherished, and valued above all else.*

Each and every spirit and soul of man has lived thousands of lives as both genders. To move forward through the energy of soul evolution man is striving to balance those two energies within.

Balance will create an equal use of the physical energies, the soul energies, and the spirit energies within each and every lifetime. The path to balance may require thousands of lifetimes. The way the balance is approached is an individual choice.

When the spirit evolves into the Eighth Realm it will become androgynous. It will have accomplished the internal balance of the male and female energies. When the internal balance is complete within all of man, it will be balanced externally within the physical world. At this point in your time there will be no "homosexuality" within the world.

Lessons are learned by the experience of the lesson in different images. This is the path of the soul and spirit within. This is the path of evolution. Homosexuality of both male and female, and heterosexuality are some of the images of the male and female integration.

Integration of the male and female energies has a sexual influence only as it is demonstrated within the physical world. These energies are energies of love opposite to fear.

Fear is the focus of the physical presentation and love is the focus of the soul and spirit world. The sexual manifestation exists only within the physical world. Therefore, sex is seen as an attachment to the physical world in both male and female energy.

As your energies integrate you will find that you have less need for the physical gratification that sex offers. You will appreciate sex only in terms of celebrating a relationship that is integrated. In this context, sex can be a beautiful and satisfying celebration of the body, mind, and spirit of self.

# General Sexual Relationships

Your life is the story of the evolution of the soul of man. How your soul evolves through the steps or levels of consciousness and learning is the choice of the individual soul. Each life will contain multiple images of the physical lessons that you are actively learning on the soul and spirit level.

There are four cycles which each and every soul must experience in Earth life and in soul evolution. These cycles are the cycles of development, awareness, understanding, and integration.

Each and every lesson will be learned in the concept of images. Indeed, each lesson that you learn is so truly expansive that it cannot be learned with only one image. In each life there will be multiple images or roles of the lessons to be learned. The choice of the image is made by the individual spirit and soul within.

In the identical way that you snap many pictures with the lens of your camera to capture the perfect essence of clarity that you are searching for, you will create different images or dramas of the lesson which will give you the opportunity to see and understand the lesson with total clarity.

The lessons that you have committed yourself to remember by being human are the lessons of love, truth, and perfection. It is this love, truth, and perfection that is the energy essence of God. You are created in the image of God. Therefore, you are seeking to BE in the image of God. The God energy is a balanced, androgynous energy of enlightenment. This is a total integration of the male and female spirit energies within you in the physical world.

Numerically this explanation would appear in groups of three as:

1-2-3_____ 3-4-5 _____ 5-6-7- _____8

  (body)        (mind)       (spirit)

physical   intellectual   spiritual

       male-link    female-link   androgynous

    development  understanding  enlightened

         awareness     integration

      dominant     submissive   equal/balance

   external focus   inner focus   higher focus

This numerical linkage of the male is symbolized in the physical, body-mind linkage and in the female as the mind-spirit linkage. When you evolve as a soul, you learn the lessons of these seven levels of spiritual life while passing through the seven levels of physical life.

Each level is again relative to seven levels. Each of these levels is again manifested in each individual embodiment. The vibrational energy of the consciousness levels expand into infinity.

*The path to love, truth, and perfection is an individual creation of multiple images of multiple lessons. One lesson is not better than the other lesson. One lesson is not worse than another lesson. They are all simply choices of learning.*

It is when you know inside that you are imaging the love, truth, and perfection of God that you have reached a balance within. When you are balanced within you are balanced without. You will be in physical life what you feel inside. When you reach this level of balance there is no fear, sin, guilt, depression, or searching for love. You are total within yourself.

God is androgynous. God is a perfect balance of male and female energy within and without.

*Homosexuality is a lesson of balance. Heterosexuality is a lesson of balance. Each lesson will be different for each person.*

The motivation toward homosexuality will manifest itself in different ways within each and every individual in your physical world. In many individuals it will be a pronounced image of dominance and submissiveness which they will acknowledge and accept as a physical need.

In heterosexuality, dominance and submissiveness are veiled, as in the protector and the protected. When you are creating a lesson to be learned, you will expand the method of learning until you get your attention and the attention of the world.

Homosexuality is manifested as an expanded attachment to the physical body. In an effort to maintain the energy balance which is being pulled inward toward the emotional and feeling self, the homosexual focuses elaborately upon the physical self.

This can also be revealed in your physical world to a degree by the choice of professions. The influence of this soul energy also is a creative source that will encourage many males to enter some form of the arts. The male homosexual will strive for physical artistic creativeness.

In the female lesbian this will not be seen. The female is balancing out the intellectual energies and therefore will be drawn to the sciences, law, research, medicine, or any other profession that is involved in intellectual details. The female lesbian will strive for intellectual creativeness.

*There is no physical "cause" for homosexuality. It is a choice to learn balance of the male and female energies. It is an opportunity to learn to love self, God, and your neighbor. This is the lesson of unconditional love.*

Homosexuality creates an image opportunity for the individual to love self and an opportunity for the world to practice unconditional love. Unconditional love is non-judgment in your physical world. There are no accidents within the Universe. There are alternate paths but the energy of man is designed as intermingled, interwoven, and inseparable with all of man and with the Universe.

The manifestation of fear, anger, rage, hostility, hate, guilt, sin, denial, and resistance are emotions of your physical world. Within themselves they create a "concept of need" that leads man into his dramas of physical life. These emotions are reactions to thoughts that create the reality of being. It is from the thoughts of the mind that man creates the physical world in which he lives. His level of consciousness creates the details of the event.

All of you are searching for the balance that is found within. In expansively acting out the role of dominance and submissiveness, you must come to terms with these emotions within. Acknowledging and accepting the lesson facilitates truth, understanding, accepting, acknowledging, and valuing self with total respect.

The search for understanding becomes the motivation of life and will be the fiber that creates, limits, or expands all of your relationships. Homosexuality is the motivation of the subconscious soul energy within as it seeks balance with the dominant external physical energy. In the lessons of the soul and spirit, you will choose the opposite energy to learn within the physical world.

Learning to love self is the first step to learning to love God and your fellow man. You cannot learn total balance within until you know who you are and how you relate to self, to man, and to God. Learning is created by the interaction, the dramas of the relationships that you create within your world.

Your belief systems have created resistance for you to overcome before you can understand, accept, acknowledge, and value self and God. Belief systems do not change what IS in the evolution of your soul. For the soul to evolve it must pass through the cycles of development, awareness, understanding, and integration. Each cycle has multiple levels of consciousness to be mastered.

*Belief systems are the resistance created by you to your own soul evolution. Denial is the physical manifestation of spiritual resistance within the physical world. Soul evolution is seen in the physical world as change and growth.*

When God created the spirit of man, He divided that spirit into two energies, male and female. As the soul of man travels through its path of evolution, it changes from the physical focus. In the beginning man is grounded to Earth. With evolution man changes to the soul and spirit focus which creates evolution to loftier energies.

The physical focus is the cycle of development for the soul. The soul focus of man is the memory of all that he has been in his soul experience. The spirit focus of man is the inherent love, truth, and perfection that is within. The spirit of man is the Godself of man.

In the belief of man, the physical focus is supreme to all other focuses. If the lesson for man is balance, he will manifest that lesson in the extremes of dominance and submissiveness which is the role of the physical focus.

*Homosexual energies are the mirror images of the physical/male energy and the soul/female energy as it evolves through the levels and cycles required in soul evolution.*

When the soul and spirit energy begins to integrate with the physical energy of man, confusion develops within the physical mind of man which he does not understand. He will begin to feel the influence of both the energies within. This confusion may occur at any point within the physical lifetime of man. Indeed for many men it will occur in what you term mid-life crisis at approximately 40 years of age.

The term mid-life is an amusing term to this spirit as I understand the mid-life period for you differently than you perceive it. In the spirit sense you have a normal capability of living on Earth for a period of 147 years in your time. Mid-life in my terms would be around the age of 74. You yourself limit your Earth life. Indeed, that too, is changing.

The efforts of the soul and spirit to balance themselves with your physical energy creates an illusion of identity loss within the physical self. It is at this moment that you enter into an awareness cycle that allows you to sense that you are more than just a physical body. Sensing the unknown creates fear for the ego which then increases its attachment to the physical reality.

*This inner turmoil is manifested in a physical confusion of gender identity loss. This physical gender loss will inspire you to seek the physical image of self within the world because you will not feel that a person of the opposite sex could have the same sense of bewilderment. Because the individual cannot assimilate the identity loss, the reflection is transferred to a relationship of the same sex. The relationship is accepted as having the added advantage of supporting the gender identity during this period of loss. The acknowledgment of the physical reinforcement becomes an emotional reinforcement of gender identity.*

Man will generally seek the opposite energy in his physical efforts to balance self. But in this bewilderment of physical gender identity loss, man creates the relationship that you call homosexuality in his efforts to understand and love self. He will resist the merging soul and spirit influence within self by attaching self more firmly to the physical image of self.

*This is the homosexual effort to balance self and to know self. He is creating a physical resistance to integration by adding physical energy to his physical energy as reinforcement.*

In the path of soul evolution, moving from the strong physical focus to the feeling focus of the soul creates intellectual and physical disorientation. This disorder occurs because in the belief system of man the male is seen as physically and intellectually superior. The female is seen as physically and intellectually inferior, or focused within the feeling or emotional self.

In the physical world these images create roles of master and slave, protector and server, dominance and submission, strong and weak, power and control, and superior and inferior, all within the context of male and female energies.

*Changing from the illusion of the role within the physical world presents an ego threat to those energies that are attached to the perception of the role. When the energies within and without begin to integrate there is a challenge to define the role in the physical sense.*

As the soul evolves, it is involved in the process of understanding and integrating the soul memories and the spirit energy with the physical energy. Within the expansiveness of the soul memory is the energy of all the experiential learning of the total experience of your soul. In addition you have the spirit energy of the love, truth, and perfection that is your inherent birthright from God. This knowledge will integrate with the intellect.

The integration may occur smoothly within the physical world as a peaceful river flows, or it may rage expansively as a flood of overwhelming emotion. Floods will always meet resistance and denial of the path as the accepted boundaries are ignored.

As he accepts and acknowledges this additional energy within himself on a physical basis, it is suddenly man's challenge and his opportunity to maintain his balance within the physical world that he understands. It is at this time that man finds himself totally immersed within the lesson of balance.

Because of his challenge to understand himself, who he is, what he is, and how he relates, man makes the choice of what he accepts as "self" within his world. The love he does or does not feel, the fear, the searching, the loss, the interaction of relationships, and the acceptance or non-acceptance of the world around him, all become relative to his judgment process.

*It is at this time when man is truly searching for his understanding and love of self, that his focus may be directed toward the physical image of self.*

His choice has total validity for him because of the image that he is creating in his lesson of balance. He is trying to capture in the physical world what he feels that he is losing. Capturing the energy that he feels fading away from self, offers a reinforcement of self.

Not all choices will be the same. Not all dramas within the choice will be the same. Man will follow his mirror image from within. It is this mirror image of self that man sees and hears.

It is the mirror image of some facet of yourself that you reflect in a relationship that allows you to vent the emotion within yourself on your sexual partner. This reflection is consistent within all relationships, but each relationship will be different.

*As the soul of man evolves and man begins to love self with confidence, assurance, and realization, he will reflect love within all of his relationships.*

Love is the energy of the truth and perfection of self. Love IS balance. Love IS understanding. Love IS equality.

This need to balance within will be manifested in the way that man accepts balance in the physical world. For the soul that is advancing through the level of female energy with the physical gender being male, homosexuality is a frequent choice.

It is also a frequent choice of the female who is trying to balance the intellectual male energy within. This is truly a search for an understanding and integration of all that is within and without, or of self. This is the internal struggle of dominance and submissiveness manifested externally in the physical actions of life. This is your search for balance.

*Homosexuality is a dominance of the supreme physical sense of the body over the mind in the search for balance of the integrating male and female energies within.*

It is at this level of soul evolution that you function from soul memory. It is within this group of souls that the motivation of creative energy will be found. Not all souls who are seeking the lesson of balance will become homosexual. Not all creative persons will be homosexual. Not all homosexuals will be involved in the lesson of balance. Not all homosexuals will be creative. Indeed, there are too many energies to make generalizations in your world.

*It is at this level of soul evolution that the confusion of sexual focus has the opportunity to occur. It is at this level that your intellect becomes confused by the integration of the male and female energies within.*

Homosexuality is a conscious choice of coping with these integrating energies within the physical world.

All of you are learning the lesson of balance. You will learn the lesson in multiple images of gender identity. You will learn in multiple energies in one lifetime and in many lifetimes. The integration of the male and female energies internally and externally will be learned by your own design and by your own choice of images.

Creative energy is the energy of soul memory, it is the female energy within. Also within the soul memory is the memory of having been the opposite sex, of having learned the physical loves of the opposite sex, the emotions and feelings of the opposite sex. In this search for balance, you will be challenged to understand who you are physically, emotionally, and spiritually.

In your physical reality this will be felt as a puzzlement that is created between the belief that is predominant in your mind and the inner feelings that you experience. This is the ego/spirit tug-of-war or the balance within and without of the dominance and submissiveness that you feel.

As an example, you may be a male that has been taught the physical focus, the world of science, and the process of the intellectual. You may be strongly attached to your ego beliefs.

Nothing in your learning has taught you the love of cooking, of caring about people, of crying, or of wanting to decorate your home in a "feminine" manner. These needs that appear to you to be opposite to who you believe that you should be, create confusion within your mind as to who you are which impacts upon your sexual orientation.

Your sexual choice was designed into your life design and was manifested within your physical world as your physical sex. Understanding and maintaining your soul and spirit choice becomes a challenge for you. It is learning to be all that you can be, as you are.

You do not understand the feminine energies within a male body. You do not understand the beginning of your mind, body, and spirit integration. This beginning integration of the male and female energies within creates the physical confusion in your external world of the physical self.

Upon your Earth different cultures have created different belief systems that structure the world of the male and the world of the female. Homosexuality and heterosexuality have existed since the beginning of man on Earth. From the beginning of your time, man has been actively trying to balance these energies within himself.

When you find that you cannot conform to the structure of accepted cultural beliefs, you increase your challenge by guilt and fear of your separation from God. If you feel you are an outcast, if you feel you are different, if you feel misunderstood, unaccepted, judged, and angry, the fear that is within you will create disease.

In the fear of being judged, you will judge yourself. In the spiritual perspective you have outgrown the developmental structure that your culture is based upon. The structure of judgment is an ego/intellectual structure that has served a purpose in the cycle of development.

*Now that you are entering the cycle of aware-*
*ness, your understanding must evolve before the in-*
*tegration and the equalization of the male and*
*female energies can occur.*

This does not mean that each and every soul will choose to learn an image of the lesson of balance by being homosexual. How you learn your lessons is an individual choice in each and every step of soul evolution. You will always choose a path that will teach you multiple lessons as you grow.

**Only the soul that is in the cycle of awareness will normally choose homosexuality as a lesson of balance.**

This soul has developed an awareness of the soul and spirit within. This awareness will not exist on a conscious level but it is there on a subconscious and unconscious level. This is a soul involved in its own evolution or advancement. This is a soul searching to understand self.

**The ego has become aware of the soul and spirit within but it cannot as yet accept releasing the physical focus to integrate the three facets of self.**

In its search this soul may focus expansively on the supreme physical sense of self which is the issue of sexual gratification. On a physical level your search will be manifested in self-gratification externally, as the search within is focused on self-realization.

While learning this lesson of balance, the soul will also be exposed to images of other lessons. These lessons will be involved in balancing the physical energies with the soul and spirit energies in the many images of love. What is in the spirit world will always be manifested within the physical world.

# Persecution In Unconditional Love

The image of unconditional love is an image that is learned through the emotion of rejection or persecution. This is an example of experiencing the opposite in our efforts to learn.

Christ manifested His lesson of unconditional love to the world by His creation of the illusion of His Crucifixion. When the soul is choosing to learn the lesson of unconditional love, it will focus on being the opposite to the accepted belief system of man. It will create the opportunity to be judged to learn non-judgment or unconditional love.

Lessons are learned by experiencing the opposites. The opposites can be experienced by active or passive participation. The soul that chooses homosexuality has chosen to be actively participating in the lesson of non-judgment. The heterosexual is choosing a passive participation of learning non-judgment by learning not to judge his fellow man. Both images are images of the lesson of unconditional love.

Do you see the multiple images of lessons that are involved within each event within the life of man?

Each lesson is interwoven, intermingled, inseparable, and interpenetrated. Nothing remains one but becomes inseparable from the web of energy within life and within the Universe.

When you choose to learn your lesson of balance by the challenge and opportunity of homosexuality, you are creating for yourself in your physical world a role of persecution. This is your choice as a method of experience to help you learn the lessons that you have designed. The role of persecution has millions of images.

**The role of persecution is a role of not being understood.**

This role of persecution is manifested because man does not understand himself. He will choose a role that will seize his attention and the attention of the world, in his effort to understand self. Therefore, man makes a spiritual statement on an individual level, a world level, and a spiritual level.

Man is integrated, his learning is integrated, and his living is integrated. The lessons of the soul and spirit will always be manifested within the physical world just as the lessons of the physical world will be manifested within the soul and spirit of man.

**Unconditional love is the lesson of integration.**

It is because of this physical manifestation of the lesson of unconditional love that the mass consciousness of man created the disease of AIDS. AIDS is not a disease of homosexuality.

**AIDS is a disease that has been created by all of man to focus his attention upon his loss of respect and value for sexual interaction.**

AIDS creates the opportunity within the soul and spirit of man to look at self and understand his physical focus. AIDS will capture the attention of the individual, the community, the state, the world, and the Universe. AIDS will be a Karmic choice of learning for many souls on Earth.

A Karmic lesson can be recognized when the disease is accepted without the understood manifestation of creation. As an example, children with AIDS have chosen the disease as a Karmic lesson.

As children they will play a role in raising the consciousness level of the world that a sexually active adult could not play. The lessons of the soul and spirit involved with the disease will be multiple. The lessons of the world will be multiple.

As a disease, AIDS serves as an opportunity for man to balance his physical focus. The supreme physical focus is the sexual focus. When you create a sexual disease of this magnitude, you are creating the opportunity to balance the physical you with your soul and spirit within. You are choosing to raise your consciousness level of the imbalance in your physical focus.

All disease is a lesson in balance of the excesses and deficiencies of life manifested within the physical body. If you focus only upon the physical, you will create the opportunity to perceive the physical self with a different level of aware consciousness.

AIDS has served all of man by capturing his attention and focusing it upon the present day intention of sexual interaction. AIDS has raised the level of aware consciousness within man of the physical dangers of sexual shopping.

Lung cancer has raised the level of aware consciousness within man of the physical dangers of smoking. Heart disease has raised the level of aware consciousness within man of the physical dangers in an uncontrolled food intake.

In this respect AIDS is no different than any other disease within your world. AIDS is within your world to teach the balance of self, which is the balance of the male and female energies within. The balance of the male and female energies within is the balance of the physical body, intellect, and ego (male energy), with the soul and spirit (female energy).

Each and every disease that man creates focuses attention upon a belief of man relative to self. If you see yourself as only a physical being, you will create an opportunity to understand other facets of self. Man will create on a subconscious and unconscious basis an action that will develop on a conscious basis.

*The ultimate in conscious awareness for man is to reach the state of super-consciousness. In the state of super-consciousness, man creates from the integrated conscious awareness state with the sub-*

*conscious and unconscious self. As your conscious, subconscious, and unconscious minds become integrated, you create a super-conscious mind energy.*

As you live to experience lessons of learning, you will create disease after disease to seize your conscious awareness of self and the balance within. As you evolve, you will become conscious of your lessons within the experience of disease.

Disease will always be on Earth until man evolves sufficiently to understand that it does not serve him. Disease is a profound lesson in the cycle of development. It is seldom accepted as a learning experience in the cycle of integration. In the cycles of awareness and understanding, it will be used less frequently by man.

CANCER is created as a lesson by some souls to learn the balance of love because they live in fear. The fear may not be accepted as fear but may be understood as anger, hate, hostility, resistance, denial, or any of the multiple elements of fear.

HEART DISEASE is created by some souls to learn the lesson of physical balance. Heart disease occurs in man because of the abuse of the physical body through the excesses and deficiencies of physical life. Heart disease is created by the fear of loving self and of being loved.

If you do not love yourself, you will abuse your physical body that you accept as self. If you do not love yourself, you will create multiple dependencies that will allow you a veiled vision of your true self. Not loving yourself is an element of the fear of unworthiness.

Each disease is created by the mass consciousness and the individual consciousness of man, for man as part of the drama of life and learning. If you have learned the lesson, you will not attach yourself to the energy of the disease. If you do attach yourself to the energy of the disease, you may choose to do so from an active or passive participant basis.

*When man creates any disease, including AIDS, he can cure the disease by understanding, accepting, acknowledging, and valuing self by learning the lesson that he is working with internally.*

Each disease raises the level of conscious awareness within your world and creates a focus within the world of prevention and cure. Prevention and cure will have a direct action upon the behavior and belief of man. The disease itself will create a direct action upon the behaviors and beliefs of man.

Medical care should be sought in physical disease to create a bridge for man. This bridge becomes an opportunity to work with self and understand self in treating the disease. Medical treatment should be focused upon creating a balance within the physical body. Many times in your world the treatment is as traumatic as the disease. Excess in any form emphasizes the need to create balance by change.

*Medical treatment allows man the time and the opportunity within the external physical world for the change to occur within and without in the physical sense. Accepting medical guidance will create the opportunity of extended "time" to effect the cure within.*

When God created man he created both male and female. He made them equal in spirit and soul. He made them different in physical form to propagate, to create their own progeny for the continuation of the human race. He created their ability to celebrate their physical bodies by the harmony and balance of design. In this ability to celebrate he gave them the power of creation.

Adam and Eve were Immaculate Conceptions and as the Spirit of the Christ Consciousness they were divided into male and female. Jesus of Nazareth and His Mother Mary were each Immaculate Conceptions in your world as once again God divided the Spirit of the Christ Consciousness into male and female. The divided Spirit of the Christ Consciousness returned to Earth without physical conception for each to play a role in the Crucifixion.

Because the phenomena of Immaculate Conception is not the way that man enters his physical life on Earth, the true balance for physical creation will always be found with the coming together of the male and female energies.

*This does not exclude any path of learning.*

The lessons within soul evolution are choices of the soul and spirit. When they are created by man as opposites to the belief systems of man, they act as a lesson for man to learn non-judgment. The lesson simply IS.

*In the energy of BEING, homosexuality is a path to the lesson of balancing the male and female energies within the physical world of man and within self. The souls and spirits that are involved in homosexual relationships today are serving as Universal messengers for the lesson in balance for the world.*

Homosexuality has been a reality within the physical realm of Earth from the beginning of your time. It has occurred and will continue to occur as a lesson of balance of the male and female energies. When the relationship of self, and the relationship of the male and female is balanced, homosexuality will no longer serve a purpose within your world.

As each soul moves through its phenomena of evolution, it will have the choice to choose homosexuality as one possible path of learning. It is a frequent choice for those souls that are balancing their male and female energies. Balancing the male and female energies within requires that you release your attachment to the physical focus. Your sexual interaction is your supreme physical focus. The male-linkage is the physical focus.

Do you see the energy connection?

In the same manner that man chooses to kill and be killed, to be in a culture of suppression, to live in a world of war, to be angry, fearful, hostile, sick, depressed, to be a member of a cultural belief or an ethnic group, some souls will choose to learn by being homosexual. They are not to be judged. They are to be loved and supported as they learn.

The soul of the homosexual is a soul in the process of evolution. These souls are advancing forward through the cycle of awareness with an energy of understanding. Soul evolution requires an openness to change and growth. Change and growth are always preferable to remaining stuck in the energy of resistance and denial.

*The advanced soul will recognize homosexuality as a lesson in balancing the male and female energies within. These are evolving souls who do not fear what IS.*

# Roles of Lovers

The roles of the lover are multiple and will be on multiple levels at different times. The spiritual definition of love is an energy action of commitment to the growth of self and another. It cannot be defined by words because it can only be understood as action.

If your lover says "I love you" and then is unfaithful, he does not understand love. If your lover says "I love you" and then ignores you, he does not understand love. If your lover says "I love you" and then abuses you, he does not understand love.

There are many types of sexual encounters within your world that can not come within the true definition of lovers. Love is an emotion of caring and sharing. Sexual encounters are based upon physical need. Physical need is confused as physical love. The values of self, of the soul, and the spirit are not considered in this physical need activity.

All activity within your world must have acceptance, acknowledgment, respect, and value to be balanced. With acceptance both parties must accept the act and the responsibility for their actions.

They both must be willing to acknowledge to the world that they were of one intention with their acceptance. They must respect each other and the fruits of their activities by maintaining the responsibility toward each other and the Universe. What they do as an interaction must have value to themselves, their children, the family, the community, the world, and the Universe.

Physical need has expanded in the minds of many because of the strong focus on the physical body in your world. You are led to believe through sexual exploitation that sex is love. Your society invites and supports sexual exploitation of the body from the old to the young.

In your world even family members will engage in sex. This is further exploitation and confusion. When this happens, understand that your value system is out of balance and out of control. This indulgence can create expansive problems for all participants.

Sex has no boundaries in your world today which is a creation of man. Maintaining a balance in sexual activity is maintaining a balance of the physical perspective within your world. When the focus upon the physical becomes totally out of balance, you yourself must correct the imbalance by balancing yourself and your world.

**All of life is your creation. What you have created you can cure.**

When the physical focus predominates as it does within your world, it is evident that the soul and spirit of man has gotten lost within the tangle of physical existence. It is this imbalance that allows and supports sexual exploitation. This imbalance then becomes the norm for the youth of your world.

The physical focus toward sex has reached critical mass within your society and within the world. Therefore, it is accepted within your world as appropriate. When there is acceptance of an act that is surrounded with so many atrocities upon the participants, it is due for change.

*The acceptance of sexual exploitation has created the opportunity for you to examine the root cause of your many symptoms and find a cure.*

Life could be compared to a pendulum swinging back and forth. When the pendulum swings too far in one direction the "weight" of the pendulum will bring it back to the other side.

The "weight" or responsibilities that have been generated within the Universe by sexual exploitation will bring the value system back to sex only as a celebration of love. This will return the beauty, value, and respect for sex into the life of man.

Sex has become an economic issue in your business world. When sex is exploited from the business perspective, it reaches critical mass more quickly and then becomes acceptable to man. When the focus is on sex without love, your world will find sex "crimes" increasing expansively. Other crimes become parasitic to the crimes of sex.

*It is this exploitation of sex by society that has escalated the challenges of your youth. When your youth feels the pressure of society to be sexually active, it creates confusion within the soul and spirit. This in turn escalates the need for physical support for them to be what they feel they are supposed to be. Drugs and alcohol give them the support they need to create within themselves an adult approach to life.*

Sex is not free within the Universe. In the Book of God is the story of Adam and Eve. Their drama of illicit sex informed you of the dramas that you would create if you practice illicit sex. The story was revealed to you so that you could understand and avoid the perils of sex.

It is the drama of you as the teacher that will be learned and repeated by your children today. You are learning through the repetition of the Christ Consciousness path, your own exploitation of sex. You will be your child's teacher.

Because of the illicit relationship of Cain and Able, Cain slew Able. This is your historical account of the perils of illicit sex. This story is related in more detail in our book, **BRIDGES OF CONSCIOUSNESS: Self Discovery In The New Age.** I will not repeat it here.

You will do well to remember the ravages of sex upon the individual, the family, and the culture. Sex carries with it enormous responsibilities that begin with the individual and expand with each generation to include all of society. This is the rock that was dropped into the pond that sent out the vibrations to infinity.

The responsibilities do not stay with the individual. They become critical concerns for the family, the community, the state, the country, the world, and the Universe. These responsibilities then become your concerns. You do not direct your cures at the cause but at the symptoms.

When you have the courage to look within, you will find the source of sexual exploitation begins within the individual. With your scientific inventions it is easier to exploit sex to every man, woman, and child within your Universe. Now your culture teaches what the parent may ignore.

Sexual exploitation has two major roles within your world. There are those who actively exploit sex and there are those who passively accept the exploitation. To solve the problem in your culture, the passive observers must become active in stopping the exploitation. What you refuse to support in your world has a very short life. This is a condition that needs to be balanced by you and can be balanced by you.

> *Respect and value for the sexual celebration*
> *should be returned to your understanding of*
> *morality.*

All of man needs to learn the difference between sexual exploitation and love. It is essential to the growth and evolvement of the spirit and soul of man. Sexual exploitation is your most expansive example of the imbalance toward the external physical facet of man.

Inside, internal to man, is the soul and spirit that is trying desperately to be accepted and acknowledged in its desire to help balance the total mind of man.

In searching for this balance, you can reach the peace of self-realization. Self-realization is loving the total self, accepting the total self, acknowledging the total self, respecting the total self, and valuing the total self. Self-realization is integration of the total self into one balanced cognitive Being.

When you love yourself, you will awaken each morning being love. You will smile with joy at life. You will be inspired and motivated to create new and beautiful moments to remember. You will feel pure joy in the center of your physical body and your heart. You will accept and acknowledge love in your mind. You will live love each and every moment of your life with each and every person that you encounter.

When you truly love yourself, you will be able to love another person. You survive in your world on the physical attraction that you feel for another. This physical attraction is dictated by the role you are attached to in your physical world.

*The love of physical attraction is ego love. It is the love that you see as your identity survival. You cannot be a lover until you understand loving.*

Love is the action of accepting, acknowledging, respecting, appreciating, and valuing the individual that you love and the commitment that you have to that individual. Love is a validation of being and of feeling. Loving is sharing and caring mutually in a relationship. Love is totally non-judgmental in all aspects of being. Love is not limited by belief systems. Love does not respond to "if." Love is the energy essence of acknowledging truth and perfection in relationship. Love is a commitment to the growth of your partner.

*Love is motivated by the soul of you, inspired by the spirit of you, and created by the intellect of you. Love knows no fear.*

LOVE IS JOY WITHIN THE PHYSICAL WORLD.

*You have come to me*
*out of the past*
*into a reality of now.*
*You have touched my heart*
*with your smile*
*hiding the love in you.*

# Sharing
# Marriage

*All is real for us*
*the truth in knowing*
*the happiness*
*in touching and caring*
*that we are there*
*for the other to love.*

*Why did it take so long*
*to find each other*
*in our world?*
*Were we growing alone*
*to find our happiness*
*so together we know only joy?*

*The most exalted purpose for marriage of two
souls is the presence of total unconditional love
and sharing with a total commitment to soul
growth for yourself and your partner. Nothing else
has the loftiness of true soul purpose.*

Unconditional love is the awareness of advanced souls. This is an integrated love. Marriages that are based upon an integrated love of the body, mind, and spirit are marriages that have the strength and courage to endure all hardships.

Indeed, not all marriages on Earth are going to occur between two advanced souls that have reached a state of aware consciousness within. Marriages will occur for as many reasons as there are marriages. Marriage is a unique relationship of sharing between two members of the opposite sex. Marriage is the most intimate and fulfilling way of sharing in your world.

If we want to know ourselves, we create the opportunity to understand who we are by the development of relationships. The relationship of marriage is a very profound and significant relationship for man.

*It is within the intimacy of marriage that man
creates the opportunity to become self-realized in
partnership.*

Self-realization by its nature of love must create within the physical world the opportunity to love. Love is giving and receiving. Love can be given to friends, family, community, and the world on a global basis, but the most gratifying love of all is that which has an immediate and a personal return.

*Marriage allows the joy of giving and receiving
on an intimate, moment by moment basis.*

In this intimacy challenges will occur. A marriage between integrated partners will survive these challenges because both partners will be open to communication and working on the issues that have presented themselves. Integration within the partners will assure the marriage of motivation, inspiration, and creativity. An exalted level of creativity cannot exist in the same energy as fear.

Marriage provides a mirror of the inner issues within self more completely than any other relationship. You will experience those images that you support and those images that are opposite to your beliefs. In experiencing the opposites you see with total clarity what you do not want in your life experience.

*In marriages that are committed to growth and are based upon the integrated, unconditional love of the soul and spirit, there will be no judgment. Judgment is the opposite of unconditional love.*

There will be marriages that you may view as unfathomable and insignificant, but believe me when I tell you that it is all part of the life design that you have created for yourself. In the interaction with the perfect partner, or the interaction with a not-so-perfect partner, you will have the opportunity to learn.

You are born into a physical existence and you focus upon that physical existence. In the beginning you focus upon physical development. Your body grows. Your mind grows. As you reach the stage of adulthood, your interactions with the opposite sex assumes a different energy. You have developed a consciousness of the supreme physical sense and you are beginning to put that sexual sense into action within your life.

In your world, this energy is usually focused upon the physical attraction of a mate. You look for a mate who can validate the physical belief systems of your world. You try to find a partner (a husband, a wife) that will fulfill the beliefs that you have attached yourself to in your lifetime.

Indeed, your belief may be so firmly attached to your physical world that it would be unthought of to marry outside of the accepted belief system. This is your method of controlling your world with fear.

*Attachment to a belief system is denial of all else that is in existence. Control is a way of dealing with the unknown that you fear.*

The belief focus in marriage will usually be directed toward the physical, the religious, or the status level of your world. There will be some advanced souls who will have a better subconscious and unconscious integration of the soul and spirit of the partner they are seeking.

If the soul is integrated to the point of consciously understanding exactly what you want within a marriage partner, you may refuse to abide by the dictates of your belief system. Or perhaps your conscious mind has never attached itself to a belief system. You will be open to free choice.

Do not be surprised if this integration is not conscious in your mind. It is perfectly normal for man in the cycle of development to focus upon physical attraction. Once you have gone beyond the cycle of development you may find yourself loving someone who does not conform to your belief in physical attractiveness.

When this love happens to you, you will either accept your love on a different basis or you will be captured in the fear of the unknown. This fear will allow you to slide back into the cycle of development as you attach yourself once more to a person that you find physically attractive.

In the cycle of development man will frequently experience devolution as his ego belief system captures him in fear. He will become self-conscious in his relationship and begin to deny the feelings that he is experiencing. These feelings can and will create panic, fear, depression, anger, despair, control, defenses, denial, resistance, and on and on.

*The cycle of development must be repeated in each and every embodiment. It will always be repeated within the physical sense, and it will be repeated to varying degrees within the energy of the soul and spirit.*

The repetition that is required depends upon the openness of the rational and intuitive mind that is retained through the physical development cycle. Openness of the individual can be defined by the level of attachment to belief systems within the physical world.

If a person is open they are first and foremost accepting of the energy of daily creation. They have strength, courage, independence, and they are self-sufficient. This positive creative person will strike fear in the heart of one who does not have these character traits. This positive energy will make a negative person feel that they are losing total control. It will create excessive judgment and attempts to control.

Indeed, these two people will have energies of such opposite polarities that the negative person will not be able to be in the presence of the positive person for very long. This is the ego fear of survival that will become dominant.

When an individual focuses totally upon physical attraction, you may find yourself, in some instances, with a partner who is not willing to look at themselves and to grow at the same level that you are working within.

When this happens, do not blame the partner. It was and is your free choice to make. You chose the relationship for a lesson to be learned. Once the lesson is learned the relationship has no purpose without joy in the sharing.

Unless your partner is willing to grow, your choice will not be perfect when you continue to grow. Accept the fact that you have gone in alternate directions. There is nothing wrong with going in opposite directions. You have simply outgrown each other. An integrated, self-realized person will accept this change willingly and will continue in their self-sufficient, independent manner.

*It is better in life to accept change than to find yourself stuck in a belief that does not allow you to open and to expand to continuous growth.*

The reason that you choose a mate that may not be perfect for you for a lifetime is that you do not understand in the beginning of your life what it is that you truly want. If you do not understand what you truly want for a lifetime, it is a true challenge to make a perfect choice.

When you can understand that you are not just a physical body, that you do have the energy of many soul memories and that you do have the eternal spirit within, you will begin to look for a mate who can grow personally and who is willing to be open and committed to growth in a marriage.

*Growth that is being shared and understood by two souls is truly a joyous, inspirational, motivational, and creative experience.*

When we speak of "open" in a marriage, we are not speaking of sexual promiscuity. We are speaking of the mind being open. In your world, open marriages have a different meaning, and I want you to understand, that is not our meaning.

*Sexual shopping during the married state is an indication of the confusion that dwells within the mind of man. This is a symptom in your world of immaturity and a poor self-image. It is not conducive to growth, happiness, or marriage. Indeed, this is the opposite behavior to love, truth, and perfection which is your spirit energy.*

Sexual shopping is an indication of the focus that you put upon physical massaging of the ego. It reflects the individual's attachment to the physical, material, self-gratifying, and external world of man. It is devolution in terms of the soul and spirit.

Man in his physical attachments and mental confusion slides back and forth in the path of his soul evolution. Sexual promiscuity is a physical exhibition of the devolution of the soul and spirit.

*Sexual shopping is a physical manifestation of not truly understanding what you want in a partnership, therefore, you are still searching. You are searching in the realm of physical gratification. This confusion will indeed continue until you integrate the soul and spirit understanding with what you see as physical need.*

When there is a relationship that is leading to marriage, sexual shopping is a danger sign of the dramas that one or both partners will be creating. Sexual shopping is the opposite of commitment in a relationship or marriage. If both partners choose to become involved in this denial of commitment, it is their free choice to confront the issues to be learned.

Marriage is a physical creation that does not change the maturity of the spouses by the recitation of the wedding vows. In the same way that death does not create a perfect spirit, marriage does not create a perfect partner. Perfection takes work, commitment, love, truth, and creativity.

*Marriage requires a commitment to work through in partnership all issues that surface between you. Marriage is a partnership not a dictatorship.*

Within a well-balanced partnership, there is unlimited potential for growth, because marriage gives you freedom. This is not understood by your world because you perceive marriage as taking AWAY your sexual or physical freedom. This belief validates that your focus is exclusively directed toward the physical understanding of marriage.

*Marriage does NOT take away freedom. Marriage gives you the freedom of not "needing" to search for a partner. Marriage gives you the freedom of communication, of beautiful exchanges, of*

*sharing, and caring. Marriage gives you the freedom
to love and be loved. Marriage gives you the freedom
to give and to receive.*

**Marriage IS a commitment to growth for both partners.** In your physical world most of you see your commitment only in terms of physically providing for or of being physically present for your partner. You do not think in terms of soul and spirit growth. Your focus is directed toward the physical commitments of the relationship.

Have you ever heard a statement such as this, "I give her all the money she needs, a good house, and a fancy car. What else is there?" Or "I give him my body whenever he wants it. I keep the house nice and I am home when he gets here. What more does he want?"

These are statements of belief in fulfillment of the physical needs of marriage. If you view marriage only as having physical needs, then of course you would feel that you are being all that you can be in the marriage when you think that you are fulfilling those needs.

Multiple levels of sharing of the body, mind, and spirit are essential in a good partnership. If you do not share the inspiration and motivation of the mind with enthusiasm, you do not communicate your true self. If you do not share the inspiration of the soul and the motivation of the spirit, you do not communicate and nurture the spirit within.

*It is when you share your intellect, your soul,
and your spirit as well as your body that you create a glorious partnership.*

Physical sharing is also essential because it is representative of the integration that you have learned. It is in sharing the physical that you validate the integrated sharing and nurturing of the self and the partner.

*Physical sharing becomes the celebration of the integration that has occurred.*

*Sharing of each and every facet of your being
will occur daily and it will occur on various levels
of consciousness which will be apparent in multitudinous ways within the physical world. This is the creation of partnership bonding.*

When there is partnership bonding, which is a commitment to growth between both partners on all levels of consciousness, there are no "problems" in the marriage, there are only challenges to grow. It does not matter how expansive the drama is or how traumatic the drama is, it is accepted as a challenge to grow. The challenge is shared together and the nurturing is shared together.

On your Earth one of the belief systems that creates confusion in marriages is the belief that man and woman are NOT equal. Indeed, let me remind you, that you ARE equal. The equality is of the spirit. It IS the eternal spirit that truly matters. It is the spirit that is on Earth to grow and to evolve by virtue of the physical experience. Your physical body is finite. Your soul is infinite. Your spirit is eternal.

*All things created by God are eternal. All things not created by God are illusion. God created the soul and spirit of man and they are eternal. The energy of man creates his own physical body and it is illusion.*

The physical body of man is illusion because it is the manifestation of energy created at Earth speed. When you see the physical body of man, you do not see man. You see only the slow energy of the physical not the energy of All That Is and not the eternal spirit which is the true self of man.

*When you focus upon the physical body in marriage or in life, you are focusing upon an illusion. This validates your attachment to your cycle of development.*

Your physical intellect is responsible to the spirit of you for maintaining the credibility of the cellular structure known as the body. The body is the chosen dwelling place of the spirit.

If you look at your physical body, it is true that many men are physically stronger than women. Women will generally have a stronger emotional and feeling sense than men. What the female lacks in strength she creates in ingenuity and endurance because by choosing to be female she is acknowledging and accepting the soul and spirit within to a greater degree than the male.

*Accepting the female gender within your culture, is accepting the challenge to live from more than the physical perspective.*

Physical strength is not the focus of the female. Indeed, it is your culture that has created the physical disparity in strength. In other cultures the female may be physically stronger than the male.

*Accepting the male gender within your culture, is accepting the challenge to overcome your singular focus and attachment to the physical world.*

When God created spirits and decided to show them a path of learning, He took the spirit and He divided it into male and female. He made the body complementary to each soul. The male was given the energy focus of the physical and the female was given the energy focus of the soul and spirit. Thus God focused upon the head of man, and the heart of woman.

This energy focus was illustrated within the physical body by the sexual design of external and internal focus. Indeed, in all aspects the male and female were created as a complement to each other, a completion of body and mind when joined together.

You do indeed change genders with your twin soul during the path of soul evolution. You work together on a subconscious and an unconscious basis to evolve your souls. You are separate, but you are one. Your energies are complete in each and completed in each other as you integrate.

When both souls are perfected, they will join together with God to integrate once again with the spirit energy of the Creator. At this moment you will become a trilogy of energy. The energy of you was created to expand the energy of God. This is shown to man as the Holy Trinity. You will become male, female, and God in your own union of perfection.

The union of man with God in his state of perfection was shown to you by the union of the Virgin Mother Mary and Jesus of Nazareth. These twin souls that lived on Earth as the Christ Consciousness became a trilogy with the Creator when they reached their state of Unconditional Love. This path of learning was defined by the Creator for man through the example of the Christ Consciousness.

The gender focus that exists upon earth creates a variety of restrictive beliefs. For many years it was believed that women were not as intelligent as men, in the same way that it was believed that men were much stronger than women. You see, each and every thought is a belief.

Beliefs are true only for you and only if you believe them to the point of living them. When you believe them and live them, you create the belief as truth for you within the physical world. Your truth as you accept it is used to create a structure of dogma for you to live by. These are physical beliefs and physical structures which you have created as truth.

*Your creation of your physical truth is not truth within the Universal system of energy. Your truth is created by your belief in the past, not your belief in the NOW that is.*

Your structure of beliefs is accepted as the basis of all sciences within your world. Science is a technique where uncreative people use the facts of the past to create. The creation is the result of building upon the past that is known until the present discovers itself.

There is minimal inspiration and motivation that is involved in the creation of your science. Science is focused on the intellect, structure, discipline, and hard work of your physical world. It does not deal with integration of the rational and intuitive minds.

Indeed, science could learn from the partnership bonding that is shared in an integrated marriage. Many marriages function more from the structure, discipline, and intellectual beliefs than they do from the nurturing, sharing, and love of the rational and intuitive minds.

It is through your attachment to the belief system that you create your world. If you believe in equality, that is what you will create by the way in which you live. If you believe only in scientific theory, that is all that you will accept in your life.

Your belief in the intellectual process will influence the mates that you choose as marriage partners and it will influence the growth within your marriage. Your marriage will be a marriage of the physical world that is controlled by the beliefs of the physical world.

If you do not believe in equality of the male and female you will not choose a mate that you see as equal to or smarter than you believe yourself to be. This would create a personal threat to your ego and your belief system and therefore to your physical comfort as you believe it to be.

*If you are functioning from the ego level and you are attracted to a person of equal understand-*

*ing, as soon as you physically acknowledge that*
*equality you will end the relationship. This image*
*of equality will appear as a threat to your image of*
*self as created by your ego belief system.*

Let me use an example: If the male is concerned about being stronger than the female, he will always choose a mate that will create this feeling of physical strength within him.

The opposite is also true of the female. If the female believes that she is not as smart as a man, she will always choose a man that she feels is smarter than she is. She will continue with this energy of unworthiness, just as the male will continue in the energy of being the sole protector, the decision- maker, the provider for the marriage.

The male will accept his role as the master of the house of marriage. In this example the male will choose a child-like partner with less intelligence and strength to enhance his own image of strength and brilliance.

The female will choose a man of intellect to enhance her own image of unworthiness as an intellectual. Marriage that is based upon this acknowledgment of inequality is focused upon the physical belief system and will not provide the loving, nurturing, and sharing energy of the soul and spirit within. The marriage will validate the belief system that each partner is attached to.

Do you see how choice is created relative to the ego belief within man?

When man has ego beliefs that restrict either partner, it will restrict both individuals involved in the marriage as well as the relationship itself. This ego controlling energy will create resistances to growth more quickly than it will create sharing in the commitment to growth.

Do you see how the ego belief about self and your role in society will determine what you think you want in a marriage?

If you are in the dating process and you are thinking seriously about marriage, look carefully at your inspiration, motivation, and intention.

If you are seeking a partner for physical appearance, the right schools, the average intelligence, and the perfect family background, you should understand that you are seeking validation of self and your ego in your choice. This choice is made only by an individual who feels so unworthy, that he has an ego need for validation. This marriage is focused upon the physical needs of the ego belief system.

If each time that you are with your person of choice and you find your buttons being pushed, you may be entering into a volatile marriage. You are attached to and reacting from the perspective of your physical world.

You are seeing within the individual the reflection of the traits within yourself that you do not admire. Seeing the traits of yourself in another before you can acknowledge them and accept them will create anger, resistance, hostility, rejection, and denial within you. You have chosen the lesson of these traits and the relationship is there to trigger your soul memory. You may be creating a different image of these traits in your current lifetime or you may be repeating an exact lesson that has become a Karmic lesson.

Whatever the reason for the lesson, it will be more peaceful if you can find someone who has learned these lessons and can now help you learn them. Two mates who are learning the same physical lessons create the dramas and traumas of your world. The same lessons for two souls at the spirit and soul level will be inspirational, motivational, and creative. On the physical level the same lesson is confrontational.

You can seldom accept or allow a relationship of soul and spirit equality to develop to the point of marriage in your world because of your ego concern. Yet a relationship of soul and spirit integration would be the perfect choice for all marriages.

*A marriage that is integrated of body, mind, and spirit energy, gives you the unlimited freedom and opportunity to grow.*

If you are open to working on the challenges of the buttons that have been pushed, then you are open to growth by exploring the issues that you are triggering. It is the soul and spirit that will be mirrored. The issues that will appear will be the issues of physical attachment, judgment, fear, control, and on and on that are in the process of integration.

Having your buttons punched is better than no communication at all because it provides you with the opportunity to grow. Boredom in a relationship destroys the relationship faster than any other emotion and is an indication that the relationship lacks the integration of the soul and spirit.

*Your soul energy will always motivate a relation-*
*ship. Your spirit energy will inspire the relation-*
*ship to greater and greater heights.*

When you have inspiration and motivation in a relationship, you can integrate it with your intellect to create rewards within the physical world.

Marriage partners are helpmates within your physical world. They extend the energy of you within all your relationships. They expand your life, your friendships, your enjoyment, your loving, and your abundance. They add to the energy of self in a peace and joyful energy of nurturing and loving.

In marriage, when you create a partnership with your twin soul, you will find yourself with a commitment to growth for each of you that will be a lifetime commitment. If you do not meet your twin soul but you find another individual who is willing to be open, who is willing to grow, who is willing to communicate, then you can again have this commitment to growth.

*Openness in a relationship will escalate growth.*
*Resistances, denial, fear, anger, restricted commu-*
*nication, and/or hostility will not create growth if it*
*exists in either partner.*

Without a commitment to growth, you do not have love. Without love you will not have a marriage that is going to be satisfactory to you on all levels. An unsatisfactory marriage will be a constant production of dramas that will develop resistance to growth on the soul and spirit level. It will allow you to stay attached to the intellectual process of growth that you have brought back into this world with you as Karma.

*It is more beneficial for you to be alone, to learn*
*from the love within yourself, than it is for you to*
*be in a restrictive marriage.*

Why do you choose restrictive relationships?

You choose restrictive relationships because you do not love yourself. You feel unworthy, so you attract a relationship that is unworthy of you. Because you feel unworthy internally you focus on the external physical attraction to choose a mate. The sense of unworthiness within you is a direct result of the denial of the soul and spirit energy within.

The energy that you are experiencing will attract an energy of like vibration to you. If you feel unworthy, you will attract an energy that also feels unworthy. If you are captured in fear, you will attract an energy that is captured in fear. If you fear being controlled, you will attract an energy that fears control.

In your physical world these energies will be exhibited in different images. For instance, a woman who fears control at work will choose a controlling relationship. A man who fears being controlled will choose a relationship that he can control.

**The energy will be the same but the presentation of the energy within the physical world will occur from different viewpoints.**

If you want to have the perfect partnership at some point in your life, it is going to be a challenge for you to look deep within yourself. You must learn to love yourself, and to accept and acknowledge the joy, inspiration, and motivation of you as a creation of God.

**Truth in acceptance is found in the consistency of the words and actions of man as manifested within his physical world. Therefore, you cannot say you are the perfect partner and act otherwise. You cannot say you want a perfect marriage and be unwilling to commit yourself to total sharing with your partner.**

**If you cannot see the wonderment, the attunement of your own soul and spirit, you will not see the wonderment or the attunement of the soul and spirit of a partner.**

There is a very high divorce rate within your culture because of the beliefs of the culture. If you would focus upon finding a partner that you accept as equal, that you acknowledge, respect, and value, you would be creating for yourself a world of joy. The willingness to share and to care with a partner is a commitment to growth.

**When a marriage is created with the loftiness of a commitment to growth it knows no boundaries. This marriage will have direct access to the inspiration of the spirit, the motivation of the soul, and the ability to integrate these energies with the intellect.**

In your world your beliefs have turned to the physical attraction, the material wealth, the education, the potential within the business world, the glamour, the looks, and creating what the Jones' have. None of these are valid criteria for marriage.

Being the most beautiful bride and the most handsome groom of the season is not a reason for marriage. But it may easily be the perfect reason for divorce.

*Marriage should be accepted in the mind, the heart, and the soul of each and every man and woman as a commitment for life.*

Marriage then becomes an aware consciousness energy that maintains the focus of the energy and the intention of the marriage. For marriage commitment to become a reality within your world you must first understand yourself and what you truly want within your world.

You view marriage as expendable, "I will get married because it is better to be divorced than never to have been married." Is that a good reason to marry?

*Your intention creates the reality of your life.*

If you want to be happy, to live in peace and joy, to grow and evolve as a soul and spirit, then it is your responsibility to choose a partner that has the same intention and values.

Good intentions and values are energies that provide the direction for happiness within the marriage. If the intention is only upon the physical beliefs and the material possessions of the world, the marriage will be restricted by those same physical beliefs and material possessions.

How do you reach the point in your energy where you know exactly what you want in a partner?

*The secret to knowing exactly what you want in a partner, is found in knowing exactly who you are. The perfect partner in life is not the opposite energy, but indeed, it is the SAME identical energy.*

Understand your intentions. You will choose your partner by the energies that are within you. If you feel unworthy you will choose an unworthy partner. If you are negative and focused upon your negative energies, you will choose a partner who does the same. If you see only the physical realities of relationships, you will focus upon what the physical relationship can do for you. This will attract an energy to you that will also be focused upon what the physical realities of the relationship can do for him.

Do you see how you create your world? Are you looking for adoration or respect? Are you secure within yourself, or are you insecure? Do you acknowledge your true feelings at all times? Are you willing to share your life totally without the slightest hesitation with the one that you love? Are you willing to be open to all communication and discussion? Are you patient? Do you understand and believe in compromise? Are you willing to be supportive of your partner at all times? Do you love totally, without any judgment entering your mind? Do you accept and acknowledge your partner as he is? Do you believe that once you are married that you can change your partner? Do you believe in equality? Do you judge yourself and others? Are you interested only in what your mate can do for you in the physical world?

In your world there is an old belief that opposites attract. Indeed, they do on the physical appearance level. These physical relationships seldom create perfect marriages. When you focus only on the physical assets of the opposite sex, you have a very limited understanding of what marriage is all about and you do not at this point understand what you are all about.

You focus on the attraction of the opposite in the concept of physical appearance because you are not happy with your own appearance. Indeed, you will choose what you believe you would enjoy being within the physical world. This represents the confusion, the tug-of-war between the physical ego and the soul and spirit within.

For example, the male within your world many times chooses a woman that is younger, not self-supporting, and not of an equal utilization of the intellect to take care of because he feels intrinsically unworthy and wants to be taken care of himself. Since he does not recognize the tug of the soul and spirit, he focuses on being taken care of in the sexual sense. Since he feels unworthy he relates his unworthiness to the sexual focus, which he relates many times to age. Therefore, he feels that a younger woman will provide him with the sexual drive that he is missing.

When the male makes this decision he does not think in the terms that I have just related. He has little if any conscious awareness of why he truly made his choice of a partner. His ego is too strong to allow acknowledgment or acceptance of the energy of unworthiness that he is struggling with.

Do you see the attachment to the cycle of the sexual energy and how the physical energy resists the soul and spirit energy?

Marriage will not survive on sex alone. When you marry from the physical focus, sex is the primary reason for the marriage. But the relationship between two people who spend their days together must be fluid; it must change; it must grow; it must inspire, motivate, and create. If it does not support these energies, it will not last. Sexual attraction is as finite as physical attraction under these circumstances.

For you to understand exactly what you want, you must understand exactly who you are. Understanding who you are takes some very intense exploration of your own soul and spirit energy. When you can be open to integration of the physical with the soul and spirit of yourself, you will be making your choices with an integrated energy. This does not mean that the physical becomes unimportant. Integration simply creates a different level of balance in making your choice.

Understanding who you are means that you must accept total responsibility for your world and what you have created. In the physical dramas of life are the lessons that you are learning. If you do not learn from each lesson, you will create the lesson again and again and again. If you are living in negative energy, you will create the attraction of negative energy again and again and again.

*If you want to change your energy, you need only to acknowledge the energy attraction itself, and then it becomes your choice to change what you attract.*

The ultimate in attraction is inspiration and motivation. The presence of these two energies will give you the freedom and creativity to be all that you can be as your self. If you have friends, family members, a marriage partner, or any relationship that inspires and motivates you, that is a relationship to cherish. You will be relating on the soul and spirit level with each other. Your relationship should be acknowledged, accepted, respected, and valued because of the inspiration and motivation that it provides to your physical life.

If you are suppressed or restricted within a relationship, you are not being yourself. If you are dependent in a relationship, you are not being your truly creative soul and spirit. If you are equal, if you communicate, if you love and nurture and share, and if you grow, you have a beautiful partnership going for you.

Why do people choose the physical opposites in their partners?

The cycle of development is focused upon learning your lessons by experiencing the opposite energy. You do not have the energy of faith in the cycle of development, therefore your ego and intellect will only accept fact. Fact is found in perception of experience. As your perception or conscious awareness changes, your facts change.

You choose this method of experience to learn your lessons. In reality, the energy within the soul and spirit is more alike than the energy of the physical. In the cycle of development you are focused upon the physical. Your focus on the physical creates total dependence upon your intellect and ego judgment.

Until you learn the lesson of the cycle of development, you will continue with the same identical attraction, although it may appear differently each time on the physical level. You will not see that you have created for yourself the same situation, because you will be looking at that situation by holding your camera at a different angle. You will be seeing a new vision, a new image because your conscious awareness will have changed slightly from your previous experience.

Because of this illusion of a change of image, it is very important that man learns to understand who he is. There are no "quick fixes" in the Universe. So to understand yourself, you must be willing to work towards expanding your level of conscious awareness. If you have a mind that is closed to all but the one vision that you accept, you will resist seeing the miracles that are all around you.

Your level of conscious awareness is your choice. Look within yourself to understand your choice. Is the choice made because it supports your ego beliefs, because it is non-threatening, because it is non-challenging, because it requires no commitment from you, because it allows you control and domination, or because it gives you a sense of power?

If you decided that you were going to build an airplane, you would have to work at understanding how to build the airplane. It would not be easy. You would have to learn mathematics. You would have to learn to work with your hands. You would have to be a mechanic. You would have to be creative as a designer and an engineer. You would have to understand a lot of scientific equipment. But if you truly wanted to build this airplane, you would focus your energy upon the task.

If you truly want to understand yourself, you must focus your energies upon the task, because YOU are very complex. You are much more complex than engineering, mathematics, and aerodynamics. You are THE most complex creation on Earth. Indeed, you will never be able to understand yourself by focusing upon the external physical world.

When you focus only upon the external, physical you and you do not acknowledge the inner you or the higher you, you have put up a fence, a resistance to hide the real you. You are functioning on only one engine because you have shut the other two engines down. You have only one power source to keep you active and flying in this physical life.

You have the choice of using the soul and spirit energy within. When you use this soul and spirit energy within, you will begin to understand who you are. You will begin to love who you are. You will begin to value yourself, appreciate yourself, and have respect for yourself. When you project these positive virtues, you will attract the perfect partner into your life.

You will always attract and be comfortable with the energies that you are presently mirroring. In another, you can see yourself. If you are boring, you will attract a boring energy. If you are motivated, you will attract a motivated energy. If you are positive, you will attract a positive energy. If you are negative, you will attract a negative energy. If you live in fear, you will attract a fearful partner. If you are depressed, you will attract a depressed partner. The image of the energy will not appear in the same manner in both of you, but it will be the same energy that is displayed in different behaviors.

*It is important for you to understand your own self-worth, in order to have good relationships. The first relationship created by you is the relationship with yourself. You must have a good relationship with yourself before you can truly have a good relationship with others. You must love yourself and honor yourself with peace, joy, and happiness.*

You must understand that if you do not have a good relationship with yourself, nobody else can give it to you. Peace, joy, and happiness are the fruits of inner labors. They are not gifts from another soul and spirit.

*Peace, joy, and happiness are gifts to yourself.*
*When you give them to yourself, you will be able to*
*share them with other people.*

In the search that you generate for a marriage partner you would do well to spend the time on yourself, and allow the Universal energies to provide the energy of partnership.

If you find yourself in a beautiful marriage, cherish it; grow; allow your partner to grow; honor and respect each other; value each other; and have a commitment to each other. If you do not at the present time have a marriage, understand that you can create this for yourself when you are ready.

Indeed, you can create the perfect partnership when you clearly identify who YOU are, and what you want. Relationships that are created before you understand yourself will result in judgment, stress, anger, stasis, and suppression. The relationships will not be a happy productive energy for you.

When you were 16 and you wanted to buy a car, your taste was different than it is at 30, 40, or 50. The older you are the more you will know yourself, if you have allowed yourself to grow. Your choices will be better and your wants will be more harmonious and balanced with your own wisdom and understanding. You will choose a different car, just as you will choose a different marriage partner and a different life for yourself as you grow internally as well as externally.

As you grow in life you will choose a different partner as your level of conscious awareness expands. If you work on yourself by expanding your level of conscious awareness and your love, you will magnetize the energy to you that will be perfect for you.

As you learn to know yourself, value yourself, love, respect, and appreciate WHO YOU ARE, your choices in life and in partners will reflect the growth within you. Know the expansiveness of your self-worth. Bask in that self-worth with total humility.

*Never accept second best in a partnership be-*
*cause second best is not worthy of who you are.*

If you choose a life partner with the mental belief that your choice is second best for you, the marriage is focused towards failure. Legally the marriage may not end, but it will fail in the energy of being a loving, joyful, and peaceful relationship.

Several issues are predominant in your marriages of today. Power, control, dominance, and submissiveness are all focuses that destroy the equality of a marriage relationship. When you seek a marriage partner, you seek your ego "concept of need" if your focus is the external self.

Power as an element of attraction presents the need to be powerful and the need to be controlled by power. Dominance and submissiveness are opposite reactions to the same emotion. Each of these emotions will be interwoven, intermingled, and inseparable as they change back and forth within the individual. They are separate and they are one within the ego of man.

When these elements can be viewed within you, you are searching the realm of your physical reality trying to understand who you are. You have only an intellectual awareness that you have a soul and spirit that must balance out the physical confusion that you have created.

***The energies of dominance and control are elements of fear that are created by your ego as its survival technique.***

Dominance and control create a negative energy that can be destructive to marriage in a subtle, demeaning energy that supports unworthiness in self and your partner. Dominance and control are the opposite of freedom, therefore they restrict and suppress life in all images of their energy. If you live under the control of another, you are being suppressed and restricted. The individual that is controlling you is equally suppressed and restricted by the "need" to control. An individual that needs to control others, is extremely controlling and closed of self.

***Dominance and control is the energy of self-gratification that is functioning from fear.***

In your physical world this energy can be recognized by the changeable personality and attitude of the individual. The images of the energy force of dominance and control change very rapidly because it is manipulated by the ego. This manipulation occurs secondary to "circumstances" and produces frequent changes as the ego identifies a change in the situation.

# Twin Soul/Soul Mate Marriages

Evolved souls will find themselves living a life of internal trauma if they marry into this energy. The energy of dominance and control in a marriage creates an emotional roller coaster for life. This energy will provide resistance to soul growth.

Advanced souls returning to Earth will not be comfortable or able to evolve in this energy force field.

*When an advanced soul can follow a path with twin soul energy that has the same level of conscious awareness, expansive evolution is experienced by both souls.*

This joining together of twin souls acknowledges the freedom of the intellect to access the soul memory of infinite experiential knowledge and the spirit energy of love, truth, and perfection. This integration of twin soul energy creates lessons that are easier to understand and learn. These lessons will be seen as more meaningful and more fun.

*The relationship of twin souls in marriage truly adds bountiful JOY to living in your physical world.*

The comfort and ease with which these twin souls accept each other is a joy to see within your physical world when their conscious awareness is advanced enough to allow the union. Their commitment is exhibited in the physical world with such devout dedication that the energy of the union will be charged with a creative flow.

Twin souls in marriage will be inseparable since their joy and love will be inseparable. Indeed, this energy that God created as one will become one within the physical world. But at the same time it will be totally separate and totally free.

*Marriage between twin souls is a shared vision of life supported by the actions of commitment, integration, and unconditional love. Marriage of twin souls is a demonstrated acknowledgement, acceptance, respect, and value of unconditional love.*

Marriage that occurs between soul mates can be of any style of integration. Soul mates are souls from the same spirit family of souls that have been physical marriage mates in past energy experiences.

Marriages between soul mates can be based within the physical energy, the soul energy, or the spirit energy. Indeed, this can be a pleasant physical union or a traumatic physical union.

*Marriage with a soul mate is a choice that is designed into your life for the varied experience of learning to love within the physical world.*

Love can be experienced on many different levels. The marriage of soul mates will choose a level from which to experience their specific lessons. The expansive lesson of learning to love begins with learning to love self, life, family, friends, ethnic groups, cultural groups, the world, and the Universe.

These lessons of love will appear in all colors, all races, all consciousness levels, and in all types of people. You must learn your lesson of non-judgment, before you can live in the energy of unconditional love. Marriage of various energies, creates the opportunity of various lessons. It is the normal path of learning for you.

In the spirit energy, soul mates are two spirits that have agreed to support each other in learning lessons of various importance in their soul evolution.

*Soul mate marriages are based upon life dramas. Twin soul marriages are based upon unconditional love.*

Once the lessons are learned in a soul mate marriage, the dramas will cease and the marriage will become more of a supporting friendship than an inspiring and motivating union.

*A soul mate is not the twin energy of the spirit but a soul that is loved and respected.*

Regardless of the interaction of these spirit souls in the physical reality, they are family and friends in the spirit sense and they are committed to supporting each other in the lessons of choice.

The unconditional love is there in the spirit energy and the physical interaction is accepted as an act upon the stage of soul evolution. The soul and spirit of man understands, accepts, and acknowledges that the soul must experience to learn. The support of friendly spirit energy is there to help you create the experience. Experience requires interaction of fellow spirits in physical form.

*It is within the interaction of physical experi-
ence that the soul can learn and evolve. There is
no other way.*

Soul mates choose to be mates by virtue of the lesson, not
by virtue of the level of soul evolution. Therefore, it is common
to have spiritual generation gaps exist between soul mates. In a
physical stage drama not all of the actors have the same level of
acting experience. In the dramas of life not all of the spirits
involved in the acting have the same level of soul experience.

With twin souls there is no spiritual generation gap because
the twin souls and spirits were created at the same moment from
the same energy source. There can be a difference in the conscious
awareness, the acceptance, and the acknowledgment of the twin
soul energy in your physical reality.

*Conscious awareness is determined by the les-
son that is being learned. Acceptance and acknowledgment is determined by the level of development
that has been reached in this physical lifetime.*

Conscious awareness and development are controlled
within the external intellect by the ego.

It is this difference in conscious awareness and development
on the physical plane that prevents the twin soul from reaching
a true recognition, acknowledgment, and acceptance of its twin
energy. Truth is the consistency between your words and actions
within your physical reality.

Conscious awareness and development is controlled by the
ego belief system in man. As the spirit energy moves forward in
soul evolution, the opportunity and ability to recognize the twin
soul energy becomes more pronounced.

*Recognition of twin soul energy within the physi-
cal realm is a capability of the conscious awareness of the advanced soul.*

The meeting of twin soul energy will trigger the soul memory
and spirit energy within more expansively than any other form
of energy integration. This occurs because the integration of the
energy creates the energy force as an enlightened energy form.

*The twin energy expands beyond the human
imagination when it is integrated. This integration
of the energy of twin souls as one spirit provides a*

*loftiness to the inspiration and motivation that is unequaled within the physical world of man.*

When twin souls recognize themselves within the physical world, fear of expansion can be an immediate reaction. This fear of expansion triggers the ego fear for survival. When the ego feels that the expansion will create loss of control and survival, it will create resistance, fear, denial, and despair.

*Your fear of expansion can continue for all of your physical life span if you are unable to acknowledge the source of your denial.*

The ego/spirit tug-of-war will begin which will quickly produce changing focuses of love and fear. As your focus of love and fear shifts back and forth, you will experience internal conflict that will create seemingly unresolvable choices.

Your denial will create a resistance to the soul and spirit energy within which will affect the inspiration, motivation, and creativity of you on a daily basis. The effect will be demonstrated in your daily physical ability to be creative. Some effect of the soul and spirit energy may remain but it will be equal to the difference in operating a car with a two-cylinder engine as compared to operating a car with an eight-cylinder engine. Your power of action and accomplishment will be frustrated and obstructed.

There will be less harmony and balance to your thoughts and actions because of the vacillation of energy focus between love and fear. Accidents can occur more frequently to the physical body because the balance of the integrated self has been compromised. Despair and depression will be subtle but they will flow like an underground river. It is there, but it remains unidentified.

*All of life is a choice and when twin souls meet and understand their relationship within the physical world they will be faced with the choice to be all that they can be.*

Fear can focus on many issues. If fear occurs it should be explored and acknowledged. The ego as the intellect's judge and jury will be struggling for survival. The unconditional love of twin soul energy is totally non-judgmental. Can the judge give up judging? The unconditional love of twin soul energy is totally free. Can the ego give up the concept of needing to control?

Twin soul energy creates balance and harmony and it cannot be controlled by the ego. The ego fears for its survival. Twin soul energy is created by motivation and inspiration which focuses on humility, peace, love, joy, and happiness. The energy of the twin soul is in direct opposition to the energy of the ego which is fear, denial, judgment, resistance, depression, and anger.

The conflict of these opposite energies creates the most extreme example of the ego/spirit tug-of-war. The ego in its war strategy will intellectualize and expound the belief system in its determination to survive. Indeed, the ego will create illusion and images that will epitomize inspiration and motivation. But the ego can never create inspiration and motivation with enlightenment. It is because of the ego's inability to be perfect that the spirit will maintain the upper hand in this strategic tug-of-war exercise.

The ego/spirit in conflict will find itself frequently changing attitudes and beliefs. It will express love one moment and in the next moment will be consumed with fear. The stronger the ego is, the longer the war will rage within. Blame, judgment, and control will be directed to the ego belief system that is strongest and considered the best strategist in winning the war.

*Twin soul marriages are the most beautiful and productive marriages within the realm of Earth. When this energy is acknowledged, accepted, understood, respected, and valued by you the creations of the marriage will be known in the world as miracles. These miracles will be a physical legacy to benefit mankind on a global basis. Twin soul marriage is to be honored and revered as the loftiest of unions.*

# Children and Marriage

Marriage is a platform for sharing intimate interaction and expansive learning. When you create children within a marriage you create the opportunity to teach by words and actions. Your child may be your miracle. Your teaching begins in silent form at the moment of conception. In the beginning this is cellular teaching rather than soul and spirit teaching.

The soul and spirit can enter the body at any time after conception but it will come and go at will. In most instances, the spirit will spend more time within the spirit realm in the first two years of life than it spends within the infant body.

After two years of life there will be frequent choices to be made by the soul and spirit which will influence its desire to remain in physical form. Once this decision is made it can again be changed as new choices occur. Indeed, this choice of the spirit to leave the physical body can be made at any time by the spirit energy. The spirit can choose to leave briefly or to leave permanently. Leaving the body permanently is known as death in your world.

Death is an illusion. The energy of the spirit created the physical matter of the body. When the spirit changes its mind it speeds up the energy vibrations and discards the physical matter. The spirit is eternal and it will choose to leave for its own personal reasons of learning. The physical body becomes in effect the ash of the expanded energy as it leaves.

The power of creation is exercised in the creation of new life. With the creation of new life the lesson of responsibility is triggered. In marriage it is important to begin the parenting of the cells through your own spirit energy as soon as conception is recognized.

When you have a conscious awareness of the power of your creation you can begin to teach the cells while they are growing. This can be done with thought energy or with the verbal energy of the voice. This energy exchange will allow you to teach the infant to remain open to soul and spirit energy.

Love is an energy that is transmitted to the cells in the very early stages of development if it is the intention of the parents. Knowledge can also be transmitted to the infant before the birth of the child if it is the parent's intention to transmit this information.

*The interaction between the parents is transmitted as energy to the child. Parenting should begin at the moment of conception as loving energy between the parents.*

The most important aspect of teaching is to avoid teaching beliefs that will create resistance and denial within the physical world. If the soul memory of the infant can be free and open, expansive knowledge will survive from past experiences.

Parenting and teaching of the infant should also include a focus on physical health because the physical body is the temple of the spirit and soul. For the spirit and soul to remain in physical form the credibility of the physical body must be maintained.

Parenting is a beautiful time in marriage. With a positive perspective of the challenge and joy involved in teaching love and sharing to a developing soul and spirit, interaction will have new meaning within your life.

The soul and spirit that comes into a marriage comes by choice and agreement of both parents and the infant. The roles are determined and the agreements are made prior to entry into the physical realm. These agreements will not usually be understood on a physical consciousness level by the parents. That does not mean they do not exist. There are no accidents within the Universe.

Not all marriages will create children. That will not be the design of every soul and spirit that has chosen marriage. If the souls and spirits have spent many thousands of lifetimes parenting, they may choose to focus on other lessons in this lifetime.

You have been given the power to create all of life, not just children. The creation of children is one physical indication of the power of creation and it is the one that is most frequently acknowledged and understood by you. Therefore, it is symbolic in your mind of your power of creation.

*The creation of children proves with total clarity the cellular memory that exists within your body. You have not yet understood the expansiveness or the importance of this scientific concept within your physical world.*

Marriages that are based on verbal and/or physical abuse are not marriages of twin souls but are marriages of soul mates. It is the marriage of twin souls that was created by God. Lessons are learned with soul mates because in the joining of this supportive energy the lesson can be acted out until it is learned. When it is learned the relationship will change.

All interaction is a joint lesson. There is no blame. These are dramas that are designed to capture the attention of the participants in the relationship. Many times crisis dramas are lessons that have been worked on for many thousands of lifetimes and have returned as Karmic lessons for completion.

*When the drama is extreme, the lesson is extreme. The design is created to capture your attention so the lesson can be learned with total clarity.*

When the lesson is a true challenge and is not understood, the souls that are involved may decide to incarnate with other souls to approach the lesson through a different image. Indeed, a lesson can be repeated over and over again from the same image with the same participants or the image and the participants can change. It is the choice of the spirit.

*At times the lesson will be so intense that the spirit and soul will seek a master teacher to help with the lesson.*

This could be compared to a student in the physical world that is failing physics and chooses to seek a tutor to pass the test. Once a lesson is learned by a soul, the soul may choose to teach the lesson as a master to clarify the experience to perfection. Your physical world understands that the best way to learn a subject well is to teach it.

Learning and teaching is an integrated process that is interwoven, intermingled, and inseparable. All of you are students and all of you are teachers. In marriage the teacher/ student, student/teacher cycle is unbroken. There is no teaching without learning and there is no learning without teaching. This energy is symbolic of the creative sharing that exists within a good marriage.

*When teaching or learning is resisted or denied within a relationship there is a tremendous fear and unworthiness that has consumed the ego of man.*

Marriage is the perfect interaction to mirror the images of self that annoy you or please you. In seeing self in the reflection of another you can create change in the energy of self. A committed marriage gives you the support and freedom to view self and to change self. Marriage is the perfect energy to learn and to teach.

Children create a larger mirror of more extreme reflection for you to view self in repetitious fashion. It is the repetition that unlearns old behaviors and creates new behaviors. These reflections will create an openness despite denial. Many spirit/souls will have children to allow them to see themselves more clearly in less Earth time.

Sharing in an integrated marriage is a consistent celebration of being all that you can be. In marriage the celebration of integrated sharing is appropriately demonstrated in a sharing of the physical body. The appropriate celebration of sexual intimacy is in the joy of being all that you can be. It is in this celebration that you have the power to create new life. The creation of new life then becomes the miracle that has a global effect.

When life is created without the virtue of an integrated celebration of joy, it is focused upon the physical in the same manner that living will be focused upon the physical. It is this focus of creation upon the physical, without an expanded understanding of the intention of creation, that produces the responsibilities within your world for unwanted children.

The global effect of creation from the singular focus of physical sex without an integrated intention of responsibility and commitment, results in orphans, disease, hunger, over-population, and economic disaster. This is in effect negative energy created by negative energy. All energy will have the opportunity to change if the lesson is learned with clarity.

*The soul that chooses to enter into a body that will not share love, is choosing to capture its attention with a challenging lesson. When you choose to create without integrated intention, you will later choose to be born into that identical situation to learn the lesson of responsibility with total clarity.*

This choice of birth will become the Karmic completion of your lesson. This is the true meaning of, "Do unto others as you will have them do unto you." This describes the Karmic completion of lessons that you design into your life.

This Karmic energy has been described in your Book of God in several ways, "An eye for an eye, a tooth for a tooth." It is not a literal physical translation but an energy of lesson completion that the soul will choose.

## Sharing in Marriage

The sharing of marriage requires the opposite of control which is trust in freedom. In trust there is no fear. There is total self-confidence, courage, love, relaxation, acceptance, and receiving. You are willing to give of yourself, to share of yourself in all facets of your being.

You communicate as easily from your soul and spirit as you do from your intellect. You celebrate your communion with your physical body as freely as you share your mind. You have no denial, no resistances, no restrictive beliefs that lock you into specific behavior, no fear, no embarrassment, no suspicion, no distrust, no jealousy, and no judgment.

Sharing creates a receptivity to change, to growth, to learning, and to giving and receiving openly and honestly. Sharing creates a positive creative attitude to the marriage that gives the relationship the freedom to grow and to expand beyond your wildest physical dreams.

**Sharing is not sharing unless it is allowed to be in total equality. Sharing is not focused upon the physical world but it focuses upon the truth of you that is integrated internally as a soul and spirit and externally as an integrated physical creation.**

In this positive creative approach to sharing self, there is unlimited beauty and joy. You begin to see yourself not as a physical body that is separate but as a cellular miracle that is intrinsically related to each other, to the world, to the Universe, and to the Cosmos.

Accepting the connection between yourself and another soul and spirit in marriage allows you to see with clarity the energy web of the Universe. Sharing with a singular energy allows you to open up the gates of your soul and spirit to share with all other people.

When you fear sharing in your world either in marriage or on a friendship basis, you are in reality living in fear of yourself. If you fear yourself, you fear all of man. When you fear yourself, you fear the unknown within yourself. This fear is your root fear of separation from God.

The God energy within you is the spirit of you. You are aware of your spirit energy unconsciously even if you deny your spirit energy consciously. If you deny the spirit within you either verbally, intellectually, or through your daily actions, you deny the God within you. If you deny God, it is your belief that He will not accept you.

This belief that God will deny you for your sins, creates the fear of separation from God. Do you see how your belief system structures and controls your life in the cyclic energy of fear?

Sharing in a partnership bonding of marriage as an integrated self is the beginning of the creation of the Holy Trinity upon Earth. This is the joining together of the male, the female, and the God energy into one union. This union is symbolic in the eyes of God as the balancing of the God energy within you. Marriage must move as the world of God moves with a rhythmic fluidity, flowing into the nooks and crannies of life, finding its balance as the obstructions appear spontaneously. When there is the freedom to love in trust and joy, there will be a harmony, a balance that will allow life to move quickly, smoothly over the rocks in the same way that a stream will flow down a mountain. All movement will become as effortless as the mountain stream as it gurgles along seeking its own peace and joy.

As the demands of life emerge, the rhythm will change and adjust to the new development as a dancer adjusts to a new step. Changes will be accepted and adjusted for, as the balance and the beauty continues.

The energy and the communion of the soul and spirit will radiate from the bonded partners that are sharing in marriage. They will shine with a delight and joy that will be contagious, as they live with the inspiration and motivation of their spirits and souls to guide them.

*Partners in a marriage of the integrated selves will be beyond the physical bonds of judgment and fear. They will be free to love and to be all that they can be, together. In that togetherness, you create miracles upon Earth.*

True marriage is the action of sharing unconditional love.

*The sea*
*kisses the sand*
*while man gnaws on life,*
*creating peaks and furrows*
*in his heart and soul.*

# Sharing
# Friends

*The sea*
*rushes on*
*while man stumbles*
*and falls in the mire*
*of change and confusion.*

*Confusion is resistance*
*to seeing oneself*
*in the energy of another.*
*The vision is not loved*
*if you are not loved by you.*

*Understand you*
*to understand me.*
*Love yourself*
*to love me.*
*We are one, you and me.*

**Friends are a gift.** They are a gift that each of you give to yourself at the time that you create your life design. It is within the energy of friends that you see yourself.

Friends will be chosen to experience the image of the opposite or the image of the same. Friends will be in your world to support you, to help you grow, to love you unconditionally, and to act as a mirror image to your thoughts, emotions, feelings, and actions.

Friends are in your world to help you learn to love yourself unconditionally by loving them unconditionally. The lesson of unconditional love is the lesson of non-judgment within the physical world.

*If you choose to live your life without allowing friends to share your life, you resist looking at and loving yourself.*

The image of opposites will be the image that is a challenge for you to acknowledge. This is the image of self that you have chosen to see more clearly to give yourself the opportunity to change. If you are focused upon the physical you, it will be a challenge to be a friend to someone who is focused upon a spiritual path. In them you will image the facet of self that you deny, resist, and reject.

The image of the same will be the image of you that you accept and acknowledge. It is for this reason that you will choose your friends and partners on the basis of physical attraction.

You are choosing what you accept and acknowledge. You are choosing the part of you that makes you feel comfortable. You focus upon that part of self that is acknowledged by you. It is the part of self that you have learned to accept.

*Choosing friends and partners that mirror the image of self as you are, does not create the opportunity to change. It will create apathy, boredom, and complacency. It will create the image within your mind of powerlessness.*

If you are open to self and to all that you are, you will have friends of all images that will be reflecting the various facets of self as a diamond reflects the sun. If you are closed to understanding self, your friends will be few and they will reflect only that part of self that you can accept.

*You are truly the diamonds of the Universe. You shine in the world as the stars shine in the Cosmos. You are designed with multiple facets. If you choose to cover some facets with black paint, you will not see the reflection that you are capable of casting.*

Your life force is the spiritual energy of you. The energy of you is the power and strength of you. The energy of you is reflected outward from self and reflects the image of self back to your own vision.

If you deny your own energy, you are in turn denying your power and strength within your physical world. If you refuse to see the image that you cast within the physical world, you are denying your personal power, your personal worth, and your personal energy from within. If you deny the image of self, you deny the power of self.

The people that you see as friends within your world are the reflectors of self. All good relationships within your world must of necessity have the basis of friendship. If you understand that a person is your friend, you are open to seeing the image of yourself within that person and to developing a more intimate relationship.

If you are not open to the image of self that is reflected within a person, they cannot be considered a friend. Indeed, you will not accept them as they are but you will judge them as the image of self that you see reflected within them. Because you do not see what you can accept within yourself, you will judge them to be someone that you can not associate with or be with.

*When you judge a friend you are in truth judging yourself. Judgment is an ego action of your physical world.*

Friends may look different to you at different times. They may come with other labels in your perception. But the friends that you know on a physical basis are truly friends of the spirit and soul within.

When you are in the process of designing your Earth life, you create an interaction with different spirit and soul energies that will remind you of your path. The friends that you meet may be friends for only a very limited time in your Earth reality. This

does not in any way decrease from the importance of that
relationship as a friend.

# Brief Encounter

Indeed, there are times when you will encounter someone
on the street, and the only interaction that you will have will be
eye contact. This limited physical interaction can be a very
important encounter for you. The loving energy that you find
reflected in the eyes of another person is a reflection of self that
can serve as a reminder to you. Seeing this love reflected toward
you is a trigger for you to remember to love yourself.

You may meet a person of the opposite sex on the street. We
will use a person of the opposite sex as an example because that
is the most intense manner of relating in your physical world. If
you meet this individual as you are walking down a crowded
street and your eyes meet, you may see within the energy of those
eyes a pure and intense love for you. You may feel within yourself
a response, an exchange of love for the energy that you have just
encountered.

What you are seeing is the energy of non-judgment that
allows the mirror image of self to be reflected back to you. This
is always a trigger to remind you of the love within yourself. The
energy of the other individual is there to appreciate, value,
respect, and acknowledge your presence. This exchange validates you as a physical person from the energy of the spirit self.

*The loving energy that is found within your eyes*
*is a very important element of giving and receiv-*
*ing. If you live in non-judgment, you will reflect*
*love to all that you gaze upon.*

Once you come in contact with this love, you know how
valuable you truly are. Remember when you are walking down
the street to raise your eyes and look at the people whom you
pass. If you will do this, you will find yourself enjoying the trigger
of electrical current that passes between you and another soul
and spirit.

This is the briefest form of friendship, but it is a valuable
form of friendship. It is an energy that helps you internally love
yourself. It restores your self-image when you are depressed or
anxious. It allows you love and appreciation in the purest form
of non-judgment.

This brief interaction of friendship is truly a soul and spirit who is giving you back the love image that exists within your soul and spirit internally. Many times these friends are your own soul and spirit energies who have materialized within your physical world to help you with this understanding.

The energy of all that you have ever been or will ever be IS. Your energy has the spiritual life force within it to assist you and to protect you. This energy force is the combined and accumulated energy of all past and future soul and spirit energy.

*Your life force can become known to you as separate energy forces or as a total energy force. It is created by the experiential learning of the soul which then combines with the spirit energy.*

When the experience of a brief encounter occurred consciously to my conduit one time, she was overwhelmed by the energy that she encountered. This happened to her in the year 1968 as she was walking down a street in New York City. The street was packed with people and all of a sudden, the eyes of this individual held her absolutely spellbound.

At that time she was going through marital problems and considering a separation. It was a difficult time for her and she was not feeling too good about herself. She was dealing with the conflict and confusion that always accompany a major choice within Earth life.

This spirit energy (which was myself as a part of her own energy) spoke to her on a spirit level. It was the electrical charge that she needed to feel good about what she was doing. In the non-judgmental vibrations of my energy she saw the love within herself. As a part of my conduit's own personal energy, I am one with her or I can be separate from her while being one with her. This is the way that energy of the soul and spirit is projected or reflected.

Brief encounters can reflect the beauty in non-judgment if they mirror the spirit energy from within. In your physical world your belief system creates judgment of friends and lovers.

*The mirror of self within another, becomes your judgment of the other. You do not recognize or have a conscious awareness that you image the traits that you do not respect, or the traits that you firmly resist within yourself to the other person.*

Judgment is an ego reaction that you focus upon as you choose your friends and lovers. You will be someone's friend or lover if they meet the criteria that you feel reflects you.

*The closer the spirit energy is between two people the more intensely the image of self is mirrored. The more directly the sun shines upon a diamond the more intense the reflection is for the physical vision.*

This mirror image of your own energy allows you to become conscious of self. If you are resisting that facet of self, you will resist accepting friendship from another person in whom the image is reflected.

The brief encounter is a common occurrence in your world. My conduit's consciousness of this encounter was a consciousness of having been given a gift. She did not understand the entire message of the gift, but she understood the energy that she had received. This additional energy created a surge within her own energy or life force and gave her the strength to love herself despite all other happenings within her life.

An instantaneous friend is truly of the soul and spirit energy, as I was her spirit energy. There are other friends that are more physical in form, and these friends may come to you as close friends, as casual acquaintances, as intimate acquaintances, as lovers, as colleagues, or as family! They may indeed appear in your life wearing any label, any identity that you can imagine.

*Image is the spiritual understanding, imagine is the physical understanding.*

# Giving and Receiving in Friendship

When an intense reflection of love appears, it is an instant of reflection of what is within you. It is there for the purpose of support and the purpose of helping you with the lesson of giving and receiving. Be open to its presence and you will be conscious of its presence.

*If you do not have love within you, you cannot reflect love without. If you cannot be open to reflecting the love within you, you will not receive the reflection of love in return.*

In your physical world this is better understood by your saying, "If you cannot be a friend, you will not have a friend."

Friends teach you many lessons. The lesson of giving and receiving could well be considered the most important because it is an all inclusive lesson with many images to understand. The lesson of giving and receiving is a lesson of loving self, your neighbor, and God. This in turn is the action of the lesson of unconditional love.

It is a challenge for you to give and to receive if you do not fully understand loving self. The giving and the receiving will occur in degrees. It will occur in images. Giving and receiving is the energy or life force support for you and it will continue in your lifetime from the moment of birth until the moment of your death in physical form.

The concept of giving and receiving is the concept that is involved with every moment of your life. When you chose embodiment you were given life in a physical body. This is your life. You were given a spirit by your Creator. You received the spirit that you were given into the energy and the body that is you. Each and every thing in your life has been given or received.

This is a very expansive concept that you see and understand from a very focused and linear view. The reason that you view giving and receiving so narrowly is that you have three minds, two which you may not acknowledge. You have the intellectual mind, the rational mind, and the intuitive mind.

The intellectual mind is the mind of the physical. The rational mind is the mind of the soul. The intuitive mind is the mind of the spirit. Each of these minds operate on different levels of consciousness. And again within each level of consciousness are other multiple levels of consciousness.

*You give and you receive throughout your daily existence dependent upon your consciousness level and the facet of the mind from which you consciously perceive your life.*

If you see yourself only as physical, if you function only from your intellect, you will receive and you will give only from the physical concept. You will indeed focus your giving on the material and you will focus your receiving on the material. You will be living primarily from the physical world that you consciously understand, acknowledge, and accept as your reality.

Within each facet of the mind are seven levels that are again relative to seven. This means that you have multiple levels within each facet of the mind.

Each level of the mind operates from a different level of consciousness. The intellect operates from the physically aware consciousness which has within it multiple levels of consciousness.

By the natural movement of your life force, you will move from the physical concept of development through the levels of the cycles of development within the intellectual mind. As this level becomes accepted and acknowledged, you will move forward into the multiple levels of the cycle of awareness. As you move into the cycle of awareness, you become conscious that you are more than simply a physical body in a physical world.

You begin to see life with a different level of conscious awareness and you begin to give by giving more of yourself. You begin to give with the energy of your soul and spirit.

As you learn to accept your new found awareness, you begin your search to understand who you are and all that you are. Moving into this cycle of understanding will create the physical need to balance the external energies with the internal energies. As you begin to understand that you are a complex, multifaceted, trilocular being, you will sense the desire to balance these different energies.

This balancing act that is going on internally will create a more expansive conscious awareness of the true self. As you seek to understand yourself, you begin the process of integrating the energies of self. As these energies merge together you will suddenly see yourself with a clear realization of all that you are.

This self-realization allows you to be physical, intellectual, to have soul memory, and to accept your spirit energy. You are aware of and you accept it all. You understand and you acknowledge it all. You respect and you integrate all that you are into your everyday life. You value yourself and all that you are as you realize who you are. You are at that moment all that you can Be while on Earth.

In your physical world you are structured by your belief systems. You see your physical world relative to your beliefs about yourself and your relationship to your physical world. The physical world is different for each man. You give and you receive relative to your beliefs.

*If you want to expand yourself, you must release all attachment to the fear that you imagine exists in the other facets of your mind. You must allow*

*your soul and spirit to join in the giving and to join*
*in the receiving. It is the fear within your ego that*
*resists your soul and spirit. Your ego fears for the*
*survival of the physical self. It is your design to cre-*
*ate the physical self as finite. If the physical body*
*were eternal you would never access your soul*
*and spirit energy.*

In the physical world you give with fear and you receive with fear because you do not trust, you do not have faith, you do not believe in the value of friends. You do not believe in your own self-worth.

*In each relationship, in each and every encoun-*
*ter, and in all exchanges of energy, the level of*
*aware consciousness determines the method of giv-*
*ing and the method of receiving in relationships.*

In the beginning when you were created as spirits you were given as your inherent birthright the love, truth, and perfection of the Father. In addition to this you were given the power of creation.

How many of you have accepted these gifts knowingly, used these gifts consciously, and understand your own power of love, truth, and perfection that you have been given? How many of you understand that you have total power of creation? Have you accepted this power, and utilized this power which establishes having received the power?

Giving and receiving began at the moment of your creation as a spirit. You receive physical life, physical bodies, and you acknowledge on the level of physical, intellectual understanding what you have physically received. You will also acknowledge what you feel that you may not have received on the physical level.

*It remains a challenge for you to understand, to*
*acknowledge, and to accept that you receive the*
*soul memory and the spirit energy at the same*
*time that you receive a physical body.*

This understanding is not part of your intellectually accepted belief system. This level of understanding has been covered up by false teachings through your embodiments on Earth. Indeed, many will experience death within your world today and feel that one life is the limit of the opportunity offered by the Father for you to understand yourself.

> *God does not limit your opportunities for multiple lives or multiple lessons. You provide your own limits of understanding the reality of your multiple lives and the complexity of your multiple lessons by your belief systems. Your belief systems then control your level of conscious awareness within your physical world.*

In the same way that the Christ Consciousness had multiple lives upon Earth, you have multiple lives upon Earth. This is the design of life as created by God.

> *No human can reach a state of love, truth, and perfection in one Earth life. Your lessons are not given to you by God, you design your lives, and you create your love, truth, and perfection within yourself. You receive balance and growth by accepting the responsibility to work upon understanding your total self. You create your own reality and your reality is your total responsibility.*

Accepting the integrated self has been the challenge for my conduit in acknowledging me. I am an energy within her spirit mind. I am the Heavenly Spirit within her that she has resisted, denied, and rejected. It has been a challenge for her to acknowledge me as playing a role in her physical life for many years of this lifetime. Yet I have played this same role in all other embodiments of my conduit.

In this lifetime my conduit had to become consciously aware, accept, acknowledge, understand, and integrate me into her physical world to accomplish her life purpose on Earth.

By acknowledging and integrating me she completed her path to self-realization in this lifetime. This gives us the freedom to work within the expanded energy of enfinite knowledge to bring our spirit message to the world. This is our life purpose on Earth.

In each physical embodiment you must begin the cycles of physical life again. You must develop, become aware, open to understanding, and then accept integration of your intellect, soul, and spirit. The more soul memory and spirit energy that remains within the intellect, the easier it becomes for you to cycle through the consciousness levels to the level of integration.

*At birth the memory is strong. The resistance to the soul and spirit memory is created within the belief structures of your physical reality.*

It is easy to say "I am an intellectual," and acknowledge within your physical world that you possess an expansive intellect. You accept this gift as your rightful heritage without true acknowledgment.

Do you acknowledge that you were given this intellect and that it was your choice to receive it? Do you acknowledge that you are love, truth, and perfection? Do you acknowledge that you are an individual that has the power of creation? Do you acknowledge that you have energies within you that you can communicate with? Do you accept that these energies within you are energies of your own being?

*You are separate but you are one. You are physical man with an intellect, a soul, and a spirit. Each facet of self is an expansive multi-faceted energy that you were given and that you received.*

Can you acknowledge the gift? Can you acknowledge that when you accept the magnificence of yourself, you have agreed to receive the gift of your Creator?

It is easier for the physical mind to give than to receive. You can focus your giving within the physical world. Receiving within the physical world carries with it the responsibility of acknowledgment of the giver. Receiving makes us responsible, it acknowledges the relationship.

Giving and receiving within your physical understanding is focused more upon self-gratification than the self-realization of unconditional love. Acknowledging that you have a soul and spirit makes you responsible for acknowledging the giver. Acknowledging that you received and accepted the gift gives you the responsibility for understanding and using the gift within your daily life.

In your world you share physical sex, not to give or to receive the gift of love and sharing, but as self-gratification for the "concept of need" of the physical body. It is this physical self-gratification that refuses to acknowledge the giving and receiving of the responsibility of friendship.

You accept gifts of love, of sex, of the soul and spirit, of material possessions and you are so immune to giving and receiving that you will not acknowledge with thanks what you have willingly accepted. Indeed, you are not consciously aware of the gift of friendship and in your unaware state you are discourteous to the giver.

In friendship it is easier for you to receive than to give. Your ego allows you to accept the gift of friendship as your rightful heritage.

*Man has no more of a "right" to accept friend-ship without acknowledgment, than he has to accept a million dollars without acknowledging the giver.*

# One-Night "Stands"

In your world of sexual promiscuity and one-night stands there is frequently a soul and spirit connection between sexual partners. Yet the encounter is focused within the physical concept and frequently no acknowledgment is made of the gift of the physical. Your attachment to the physical allows you to take what you feel you need without giving of emotion or feeling. This energy of "taking" that is apparent in sexual encounters, is repeated in the world of crime. This is the energy of self-gratification. The energy is the same.

If the encounter is observed from the concept of initial attraction you will understand that an energy existed. This energy is the energy of friends on the soul and spirit level. You are in the lesson of giving and receiving. When you learn the value of giving and receiving between friends, you will not practice sexual encounters for the purpose of physical satisfaction. Exploiting physical satisfaction is the base level of the energy of the cycle of development.

*It is man who creates the limitation of the sexual encounter to the base level of physical energy out of his own fear.*

The male is more satisfied with this form of self-gratification without responsibility or commitment than the female is. It is the male energy that reduces the encounter to physical gratification without acknowledgment of the friendship that could exist.

In many instances, a sexual relationship will continue through the years with no emotion and no feeling for the male. There will be only the purpose of physical gratification. This is ego gratification. For the female this relationship will be a longing for emotion and feeling but the energy will not be addressed because of the fear of losing what IS. The giving and the receiving in this friendship are not equal and are coming from opposite energies.

The male energy within the human being is the energy of the physical focus. The female energy within all humans is the energy from the soul and spirit. The giving and receiving energy within you comes from the female energies of you. The self-gratification of the physical body for physical purposes comes from the male energies within you.

When two individuals are involved in giving and receiving with the supreme physical sense, their focus will frequently be from different consciousness levels. If they develop a true friendship and appreciation of each other before the giving and receiving of the physical self becomes part of their world, the relationship will endure much longer. It will endure because of the soul and spirit energy that will be involved with the physical energy.

These casual physical relationships are not based upon mutual giving and receiving with love. Love is inseparable from truth and perfection. Therefore, a relationship that is based upon love is by its inherent nature based upon commitment and responsibility. The level of the relationship will be seen within the thoughts, words, and actions of the participants.

**Truth is the living spirit of love as manifested in the physical consistency of the thoughts, words, and actions of man.**

If the truth of love is not seen within the relationship the encounter is based upon the self-gratification of the physical body. If the energy of the relationship is the same for both male and female, they are coming from the same energy internally. This energy could be from the male focus or the female focus. As long as the energy is mirroring the same in each participant, the giving and receiving is equal. If the energy is not the same, the encounter is not equal. There is no communication and responsibility involved if the energy is not equal.

*This phenomena of self-gratification is exploited by man daily in millions of instances because man refuses to receive and acknowledge the soul and spirit within.*

You have an attachment to the physical focus of self- gratification and you cannot release this attachment and be open to receiving the image of your own love being reflected back to you.

*In the physical belief of the male ego, he is giving the female what she wants in the physical encounter. He judges what she wants by the image reflection of what he wants. The male and the female have only a veiled image of who the other truly IS.*

The purpose of the male and the female upon Earth is to learn the gender lesson that is opposite to them and to provide levels of consciousness in the path of learning. Until you begin to understand that what you acknowledge and accept is the image of yourself and not the other person, you will not understand your search.

Understanding your sexual partner is a step forward to understanding yourself. To understand the sexual partner there must be communication from the soul and spirit level. There must be acceptance and acknowledgment of each partner by the other. There must be a caring and a sharing of love and activities. As you can see, the casual encounter of the one-night stand does not allow you the friendship that is needed to grow.

Indeed, sex without love exists within your world only as a physical/emotional confusion. It is indeed, traumatic to the female energy and should not be considered as an alternative in life. Honor, respect, and value yourself in accepting only that which is worthy of your love.

Trauma occurs for the female because the focus of the female is the emotional, feeling focus. When the female allows self-gratification for the male without receiving equal to what she is giving, she is contributing to the male energy remaining captive within the physical world.

*Rewarding ego self-gratification is a silent message to the male, physical energy of your world that they are perfect as they are. If the male ego receives the message of perfection, there will be no motivation or inspiration to change. The male energy will remain comfortable and accepting of self, which will continue to capture the energy of humanity within the energy forces of the physical.*

If one participant is giving in a relationship and the partner is only receiving, the giver has a concept of need to give under any circumstances. The giver is reflecting their own spirit energy. The partner with the physical receiving focus is reflecting only self-gratification, not love.

*Man will always give and receive from his own consciousness level which will be reflected back to him. In this instance the person who is only receiving will feel that the partner is only receiving. The giver will continue to give because the giving is reflected back to the giver.*

It is because of this reflecting image that occurs that man does not truly know the feelings and emotions of the partner unless they are communicated with consistent words and actions. This is the creation of truth in a relationship.

In this drama of physical relationships there will be giving and receiving, but the individual perception of the gift will be determined by the image of the individual's energy. If you feel that you give but do not receive, look again at the openness of your giving. Seek confirmation of your feelings with verbal communication.

*When giving and receiving of your physical self is enjoyed by two people open to all facets of self, it is a glorious experience of celebration on Earth.*

# Critical Mass Energy

Every individual that you meet has a purpose within your life. It is because of this basic lesson of giving and receiving that man must learn to be a friend. In your world you may learn to receive or you may learn to give. You may be in a lifetime that is focused more upon one than the other.

Giving and receiving, to be perfect, must be integrated and balanced in the physical world. Balance for man can only be achieved through openness within man. Giving and receiving is the balancing energy within human interaction.

When you can understand that you can also give from the soul and spirit within you, you will be acknowledging the capability of balance. With an energy balance you can give love that is pure and unconditional and you can receive love that is pure and unconditional. You will have taken away the fear of interaction that clings within the physical intellect and ego energy.

*When you fear as you do within the physical consciousness, you cannot accept unconditional love. You cannot receive and you cannot give from the spirit energy of self.*

The spirit of man knows no fear. The spirit is pure in its love, truth, and perfection. It is the ego belief system of man that focuses giving and receiving in the physical world within the energy of fear.

*It is symbolic of your belief system that you celebrate the birth of Jesus with material gifts. You would do better if you gave love to all around you.*

Loving your family, the Earth, and the world will have an impact in giving and receiving positive energy. When you are able to radiate your positive energy into the Universe to add to all the positive energy of other individuals, you will be creating the critical mass of positive energy that is important to your world.

When energy reaches critical mass it affects the Earth that you live upon. If you live in the energy of unconditional love of self, of being worthy of the love, truth, and perfection that is within you, you will allow this positive energy within you to attract other positive energy.

*When this energy builds to a state of critical mass it will be understood by all beings within the Universe. At that moment all beings within the Universe will accept the understanding of friendship as unconditional love.*

When you give physical, material presents you limit the energy of giving and receiving to the physical world. The energy of a physical gift remains a physical energy unless it is surrounded with the pure energy of unconditional love. If it is given to receive, it will not reflect the energy of unconditional love.

There will always be an energy reflection of intention and it will be understood on a soul and spirit level.

Let us use an example of giving and receiving. We have a man and a woman in an intimate relationship. They give each other their physical bodies but they withhold from each other the energy of the soul and spirit. They talk to each other in terms of physical actions but they do not give of the energy that is in their hearts. They cannot speak of their feelings.

It is within the heart of man that his feelings dwell. The heart is the focus of the energy of unconditional love. Until you can give to your partner this unconditional love, you have only a physical relationship which may or may not be a friendship.

*The lesson of the heart for man is the lesson of integration for man. The lesson of integration creates the action of understanding self.*

When you as an individual can give from your heart, give from your soul and spirit as well as your physical body, you have integrated the three facets of your mind.

All energy originates within the mind of man. It is the energy of the integrated mind that slows down the energy to create the physical body. The energy of the intellectual mind relates to the physical body and is therefore more understood by the conscious mind of man.

*It is the belief of the male energy that if he shares his physical body he is sharing all that he is.*

The offer of the physical body for male energy is their understanding of the offer of friendship. Of course, the energy of friendship is understood only as the offer of their body. There is no integration of self involved within this physical process.

*Indeed, the ego of man sees his physical body as a gift which he has given and he believes that the female accepts his gift with gratitude. The female is searching for emotion and feeling and is not fulfilled with a physical encounter.*

# Soul and Spirit Energy

The energy of the soul and spirit is more of a challenge for man to understand.

*Soul and spirit energy cannot be intellectualized.*

Soul and spirit energy is displayed in physical reality by the feelings and emotions within. It is there to share, to give, and to support the unconditional love within. It is an energy that must be understood on faith. It is not a tangible physical reality that can be scientifically studied and understood.

Your belief system focuses you within the physical consciousness where you feel rejection and resistance if the physical pattern of life that you have accepted is not consistently repeated within your daily activities.

*Change creates a feeling of unworthiness in you. Spontaneity is viewed as a crisis by you. Change and spontaneity are opportunities for growth and celebration within your life.*

You are focused upon giving and receiving from the physical level of consciousness. Your fear of rejection is a hidden feeling from a physical level of consciousness that is focused upon denial of the soul and spirit within. This consciousness is reflected back to you as resistance and denial from other human beings within your world.

*It is because of the fear of rejection that the male who is focused exclusively in the physical world will have few friends to support him.*

It is from this unacknowledged level of physical consciousness that fear dwells, that unworthiness dwells, and that anger dwells. When you can go beyond this physical consciousness and integrate the soul and spirit energy, you will learn the lesson of the heart. With this integration you will become open. You will give openly and you will receive openly. You will reflect within the world the love that you are within.

The challenge for male energy in integration is his focus upon intellectualization and physical gratification. When he first becomes aware that he is more than a physical body and he begins to accept the awareness of a soul and spirit within, he will focus upon the soul and spirit from the concept of the intellect.

*The intellect/ego mind is the external focus of physical energy. You attach your perception of your soul and spirit energy to your understanding and perception of your physical energy. Your soul and spirit energy cannot be understood from the perception of your intellect. It can only be under-*

*stood from your energy of faith. In your physical reality, your soul and spirit self is an energy of faith.*

The energy of faith is the energy of inspiration and motivation that is created from the soul and spirit within. The soul and spirit of man are energies that are beyond the comprehension of the intellect because they will not conform to the scientific concepts of your physical reality that you "think" you understand.

When man can integrate his soul and spirit with his intellect, he will be inspired and motivated to create within the physical world from his intellect. Many humans upon Earth do indeed function from an integrated mind even when the ego accepts all acknowledgment of success for the intellect alone.

*The more soul and spirit energy that you integrate into your intellect the more humble you become.*

The humble man consciously recognizes that he created from other than his intellect. Subconsciously and unconsciously he feels the integration of the soul energy of infinite knowledge and the spirit energy of enfinite perfection with the intellect. This conscious understanding and acceptance of an integration of force beyond the intellect balances out the energy of the ego/intellect.

Man's fear of integrating the soul and spirit energy with the intellect is symbolic of man's fear to integrate his energy with the energy of other humans on the physical level.

*This ego fear of integration in man that resists receiving the inspiration and motivation from within, is mirrored in his denial and resistance to friends within the physical world. The energy within the mind of man, creates the outer world of man.*

The soul and spirit within you accepts integration which creates the activity of giving and receiving with the intellect.

If you are not conscious of the soul and spirit energy, this interchange will continue on a subconscious and unconscious basis. If you resist the giving and receiving of your soul and spirit with the intellect internally, the resistance will be manifested in your physical ability to give and receive of yourself with friends and lovers.

*Denial of integration will always affect man's*
*ability to be all that he can be within the physical*
*world. He will deny and resist his own inspiration*
*and motivation because he will not trust it or*
*believe in it as part of his reality. The lesson of*
*integration is the lesson of the heart.*

All humans function from both male and female energy. It is a greater challenge for the male to integrate female energy than it is for the female to integrate male energy. In your culture of today you can see the action of these two energies as they create dramas of life in their efforts to balance their energies within.

*This lesson of the heart will continue to be an*
*issue for man until he develops a conscious aware-*
*ness of all facets of his mind. This awareness will*
*trigger a conscious willingness to accept the inspi-*
*ration and motivation from within. This accep-*
*tance will create a total faith in the unconditional*
*love of self.*

In the physical world words can be used without the support of action. People can say things but not mean what they say. They do not give and receive. They do not act out their thoughts and their words.

When you accept the lesson of the heart you will find yourself being emotional and having feelings. You will integrate these emotions and feelings into your everyday relationships and friendships totally without fear or hesitation. You will become what you say that you are.

As you integrate the soul and spirit energy you will find truth in the consistency of your words and actions. You will be love, truth, and perfection. You will not just say, "I love you." You will allow each and every action to BE love in motion. The energy of your love will create the action of your love.

*For man to truly know the meaning of love he*
*must integrate his feelings, his heart, and his emo-*
*tion into the intellectual physical consciousness.*
*Love will be the active integration of all.*

When you have trust and faith that love is indeed happening in your world, you will have more trust and faith in yourself and in each other. You will begin to understand on a different level, not just from the consciousness of the intellectual, physical level.

You will begin to feel the love, truth, and perfection within yourself and in all of man. As you feel love, you will reflect love within your actions.

*It is at the moment when you become living truth in action that you learn to be a friend.*

The love that you feel within will be reflected to other men and to Mother Earth which is the source of your physical body. You will be a source of love to your friends in life. You will share your love as freely as you breathe. You will act in a loving way to protect the Earth and the Universe from which you came. You received a physical body from Earth. You received the life force of energy from the spirit energy of the Creator.

*You have received. In being the truth of love, you will give love.*

It is now time for man to give life back to the Earth. Giving is an action of friendship within your physical world. What man is, is what he gives. If man is the image of anger, hate, and resistance, he will give anger, hate, and resistance. You give to the Earth and to all of mankind, the energy that you are.

*Energy is your image that you reflect. This image is the energy that you radiate to add to the accumulated energy of the Universe. If you want to protect yourself, the Earth, and the Universe, be only positive energy.*

When you can open yourself up to the energies within, you will open your energies without. You will give of yourself to your friends and to your lovers. You will give love, because you are love. You will be a friend because you are a friend.

If you have a friend, you must BE a friend to keep the friendship alive. You cannot expect a friend to do all of the interaction. What you learn from friends is giving and receiving, interaction, sharing, imaging your own self, perceiving your own self, and you learn love. These are the primary reasons for friends. Without the interaction of friends, you cannot grow.

# Understanding Friendship

The subject of friends is a very expansive subject, on which we may someday do a book, so you can see that what we can cover in this commentary will be an overview. But I do want you to be able to see with clarity how important friends are in your world.

We also want you to see with total clarity that your friends are the energy of you reflected from you. As you choose your energy, you choose your friends. It is the energy of self that you perceive in others. If you do not like someone, it would serve you to understand why you do not like them.

If you decide that you want to get rid of a friend, you can understand that you will have the same image occur in friend after friend. The situation will repeat itself because of the energy attraction, until you learn the lesson of the interaction.

The lessons that you design with special friends will continue to attract the return of the same friend until you learn the lesson with total clarity. Each return will create a different image of the lesson.

When you have a friend, it becomes your responsibility to yourself to be as good a friend as you can possibly be. To be a good friend, you must be a friend who does not judge. You are there to give and to receive. You are a friend, to love your friends unconditionally.

Judgment is the opposite of unconditional love. The energy of friends must be accepted as they are and understood as they are. When you judge a friend, you are in reality judging yourself.

When you find yourself thinking, "This person is bothering me," you need to look within, and find a new perspective with which to view your friendship. This new perspective will help you understand the energy within you that you saw mirrored within your friend. It is the energy of self that you are resisting and denying that pushed your buttons. Because you see, life is like a gigantic jigsaw puzzle and it is very carefully designed.

You have created the design. You have created the interaction. You have created the relationship because of your desire, your wish, and your want to learn a lesson. When you imagine life as just one big lesson, you may find it boring in concept.

In reality, life is the most exciting and expansive action that you can involve yourself with. It is because of the creation of these lessons, through the concept of a total design of multiple interaction, that you allow yourself to see and to remember who you are in all of your beauty.

*Envision life as a master chess game. Each move dictates the next move. Nothing is known, and all is known.*

If you look at a friend and you do not see beauty, then you do not see beauty within yourself. This may be a challenge to understand for some of you who say, "I know exactly who this person is and he is driving me nuts."

Yes indeed, you will create irritating relationships, and when you create these relationships it is for your benefit. These relationships allow you to see yourself with total clarity within the actions of another.

In understanding your friends, you will clearly see either how you **want** to be, or how you **do not want** to be. When you understand the lesson with total clarity, you can release the attachment to the relationship if that is your choice.

When you can see yourself with total clarity, you can then perceive your relationships differently. Your friends will also be working on a lesson. Once you see any relationship differently the relationship will change. When your friends see the relationship differently, the relationship will change again. It will be because of the interaction within the relationship that you both have grown.

How do you adjust your perception of your interaction so that it can become productive, rather than destructive?

You perceive relationships differently by looking within. Looking within allows you to see the lesson that you are trying to learn in the relationship. Focus upon learning the lesson and not upon judging the relationship. The lesson is different for you and your friend. If you judge the relationship, you have created resistance and denial to the lesson that you are attempting to learn.

Are you expecting your friends to be something other than what they are? Are you judging them to be less than what they are? Are you expecting them to live by a belief system and a role that they are totally unconscious of existing? Are you wanting them to be as you see yourself? Are the irritations that annoy you with your friends, also habits that you are presently attached to in your life? Are the characteristics that upset you, threatening to you? Do these traits create an emotional response within you? Do you fear emotion? Is there a balanced giving and receiving in your interaction and in your communication?

You see, the way to have a truly beautiful friendship is to have total, truthful, and open communication. If you function by belief, by judgment, or by assumption, then you are not communicating, you are not interacting truthfully and openly with your friends. You are only interacting with yourself through the energy of judgment. Your friends are unaware of your feelings unless you communicate them openly and truthfully.

**Friendship requires a commitment to give and to receive as freely, openly, and truthfully as an intimate relationship does.**

Judgment creates the opportunity for destruction of the friendship because when you interact with yourself on the basis of judgment, assumption, and physical perception, you do not truly understand the feelings in the heart of your friends. You are not communicating.

Interaction means communication by feelings, emotions, words, and actions. It means to interact on all levels of the integrated self. The image of your friends when seen with clarity, will be the image of self seen with clarity.

What is the way that man has chosen to interact primarily? You have chosen to interact primarily through the process of speech, through the process of verbal communication. This art of physical communication is manifested in your physical world by radio, television, movies, operas, plays, books, newspapers, speeches, schools, and on and on.

**The reality of communication is so common to your intellect that you forget to communicate unless it is a planned event.**

In the spirit world communication includes interacting from the physical, intellectual, rational, and intuitive mind. Communication is the intermingling of physical, intellectual, soul, and spirit energies. It is interacting physically, mentally, and emotionally with the feelings of the heart.

If you truly want to be a friend and to have a friend, you have to learn to give and receive from the energy of self. You must learn to listen as well as to speak. You must allow the energy and the emotion of your feelings and your heart to be transmitted with your words.

You must do as your politicians do and offer equal time to your friends. If you cannot listen to a friend, you cannot hear a friend, and you are denying and resisting the friend and the friendship. Allow yourself to care about how your friend feels. Communicate your feelings not simply your words. Communicate with follow up actions that show your caring and your sharing of emotion.

*It is when you are willing to give of yourself to your friends, to interact on all levels, that you will receive more than what you give.*

Is this "equal?" Yes, indeed, it is equal because when a person has your attention and can speak to you, you have given them your most fabulous gift of self. You have given them a gift of acknowledgment, a gift that says, "I appreciate, I value, I respect what you have to say." When you appreciate, respect, and value the words of your friends, the energy of your friends, you truly respect, appreciate, and value yourself.

This primary role of friend is an image of the lesson of unconditional love. This is the beginning of a lesson that returns you to the energy of the Father.

When God said, "You must love ME, and love yourself as ME, and love your neighbor as yourself," He was saying that we are all equal; we all deserve equal unconditional love. In equality there must always be a balance and harmony of the energies.

If your friend happens to be your lover, as well as your friend, you will find your lessons of friendship becoming even more profound.

*The closer the friend is, the more significant, the more expansive, and the more focused your lesson is with that friend. Close friends will not all be lovers. They may be of both sexes that enjoy the celebration of friendship. Friendship celebration is the action of giving and receiving.*

This does not mean that friends who are not lovers are not important. Lovers are friends that you have chosen to work more intensely with on the lessons of the heart.

Unconditional love is truly a lesson of friendship. It is a lesson of loving the soul and spirit energy that exists within your world, regardless of where it is, who it is, what it is, or how good or bad you judge it to be.

Friendship energy is simply part of the energy of unconditional love. Friendship creates for you the images that all of you must experience in varying degrees to learn with total clarity the lesson of unconditional love. If you fear friendship you fear the lesson of unconditional love. You fear the Godself within. You fear the emotion of love.

This lesson of unconditional love is the lesson of giving and receiving. It is the lesson of sharing and caring. It is the lesson of the heart. It is the lesson of integration. It is the lesson of balance. It is, indeed, the root of all lessons for mankind.

> *Friends who are your close friends in life are the most valuable assets in your world. Friends are your gift to yourself.*

I want to emphasize this gift of friendship because it is where you will consistently interact, consistently receive support, consistently give support, consistently find the ability to grow and understand yourself, and consistently be able to value yourself.

> *Friendship is the living spirit of love in action. True friendship is the energy of unconditional love in action within your physical world.*

There is nothing in human existence that is more important than friendship. In friendship you can learn every lesson there is for you to learn, if you focus upon communication and interaction. If you resist communication and interaction, you are indeed resisting the friendship and the growth experience for self.

If a friendship feels too complicated, getting rid of it will only create another exactly like it. If you have a problem with a friend, work with the friend to see yourself with clarity and solve your perception within yourself. This is your opportunity to grow. Make that friend someone you can truly love, appreciate, and value.

If you reach the consciousness of communication and interaction and the friend does not, release your attachment to the closeness of the relationship until the friend can grow in the lesson of loving and accepting self.

> *You can unconditionally love a friend and not be in their physical presence. This does not create mutual growth at the same level but it will allow the friendship to continue.*

In your world you spend a large amount of time with the people with whom you interact in the business world. If you want to learn how to create abundance in your life, you must treat each of these relationships with friendship, with love, with understanding, with true appreciation, respect, and value.

It does not matter to you if someone exists in negative energy, because you do not have to perceive that part of the individual. You can choose to carefully select out the positive energy and focus upon the positive energy. When you continue to give positive energy to the friend it will be returned.

You will create for yourself a truly valuable friend. This friend will be with you, to interact with you, for all of your lifetime. The strength of the friendship may not be apparent to you in your physical world. But, you see, the interaction of friends is not limited to the physical level.

When you have a friend, you have the capability to interact with this friend whether or not you are enjoying each other's physical presence. You can communicate, you can send them loving energy, you can send them words, you can send them pictures, and you can indeed join them through spirit energy.

Through this energy interaction, you can continue with your soul and spirit work together. This spirit interaction can heal the energy of a negative individual. You can support your spirit energy by focusing on the positive physical energy within your colleague.

Spirit interaction occurs during sleep time and is an excellent way for you to move forward in your soul evolution. If you do not want to interact on a physical level with a friend, you can consciously choose to communicate with the energy on a soul and spirit level during sleep.

If you have relationships that are creating dramas in your life after you have learned your lesson, make the choice to interact with the energy in another manner. Look within yourself and find the judgment or the resistance to the relationship that is within you. On a conscious basis perceive the good energy, the positive energy that exists within your friend. Release your attachment to judgment.

There is always positive energy within all of man. When you learn to focus upon the positive and allow the negative to become neutral, you are making progress in your soul evolution.

> *The challenge for man is to understand that he chose the Earth experience to cleanse and heal his soul energy. This is created in the physical world by cleansing and healing the physical body and the physical mind. Life and the interaction of relationships is the physical process of healing and cleansing.*

It is by the lessons that you learn that you cleanse and that you heal yourselves. As you work internally upon yourself, you begin to radiate a very positive energy that heals other souls and spirits within the Universe.

Do you see how the magnetism of energy works?

# Friendship and Marriage

In your world marriage is a common event. This event, if it is begun with the basis of friendship rather than physical attraction allows the healing and cleansing of both parties to be expansive. If a relationship begins with a basis of only physical attraction, you will find yourself stuck within that energy. Marriage will become a daily challenge to rise above the negative perception and allow the healing and cleansing to occur.

Many friendships last longer than many marriages, because friendships do not usually begin as physical attractions. Friendships begin with a sense of appreciation, a sense of value, and a sense of respect for an energy within you that is reflected within the friend. This is indeed the perfect energy to begin a friendship and to sustain a friendship. Indeed, friendship is the best energy from which to begin a marriage.

> *It is possible at times for people to grow more expansively through friendships than it is for them to grow in a marriage. This happens because it is easier for you to cope with your reflection, if you do not constantly have to deal with it before it is accepted. Occasional exposure gives you time to process the lesson at your physical and intellectual pace.*

I am not suggesting by any means that anyone should not get married or be married. I am only suggesting that if you are married you should develop a lasting friendship with your partner that will balance you during your periods of growth.

A friendship of total communication and a friendship of expansive interaction will create a stronger marriage. A marriage of strength is an integrated marriage that allows the physical, the intellect, the soul, and the spirit equal balance.

*It IS the mind that builds your world. Your body and your life are the results of the activity within your mind.*

It is our purpose to help you understand your life activity and to heal any bruises that you may be attached to. Releasing the fear from your life will allow you to understand the wisdom of integration and balance.

The mind has been created by what we call the physical mind, which is the intellect and the ego; the rational mind, which is the soul memories; and the intuitive mind, which is the spirit energy.

You visit each space individually. They are your interior castles, the mansions of your mind. As you grow in wisdom and understanding you integrate these three facets of the mind until you have a smooth flowing channel of energy that circles through them all. This is known as integration. Friendship is one image of the lesson of integration.

It is my wish to encourage each of you to make friendship a very important energy within you. Be willing to communicate freely, openly, and truthfully.

*Understand that giving and receiving in friendship means to give the energy that you wish to receive in return.*

Being a friend is being willing to give and to receive openly, without judgment, and without resistance. If all of your relationships can begin with a very solid, truthful friendship, they will last you through a lifetime.

Relationships that are lasting have their own special benefits in the physical world as well as in the spiritual world. Knowing that you have a true friend that you can talk to when you "need" to talk, will many times help you maintain your balance within your physical world.

All relationships will benefit you in your soul evolution in a way that will be impossible for you to perhaps comprehend on a conscious level. The energy of friends is interwoven, intermingled, interpenetrated, and inseparable.

*The friends that you know in the physical world
are truly friends of soul and spirit energy. They
are part of the design of life that you have created
and they are there to play their roles as they
agreed to do.*

The affect of energy with energy is not understood on your level of physical consciousness in your cycle of development, but it will become a new awareness within your world as you evolve. When the superconscious energy of the mind is acknowledged and accepted in the physical world it can be utilized with a different intention and a different understanding.

The value of non-judgment is a lesson well worth the energy that is expended. Non-judgment is the most important energy of interaction, and it is the basis of all loving interaction. When you can actively practice non-judgment in all relationships you will have climbed several steps of the spiral stairway to Heaven. The physical manifestation will be a releasing of fear, anger, and resentment within the physical world.

Judgment is a value energy of the belief system that you burden yourself and your friends with in each physical lifetime. It is judgment that creates differences and differences create war, killing, divorce, fear, anger, hate, abuse, and unhappiness. Judgment turns friends into enemies and creates loneliness within and without. Judgment destroys marriages and intimate relationships.

# Family and Friendships

Your family should be a source of strong and lasting friendships. The family is a network of spirits that have agreed to be your safety net within this physical lifetime. They love you unconditionally in the spirit world. Because of this strong and enduring spirit energy it is easier to be friends with your family members than with any other person.

The family exists for you in multiple levels. Understand that all levels of your family are there by design. You can create long and lasting friendships within any level of the family network. This network includes the extended family of husbands, wives, in-laws, cousins, aunts, uncles, and all other levels of family relatedness.

If you marry and divorce, try to maintain a friendship with the former mate and their family. It is understood that friendship must be accepted by both parties. If that does not seem possible at first, continue to send loving and supportive energy to the former mate. Divorce is normally created by a lack of understanding and communication between the individuals. When that energy can be healed, the friendship can be very valuable to the family unit.

Children can become the best friends that parents can ever have. Just as parents can become the best friends that children can ever have. On a spirit level these relationships are intermingled, interwoven, and inseparable. The challenge for you is to create a truthful and open communication on a physical level so that the support will exist with a conscious awareness and love.

Parents must also understand that they only agreed to be involved in the energy of the child for love. Abuse and control that continues from childhood into adult life is a lesson that should be perceived, healed, and cleansed.

If there is fear, anger, resentment, and hostility that is left over from a poorly communicated issue, there cannot be unconditional love. Allow the anger, fear, hostility, and resentment to be communicated. Allow it to be freely and openly discussed.

Many times the perspective of the child is totally different than the perspective of the parent. Perspectives are created in children by a lack of information and understanding that would surprise the most perfect parent.

Siblings are another source of friendship within your world. Brothers and sisters are in your life because they have chosen to be in your life. They are part of the spiritual safety net of unconditional love that exists for you whether or not that love is demonstrated within your physical world.

In all circumstances of relationships, the most common constraint to true friendship is a lack of understanding and communication on a truthful, open, and accepting basis. Your mind creates images of your own energy to reflect to all other individuals.

The beliefs that you each hold may have little similarity. Indeed, you could be in total agreement with each other and still perceive that you do not think alike or understand each other. If you do not communicate your feelings and your emotions along with your beliefs, you may still not fully communicate.

It is important in communication to express your feelings clearly and precisely. Do not expect that the friend is going to "know" what you think and how you feel. Spend time together with a total willingness to explore your relationship. If you fear and resist any form of interaction you will loose your friend.

*If you choose to listen and not speak, you are not communicating. If you choose to speak and not hear, you are not communicating. If you choose to ignore the issues, you are not communicating. If you will not devote time to the friendship and its survival, you are truly not interested in having a friend.*

It is important in friendships not to send mixed messages. If you want to be a friend, then be a friend. If you want someone to listen to your troubles but you are not interested in any further communication, you do not want a friend, you want a counselor. It is appropriate for you to pay for counseling and you should in this instance seek out a professional.

It is more valuable to have a friend. Friendship means that you give and you receive. Friendship is a two-way street.

*The rules of friendship apply to all levels of friends. These friends might be family, acquaint- ances, lovers, close friends, colleagues, and/or part- ners. The level is unimportant. The unconditional love, the giving and receiving, the understanding and communication, the sharing and the caring, the accepting, the acknowledgment, the respect, the value, and the expenditure of time to be with a friend are the most important issues of all.*

In following these rules, you validate the importance of the friendship and the friend.

The most destructive energy that can be imposed into a friendship is the energy of judgment. Judgment is a belief stan- dard that you impose upon another. It allows you to perceive a friend as you perceive yourself.

*Judgment perception is not a true picture of the friend. It is an image of your own sense of unwor- thiness reflected from within you.*

Judgment is an action of the ego that is supported by your intellect. It has no validity in friendship and indeed its presence nullifies the concept of friendship. Friendship is the energy of unconditional love. Judgment is the opposite energy to unconditional love.

If there is a friend within your life that you are judging or have judged, examine the energy of your beliefs. This friend has agreed to help you with your lesson of unconditional love. Understanding the energy of your judgment will help you understand the opposite energy of unconditional love.

Your energy may change, and the energy of your friend may change but if you are unaware of the change within yourself or your friend, your consciousness of the relationship will remain unchanged.

Once the exploration of the energy and the lesson has begun, call your friend and communicate your intentions. Working on friendships together creates the interaction of friendship. Interaction is the only productive way for you to grow and to learn within the physical world.

Interaction within relationships will create a clear image of yourself and who you are. It will allow you to see the total you as you were meant to be. When you can recognize with joy that the physical, the intellectual, the soul, and the spirit are integrated and balanced, you will understand who you are.

When you can understand the value of non-judgment, you will find the joy of unconditional love in the interaction. This will be the beginning of your self-realization.

Self-realization allows you to create beautiful friendships that will be rewarding, productive, supportive, and loving for a lifetime. Friendships allow you the interaction to grow in soul evolution. Friends are a gift to cherish.

# Cultural
## Relationships

It is important for man to understand the cultures of families and the cultures of relationships. Do you know what a culture is? A culture is when man focuses on behaviors and beliefs in a like manner. This focus upon behaviors and beliefs in the same manner is a culture in your terms and a consciousness level in spirit reality.

Cultures essentially exist in levels within your society. You could call groups from one country one culture and groups within that culture, subcultures. Let us use, for instance, the ethnic group of Italians. For many years some individuals in this culture have been involved in drug cultures, and in behavioral cultures of prostitution.

These are subcultures within a culture. Not all Italians are involved in these activities. Many Italians will spend their lives in a personal effort to change the activities of these subcultures. Italians are also blessed with many advanced souls who pursue the creative arts such as painting, music, sculpture, inventions, and many other artistic endeavors.

These subcultures within a culture exist side by side but they exist from a different consciousness level. Those souls that are involved in crime are captured within a physical consciousness level that is in the early cycles of development. The creative souls that focus upon the arts are living from soul memory which places them within a different level of consciousness.

All cultures have infinite levels of subcultures that are never classified within your world. Any group of people with divergent beliefs or behaviors creates a subculture within a culture. If you have a culture that is a drug culture or a culture of prostitution, you have a group of people whose behavior and whose belief systems are focused upon the activities of their world.

So you see, cultures are created by man and they exist as group beliefs and behaviors. They share a conscious focus upon a specific energy level. When groups of men focus upon similar beliefs and behaviors within your world they develop a culture which is a focus upon a specific consciousness level. In these cultures you will frequently resist all exposure to other consciousness levels because your focus is so intense.

In professions, cultures are again created. If you have people who are in the computer world, they speak the same language, they have the same behavior, they have the same belief systems, and they focus upon these beliefs and this behavior the majority of their day. This creates a culture within itself.

The important thing for you to understand is the power of the belief system, because it is your belief system that is created by groups of man. These various levels of culture then grow from each other and they collectively produce the energy that structures and controls your society.

In our example for instance, the drug culture supports the culture of prostitution and the culture of crime such as stealing, murder, and rape, which in turn supports the medical culture, the judicial culture, the law enforcement culture, the corporate culture, and on and on.

These cultures become dependent upon each other. If you did not have crime you would not need the law enforcement community and you would have less need for the judicial and legal cultures.

If you look at the medical profession you can recognize a culture that sees itself exclusive within its realm of science. The focus of the medical world is disease and trauma. If you look at the legal profession you find a culture that is focused upon judgment.

When two cultures join each other within a cycle and exist in opposing energies without integration, such as the medical world and the legal world, they capture man in this dichotomy of energy exchange. Being captured in the energy of the judicial and medical world creates dramas within your world that are profound. As these business cultures feed upon each other, they control your world. They hold man captive in the energy of the consciousness level that is generated.

Let your mind wander through the professions that you know. See how the behavior and the beliefs within professions are similar and how they create similar worlds. Do you see? The irony of these business cultures is they are created within your world with the intention of self-gratification.

Self-gratification for one man is frequently exploitation of another man. You create personal gain by the opposite energy. Personal gain does not guarantee growth and happiness within man unless it is created secondary to Universal intention. Indeed, self-gratification will constrict man, not expand man.

In the medical world or the legal world if your intention is to help man, then you function with intellect, feeling, and emotion. If your intention is the self-gratification of financial reward, you function from the intellect and ego which is focused toward your own material needs.

Using this example should help you to understand that even in instances where cultures appear Universal there are subcultures that are delineated by intention. In the world of law enforcement there are subcultures that are easily recognized.

There are law enforcement individuals who enter into this profession because the power and control over people both with firearms and without firearms is a boost to their ego-self. Others will enter into the law enforcement culture with the intention of helping other people.

In your world each culture is then judged by certain standards of right or wrong, good or bad, or caring or destruction. These cultures will change their level of acceptance by the people themselves in waves of energy that have a Universal impact.

If you look at people who own restaurants, or you look at people who are nurses, or you look at people who are publishers, and I wish to include all of you reading this text because I want you to see within your own experience how your behavior and your belief system controls your life. Do you see within your own experience how your belief system, your activities control your world? Your life is an energy design that you created as your reality in the physical world. You function from a specific level of conscious awareness.

If you believe that you need to serve other men, you will work in a service culture. If you believe that you must serve yourself in terms of intellectual involvement, you will choose to be in a group that will allow you to fulfill your need.

Each and every facet of your life will be focused within the behavioral pattern and within the belief system of your chosen structure, if that structure is all that you accept as your world. This is your choice. This is the culture of your physical belief system.

This culture of beliefs that you have developed around your perception of reality becomes an attitude towards life and living for you. You accept what you believe as the only belief that is right. Your belief in your own invincible perception of the world becomes your bastion to defend.

Have you ever seen a glass jug that has a ship totally reconstructed within its interior? When man creates a structure of beliefs and lives by them, he reduces his potential in the identical way that the ship's potential is reduced within the bottle.

The beliefs of man create a glass jug around him. He can look out but his vision is limited by the reflection of the light on the glass that protects him. He lives his life encased within this shield that does not allow him the freedom to go beyond where he is. His growth and his exposure to activity and relationships is confined by the glass jug that surrounds him. The walls of the glass jug become his life restrictions. He must remain a miniature of self to exist within his tiny world.

The small ship that is constructed within a glass bottle will never sail in the water of a lake. When a man creates himself as a captive of belief systems, he creates a life in a glass jug. He will never allow himself to sail the seas of life to experience and to grow in the manner that he intended to grow when he created his life design.

Human cultures are intermingled, interwoven, and interrelated to the point where they cannot be separated. Man sees himself as separate but in reality his entire life is dependent on the energy of others in your modern culture. You watch television, drive cars, eat prepared foods, seek medical attention, use policemen and firemen, read books, buy your clothing, go to movies, fly in planes and on and on.

In the spirit world, we also have cultures. We have cultures of spirits that choose to come into their Earth existences to serve man, to provide music, to be mathematicians, and scientists. Do you see?

When a spirit is created in the very beginning of their creation, they may not be in the same spirit culture that they are in today. So you see, what the spirit does and what man does is identical. As man grows he changes his focus, his behavior, his beliefs, and many times he changes his profession within a single lifetime. As he evolves through the embodiments of the soul, he visits and challenges many different cultures of your world. These cultures offer you the opportunity for growth in your soul and spirit energy.

At one point in your life, you may find that riding a motorcycle and being with a motorcycle gang your culture. Twenty years later you may not want to even see a motorcycle. The experience was there for you to learn and to evolve. In your participation was a lesson of that particular culture.

You grow from the experience of living. It is the culture, the personal relationship with your behavior and your beliefs and those of like behavior and like beliefs, that teaches you.

You may choose to be with a certain culture in order to experience the opposite. It is when you experience the opposite that you learn what you do not want. If you do not allow yourself to experience the opposite some place in your evolution, you will not be able to perceive in a comprehensive way where you are in relationship to certain issues.

Cultures are created by you for the purpose of soul evolution. When the spirit decides to be born into a culture of a certain land and focus upon certain behaviors and certain beliefs, it is because that is the lesson that you have chosen to work upon.

Each of these lessons must be learned in turn. If you do not learn, you do not grow and evolve. Nothing that you do is wrong; it simply IS. It IS the way you have chosen to learn a specific lesson.

> *You create your world from these behaviors and from these belief systems. When you find yourself in a situation where you are not happy, peaceful, and joyful within, you have created the opportunity for change.*

Change is growth. If you focus upon only one belief system and one set of behavioral traits, you will never grow. You will be stuck in the energy of the culture which you have adopted as your choice in life. Life that knows only one facet is restrictive to growth.

I am sure that some of you have heard the word "cult." "Cult" is simply short for "culture." In your world cults are considered to be people who focus upon a certain behavior or belief normally focused toward the spiritual or the occult. This definition is not truly comprehensive, because the word "cult" signifies culture which is the basis of your physical world.

People within what you would term cults are indeed focusing upon a set of beliefs and a set of behavioral actions. They are living their culture. When you can understand the importance of the culture, the importance of the belief system, and the behavior of man, you will understand the wisdom of change.

In the spirit world the soul learns from the dramas that are designed into an earthly existence. Earth is indeed the schoolroom of man.

*If all souls grow and develop on Earth as humans and believe that they have only one life, that is the beginning of a culture.*

All humans that believe in only one physical life create a cult. The binding of each human to this culture by the singular belief in one lifetime, could then make it applicable to your vision as a cult.

*A cult is the sharing of a singular belief within a culture.*

If you live within a culture that focuses your belief upon only one physical life, that belief will affect the entire structure of your life.

*Believing that you are born only once creates a belief that you have only one opportunity to become perfect within the eyes of God. When you believe in the concept of time and space, this belief can create panic and despair within the intellect and ego of man.*

Indeed, the panic can become so acute that you fear to live because you fear that you will be found guilty of sin. This panic can lead man to suicide in your physical world because death will be viewed as a release from the opportunity for guilt and sin.

The opposite reaction to the panic of living and creating sin, is the focus on the impossibility to achieve perfection. If man believes that it is impossible to become perfect in one life-time, he will accept the approach that it does not make a difference how he lives. He will then create multiple crisis in your society because he thinks he is doomed to "hell" and he is paying society back before he goes. He is seeking revenge on the world that he blames for his life circumstances.

Another approach to achieving perfection is doing exactly what you want to do, and then believing that God will forgive you. This is total avoidance of responsibility for your personal actions. This is the belief that allows you to be as sinful as you like and God will take care of it for you.

Your behavior becomes part of your cultural beliefs. The behavior that results from these beliefs creates the dramas and crisis of your world.

Do you see how beliefs structure your world?

The belief in the judgment of God after one life that is being lived in a world of sin, creates a desire to leave that world before guilty behavior eternally separates you from God.

*This fear of separation from God is responsible today for many suicides especially in your children. This is a belief that removes hope from life and creates the ultimate vision of failure in living.*

It needs to be understood in your world that you have an eternal spirit within that has an infinite time to become perfect and return to God as an integrated energy.

*God does not judge you. You are your own judge by virtue of your belief in judgment.*

God created you. You have the inherent God energy within you. Your behavior and your beliefs are your responsibility. You have multiple opportunities to grow through your own levels of consciousness to perfect, to heal, and to cleanse your soul to spirit perfection.

*Your culture that focuses upon one life for man is focused upon a belief system, a culture that was designed by men for the control of man.*

This belief is frightening to all humans because it instills a hopelessness that man cannot see beyond. This hopelessness creates alcoholism, drug addiction, adultery, crimes of all manner, and other dependencies because the man who experiences no self-worth will see no future beyond today.

This belief is the opposite belief to eternal life. It is a belief that controls a large culture within your world. Learning to Be unconditional love, truth, and perfection in one short Earth existence is an ego issue for man on Earth.

The Christ Consciousness required many thousands of years in your physical time to reach His state of perfection on Earth. He came to Earth to show man the path to perfection. He experienced thousands of lives as man living within your cultures of Earth.

As spirits, you have all been around for many thousands of years and for many thousands of lifetimes, because you see, as spirits, life is truly eternal. When you slow down the electromagnetic energy that is you as a spirit, you create physical matter. That physical matter is called the human body.

When you have learned your lessons in this body in this lifetime, you will speed up the electromagnetic energy of you as a spirit and you will simply lift away from your physical body. You will make the choice to leave your body because you are going forward, you are evolving in the total concept of soul evolution. You will choose another body and come back to Earth to live another lifetime.

It is always your choice as to which culture you choose, which set of beliefs that you choose, and which set of behaviors you choose as your dramas in a lifetime. Because of the design that you have created for yourself, you will choose to create certain dramas that will allow you to learn the lessons you have chosen to learn.

In this schoolroom of Earth, you choose your culture as you would choose a college, dependent upon subject matter. The subject matter of a culture is the belief system and the behaviors involved. This choice is determined by what you want to learn. You have signed up for certain courses and you will focus on certain subjects with intensity, to learn the lessons that have taken you into another physical embodiment.

When you decide to come to Earth, you have decided to enter the "college" of Earth. You have chosen your personal opportunity to learn. Your experience will be the dramas that you create within your physical world. These dramas will be structured by your culture, your belief system, your behavior, and your chosen relationships TO SUPPORT what you want to learn.

When you go to college, you will pick out the books that will support you in the classes that you are going to take. In the classroom of life, you will also choose the beliefs and the behaviors that will support you in your lesson.

In college you will choose to be with a specific group of friends. In your choice of life, you will develop specific relationships to support you. There are no accidents within the Universe. There are only committed and diligent spirits who are focused upon their own soul evolution.

*Growth requires the interaction of relationships
with other spirits and souls in order to create the
dramas of experience.*

Cultures within the physical world are created by the level
of conscious awareness within man. If man is focused only upon
the physical, he will believe that he is finite. He will not be able
to envision beyond the physical concept of his accepted reality.

This attachment to the physical world will also create fear
within man as he perceives his role of responsibility in the
concept of being finite. Indeed, his relationship to life in general
will be one of failure to accept responsibility.

If you fail to accept the responsibility for self, you will not
see that you are responsible for your world, too. This fear of
responsibility becomes interwoven and inseparable from the fear
of separation from God.

This fear of separation from God has been exploited by man
since the beginning of Earth time. Indeed, the writings that
clarified this relationship of man to Earth and to God were purged
by man thousands of years ago in their own fear of losing control.
It was your males that chose to maintain their attachment to their
physical reality by their vision of control.

This is part of the lesson found within the cycle of development for man. Control keeps man attached to the physical world.
This is part of the male role as the physical linkage to Earth. This
is the ego role in the tug-of-war with the eternal spirit within.

*Decisions have been made by males throughout
history to maintain their physical attachment by
controlling the evolution of man.*

The female energy is the energy of the heart which is the
energy of the soul and spirit. Because of this understanding and
the perspective of the heart and feeling energy as a weakness,
man has also seen fit to control the female throughout history.

*The male need to control the female culture is
symbolic of the male need to control the energy of
the soul and spirit within himself, which his ego
identifies as a weakness.*

This external need of the male to control the inner self has
always been symbolized in the physical world by controlling the

female culture. Controlling and denying within the physical world are symbolic of controlling and denying the inner self.

*When man or woman controls or denies the inner self within any culture, they are actively learning the lesson of balance through the integration of the male and female energies.*

It is through dramas, through the art of living, that man learns. No matter what the lesson is, it is there for a purpose. This becomes a true challenge for man on Earth to understand. When you are an observer to another man's drama, you will feel emotions of sadness, anger, and fear for the person that you love.

Do not concern yourself with this fear. You must remember that you are in this drama with this person as support. You are the textbook that is helping with the lesson. You are there to love the individual, to support them, and to play your role in the drama.

*The interesting thing about dramas in your life is that there is a lesson for each party involved in the drama. But no two lessons are identical. Your lesson will not be the same as the lesson of your lover, your friend, your sister, or your mother.*

The relationship between you has to do with your lesson on an individual basis. But you have agreed, when you came into this culture of humanity, to support, to love, to interact in relationships that will help not only you to learn, but other spirits and souls to learn.

In your world your dramas are primarily structured within the cultures of Earth with some influence from the spirit world. As human beings, you are attached to the beliefs of Earth which create dramas that are symbolic of the spirit world but translated within man by his culture and his belief system.

*You are evolving at the time of the dramas but you are evolving within the cycle of development which is the slowest energy cycle for man. The cycle of development is firmly attached to the physical reality of man.*

# Cultural Beliefs

When you sleep you spend your time traveling and working in the soul and spirit world. This information is then translated through your intellect and ego into symbols that are understood by you intellectually. If the ego and the intellect find the sleep experience threatening, they will translate the sleep experience into a threatening physical experience.

You work with your soul and spirit while asleep because you deny the activity of the soul and spirit while you are awake. If there is expansive denial, you may find yourself needing more sleep. If you work comfortably with the soul and spirit while awake, you will need less sleep.

Your soul and spirit are integrated as part of your total self. Denial and resistance cannot remove the soul and spirit influence. If you resist working with your soul and spirit on a conscious awareness level, you will work with it more intensely in the subconscious and unconscious levels.

Your culture as a whole believes that man needs eight hours of sleep. Have you ever considered that you believe that you have 24 hours within a day and if you divide 24 by the three facets of self, you would be agreeing to allow the spirit equal time for its work.

*In the beginning of man's time on Earth, he understood that his knowledge came from soul memory and spirit energy. He slept to remember information. Since getting information was his intention in sleeping, his intellect and ego did not translate the information into physical symbols.*

Man accepted the soul and spirit memory as visions, words, and symbols which he could use in his new life on Earth. This was his opportunity to be in touch with his soul and spirit energy. His sleep activity was his inspiration and his motivation.

Now sleep is identified and accepted as rest for the physical body. It is acknowledged, accepted, and expected as a physical need. The singular focus on the physical self increases the desire to sleep. Indeed, man is so firmly attached to his time of sleep and quantity of sleep that he believes he cannot survive without the required number of hours.

It is true that man needs sleep of some degree, but the intention of sleep is misunderstood in the same manner that dreaming is misunderstood. When the conscious focus is directed primarily towards the physical, the spirit self will demand equal time because it is working with you on an unconscious basis in its intention of love.

The belief in sleep is a cultural belief that has become close to Universally accepted as a physical "need." This is a perfect example of man creating his own reality within the physical world.

Sleeping provides man with a very supportive network of energy. As you look around you at different cultures, different belief systems, different behaviors, you will see within these cultures similarities of speech, of dress, of language, of professions, of housing, and of geographical location. You can see the support structures that man has created within his world.

**You cannot see the support structures of the sleep world that man has developed.**

You can also see, as you look at your history, how cultures are involved in evolution. When the culture of Earth was known as Atlantis, it was a culture of little defined structure but it had an expanded understanding of using infinite knowledge. The areas of the Earth at that time were known by other names but names are not important. What is important to you at all times is to understand that it is through this path of evolution within cultures that you grow.

When God created man, by dividing the Christ Spirit into Adam and Eve, He created man as you know man, but He created a man that lived in a different culture. It was by no means a perfect culture. It was a culture that lived the same dramas, the same traumas that you live today. The events were many times created with different circumstances than they would be today but the results were the same.

The Garden of Eden was a culture that had not advanced intellectually to the degree that your culture has now advanced. It was at this time that man was returned to the beginning levels of the cycle of development because of soul devolution secondary to physical attachment.

*It is imperative at this time in your culture that spirits such as I come to speak to you, because you see, man has evolved physically and intellectually over thousands of years of being. Now the time has come for man to evolve as souls and spirits WITH conscious knowledge, WITH acceptance, WITH acknowledgment, and WITH value of self.*

Living in cultures that are destructive to the human body, to humanity, to self, to your Earth, and to the Universal energy, is no longer productive for man.

*It is important for man to change the behavior and beliefs of his culture. It is time for man to value, to accept, and to acknowledge the wisdom, the ingenuity, the power of creation that is within him.*

Man cannot change his culture until he changes his belief in himself as finite. The concept of being finite interferes with man's understanding of his power of creation and in his understanding the love and peace that can be found through the integration and discovery of self.

Indeed, man is like the hermit crab. Man has this spirit that runs along the sands of time, scampering into a physical body, a temple that he can use on a temporary basis until he learns a lesson. Once the lesson is learned he scampers on through the sands of time looking for another body, another home from which he can learn another lesson.

When you think of life simply in terms of lessons, it can sound deceivingly dull. Believe me, it is your ingenuity and creativity that keeps your life from being dull. When you look at the dramas that you create, you will see how inventive you can be.

Many physical lives are required for the soul and spirit of man to move through the lessons of evolution. Accepting the BELIEF in evolution can take thousands of lifetimes for man. You have debated the theory of evolution and the "explosion" concept since the beginning of time. Would it surprise you to know that they are both true?

Each of these happenings were real in the history of the Universe and of man. Neither of them are important today except as they satisfy your physical, intellectual curiosity. Your present world is the NOW, the present moment of your reality. Your interest should be focused upon the evolution of you as a soul and spirit. The evolution of the soul and spirit is controlled by the behavior of man as he moves through his cycles of growth.

*As long as man is attached to the physical intellect, ego, and body, and focuses his belief in that energy, it will take him many more thousands of lifetimes to evolve from infancy to adulthood in his progress through the cycles of evolution. Devolution is now a reality within your world.*

Many lifetimes are required to learn one lesson because despite the intellectual knowledge within man it is not integrated into the wisdom of intelligence. The wisdom that is acquired through the knowledge integration of soul and spirit energy with the intellect far surpasses the intellectual capabilities of man.

*Man will repeat his lessons over and over and over again, until he can accept and acknowledge WITH CONSCIOUS AWARENESS what the lesson means for him. Man will not look because he is afraid to see. He will not listen because he is afraid to hear.*

Man is controlled by his own fear of self-discovery. His fear is rooted in his feelings of unworthiness in the eyes of God. Because he lives in fear, he avoids the issue. Man believes that avoiding the issue will avoid attracting the attention of God because he sees himself as unworthy of God's attention.

This is a cycle of belief that is created within your culture because man believes that God is responsible for his salvation. Man believes that if he is not called, his sins will not be noticed. This belief has the ability to capture man within the physical energy and to hold him captive for thousands of lifetimes.

*God is not responsible for your salvation. You are responsible. You are also responsible for your thoughts, words, and actions. You are responsible for learning to be love. You are responsible for self and all facets of self. You are responsible for who you are, what you learn, the health of your physical mind and body, and for your own soul and spirit evolution.*

God sent His son to guide you, now it is your responsibility to define the path correctly within your culture and to love and nurture yourself, your family, your world, your Earth, and your Universe.

Upon your Earth you have only to watch your television, listen to your radio, read your books, newspapers, and magazines, or go to your movies to find yourself exposed to the destructive actions that occur within your world as you create it and as you re-create it.

The culture that you create within your world, structures your world. Your culture and your beliefs are your responsibility. You have free choice, free will, and free intention which was your gift at the time of your creation. You have the power of creating your own reality. You use your power of creation to create your world whether or not you have a conscious awareness of what you are doing.

*It is time to look carefully at your creation until you can see. It is time to listen carefully to your creation until you can hear. Man has the power to create destruction as the opposite of growth. He has the power to create disaster as the opposite of peace. He has the power to create ugliness as the opposite of beauty. He has the power to create fear as the opposite of love. You choose your own creation of your world.*

If you want to learn a lesson, you have to understand the subject. If you are in the first grade and you are learning the alphabet, you must understand what each letter looks like. If you do not understand what each letter looks like, and how it relates to the sequence of your alphabet, you will have a very difficult time learning how to read. You will have a difficult time evolving, growing from the level of first grade through the level of your college studies.

If you do not understand the lesson that you are learning as a soul and spirit, you will have a difficult time moving to the next level. As man lives his life, he creates images of the lessons he is working upon.

Each lesson is understood in relationship to your belief system. If you are attached to the physical ego and intellect, you will judge your own creations by your understanding of the physical.

You may need to live 2000 lives to learn one lesson. It may be less. It may be more. But until you learn WHO YOU ARE in terms of the total integrated self, you cannot move forward to the next class. You will be stuck in your lesson of the physical for thousands of lifetimes. In each one of these lifetimes, you will repeat the lesson over and over and over again until you understand it with total clarity.

It will be like having your teacher say in kindergarten, "Go to the blackboard, and write your 'A' two thousand times." Your teacher wants you to learn to recognize the 'A'.

The spirit within you wants you to recognize your "self." The spirit is part of self, the soul is part of self, and the physical body, intellect, and the ego are part of self. Acknowledging these three facets of self and understanding their relationship to each other, will help you learn your lessons of life.

Have you ever seen a friend, or yourself perhaps, who is consistently involved in multiple relationships one right after the other?

In each relationship the same lesson is consistently repeated over and over again. This repetition is necessary for man to see the lesson with total clarity.

Have you ever seen a man or a woman who is focused on addiction, perhaps not just for themselves, but for those souls they have chosen to interact with? Have you ever seen a person who could not keep a job? Have you seen these same individuals repeat experiences over and over and over again in each life event?

When man re-creates his reality consistently, and it does not have to be in the extreme, he does not understand who he is or what he wants in life. He has become captured by fear. His identity has become that of the dependent energy of his beliefs.

It is because of this dependent need for a physical identity that man groups himself into a culture, a belief system, a set of behavioral traits, or a relationship. It is man's belief that he gives himself power if he BELONGS. Belonging gives man physical identity.

*Belonging is the purpose of cultures. Cultures are created by the beliefs of man for identity purposes.*

Without the power of beliefs, man loses his identity and he is not comfortable. He feels different. Because of his fear, man has chosen to create an atmosphere where he can learn and where he can feel protected within his belief system by the reinforcement of others. It is this intellectual need for belief support that has created many churches within your culture.

*Having large groups believe the same thing you believe provides validation within your mind that*

*the belief is right. It also supports you in your be-*
*lief that others who believe opposite to you or dif-*
*ferent from you are wrong.*

If you are afraid or if you live your life experiencing fear, the fear within your mind will be manifested in your physical body and within your daily life. Each and every belief system that is within your mind will have a physical reaction within your world. This is the energy reaction within you and within the Universe. If you believe in guilt, you will feel guilty.

Understanding the effect of your culture and your beliefs upon your physical body and upon your physical world is an important lesson for each of you. Understand that when man lives with fear or any of its emotional elements, he will create dis-ease and disease.

Fear WILL ALWAYS have a physical manifestation of importance upon some physical part of self. It may be the mind, the self- image, or the body. The level of severity will depend upon how long it takes you to confront the issue within.

*It is the cultures of your world that support be-*
*liefs such as fear that create support of fear within*
*man.*

Since you create your own cultures, the time has come for you to create a culture of understanding of self and Earth.

When you understand exactly who you are, you will understand the power you have to create the love that is within you. The love that is within you is inherent within you. This love is the God energy within you. It is the love, truth and perfection that is your inherent birthright.

*You should have no fear of separation from God.*
*God is within each of you. You cannot be sepa-*
*rated. You are separate, but you are one. You are*
*love, truth, and perfection.*

Each spirit and soul on Earth that is within a physical body attaches itself to belief systems, to behaviors, to groups, to languages and to geographical areas, and it structures the physical world that it knows from this culture.

Some of your cultures teach that you are separate from God. This is a belief system that you choose to attach yourself to in life. Believing that you are separate from God creates the vision of a deity to worship outside of self.

*Creating the vision of a separate deity of spirit energy creates the vision of a false God. The Creator has instructed man not to worship false Gods. Attachment to the physical body as a singular focus is in effect worshiping a false God because it is a denial of spirit energy.*

You have the power of creation. Therefore, you have the power of change if you are not happy with your belief. If you are comfortable with your belief, then you are not ready to change the belief. If you are comfortable with your beliefs, you will live in peace, joy, and love. If you do not know peace, joy, and love it is time to examine your beliefs.

Beliefs that are true for you will allow consistency in your thoughts, words, and actions. You will always do unto others as you would have them do unto you. You will BE loving, nurturing, and caring in your daily life.

*If your life does not reflect this perfection of balance, then you are not true to your beliefs or your beliefs are not true to the soul and spirit energy within you. Only you can understand your inner and higher integration. Only you can change yourself. Only you control your world.*

When you attach yourself to a culture and to created belief systems, you have chosen the control and influence of the culture. You have acknowledged and accepted the restrictions of the belief system. If these beliefs create joy and peace within your world, they are perfect for the lessons that you are learning in this lifetime. If they do not allow you to believe totally with joy and peace, then they are not conducive to your ultimate lesson of life. Beliefs are the created resistances to growth within.

When you come to listen to people like me or when you read our books, you should take with you only what works for you. You should leave the rest because not every word that I speak can be understood by each of you. So you take what you understand and you continue to build upon that.

*My purpose of communication with Earth is to help man understand himself by discovering the LOVE, beauty, peace, and joy within himself. The energy of self-discovery will allow man to BE ALL THAT HE CAN BE.*

When you discover yourself, you will create within your physical world a new set of beliefs, a new culture, a new world, a new Earth, and a new Universe. Each and every one of you have within you the power of creation. No one else can ever create self-understanding for you. You will live within the world that you create. Your world is your choice of creation.

You have personal power only over yourself. Your energy is magnetic as you interact, intermingle, and as you learn your lessons. As you learn you change and as you change, the world around you will change. Your lessons are yours to master in your own way through interaction, through relationships, and through experiential learning.

Other parties involved in relationships or interaction with you may not have any concept of life as a lesson. This lack of conscious awareness for another person does not invalidate the experience for you. Indeed, seeing another individuals level of consciousness may be your lesson.

When you come together to share cultures, you are sharing the creations of belief systems by man, for man, on Earth. If the belief system does not allow you to awaken each morning filled with joy and love, it is time for you to look at that belief system and create a new one.

When you begin to look at your belief systems, they should be examined in the same way that you examine your closet when a new season arises. Those beliefs that do not serve you anymore should be laid aside. Thank them for having served you and for helping you to grow. As your growth expands, your beliefs expand and some will truly be restrictive in your new world. Release your attachment and enjoy the freedom that you experience.

When you choose to change your belief system, it is because a new season, a new cycle of awareness, has occurred within your life. In the same way that you change your clothes with cycles of the weather, you need to change your belief systems as the soul moves through its cycles of growth.

Not many of you would care to wear your bikini if the temperature were ten degrees below zero. Why would you choose to maintain your belief system when you are changing the climate for your soul and spirit? No one else is going to come into your bedroom and lay out new clothes for you and tell you the weather has changed. Only you can feel the temperature against your skin. Only you can know when your belief systems are outdated.

In the same way that you would not choose to drive the car that you had at 16 at the age of 50, you will not choose to live by the same beliefs that you had at 16 when you are 50.

You are very familiar with changing your physical world. You throw away your clothes and buy new ones, sometimes on a weekly basis. You change your car every year or two. If you drive down the street and see a new toy, you do not hesitate to buy it. You change your house every few years. You have no restrictions if you want a new job.

But when it comes to changing the beliefs that you live by, the challenge increases. Your culture creates your self-image, your identify with its beliefs. Those beliefs create within you the image of you within your mind.

*Your beliefs create a physical process as structure from which you create your self and your world.*

You are not your beliefs at all. Your beliefs are your glass jug. You are energy. You are energy that has slowed down to physical matter that is evolving whether or not you are conscious of that evolution. You are integrated as physical body, soul, and spirit. It is your physical body that houses the intellect and the ego. Your body is the external creation of the physical self that you identify as you. You exist in physical energy as multiple consciousness energies.

*The soul and the spirit are internal and they are eternal. They are integrated whether or not you are consciously aware of the integration. The intellect/ego is your conscious self. The soul is within on a subconscious basis, and the spirit is within on an unconscious basis. An aware integration of the soul consciousness and the spirit consciousness with the physical consciousness creates within man a superconsciousness.*

You can deny the soul and spirit. You can reject it. You can refuse to admit that it even exists. It does not matter because the soul and spirit are eternal. Because the soul and spirit are eternal they are not influenced by your physical energy which is finite.

*The only energy that is altered by your denial*
*and resistance to your soul and spirit energy is the*
*physical energy of your aware consciousness.*

When you doubt the physical presence of your soul and spirit, look in the mirror and see the good that is within you. The good that is within you is the positive energy of your soul and spirit. Your soul and spirit are the beauty within you.

The belief that you have in your present day culture of focusing only upon the material, physical world around you, allows you to ignore, to be in ignorance of the soul and spirit within. Your beliefs allow you to deny yourself as you truly are.

*Your beliefs keep you from understanding that*
*you are growing consistently through your dramas*
*of repeated physical lives.*

When you can look at your belief system, change the belief, and expand your mind to a new understanding, you will begin to truly appreciate WHO YOU ARE. Knowing who you are allows you the vision of how beautiful you are, how expansive you are, and how filled with wisdom you are.

If you can understand that you have access to INFINITE knowledge within your soul and spirit, you would have nothing else to learn. You already KNOW yourself intimately.

*Because of your ego belief in your unworthiness,*
*you resist the memory of self on a conscious basis.*
*You fear the unknown as part of your physical be-*
*lief system. You also deny the intellect access to*
*the soul and spirit memory because that memory is*
*a threat to the physical ego of man.*

*The ego of man holds man captive within his*
*physical belief system.*

Man creates many cultures upon the Earth. Each one of these cultures is focused toward a specific belief system and specific behavioral traits. They also have in common many other elements of emotion and attitudes. Many of these elements are focused within fear. Others elements are focused within love.

*You will move through many cultures within a*
*lifetime. Within thousands of lifetimes you will*
*cover the entire spectrum of cultures over and over*
*again. This repetition will continue until you can*

***move forward beyond the physical levels of belief
into the soul and spirit levels of awareness, understanding, and integration.***

In each physical life all cycles exist beginning with the cycle
of development, the cycle of awareness, the cycle of understanding, and the cycle of integration. All cycles are repeated again
within the soul energy and within the spirit energy. Each cycle
contains seven levels relative to seven and seven. These consciousness energy vibrations expand out into infinity.

You are aware of all the beliefs, all of the cultures, and all
of the languages in the world. You will not be able to access this
awareness within each physical lifetime and that is as it should
be. It is not important to access every belief that you have ever
known in each lifetime because you would find yourself in
intellectual overload. Intellectual overload would create more
confusion within you and within your world than presently
exists.

What IS important is to LOVE YOURSELF, and understand
WHAT you are here to learn. This will provide for you a very
happy Earth experience.

Understanding will create within you a new belief in self-
discovery. A new family culture of self-discovery will save man
from himself.

# Ethnic
## Relationships

Ethnic families are created by souls that have chosen to come together to focus upon learning a lesson through a mass consciousness.

*The primary ethnic family on Earth is the human race. The human race has chosen to come to Earth to heal and cleanse themselves. The human race is a physical manifestation of the soul and spirit energy of the individual energy that was created by God.*

The lessons will be specific to the sub-cultures of ethnic groups which have developed from the original ethnic families of humans created by God.

Each individual in an ethnic culture will share a basic belief system. The belief systems have become such a strong influence within ethnic groups that they have reached a state of critical mass.

Once an energy has reached critical mass, it is automatically understood and accepted as a lesson by the soul. The critical mass belief is a belief system that is understood before birth and is accepted as the primary lesson of the embodiment.

*A soul and spirit will choose an embodiment into an ethnic group to awaken the physical self to the lesson of soul and spirit energy.*

Soul and spirit lessons are a multitude of expansive understandings that focus upon freedom of choice, free will, free intention, the power of creation, the inherent love, truth, and perfection of the soul and spirit, and the ultimate lesson of unconditional love. These lessons are approached in physical life through a multitude of images.

Man does not have the intellectual insight and unconditional love necessary to approach a lesson in its entirety through his physical focus of reality.

*Man learns by focusing upon the opposite energy to understand what he does not want. When he understands what he does not want, he can see what he does want with more clarity and understanding. The physical world creates reflection within man rather than true vision.*

Choosing beliefs that restrict by the energy of critical mass before birth is focusing on the opposite of soul and spirit freedom. Critical mass energy is an energy that has accumulated within the Universe to such an expansive degree that it is accepted by everyone.

This acceptance includes those souls and spirits that have not chosen that particular lesson for this embodiment. The Universal lesson for those who have chosen the ethnic energy is clearly understood by all on the soul and spirit level.

*Freedom is frequently learned through this lesson of ethnic belief, because your sense of unworthiness has reached critical mass. The spiritual definition of healing and cleansing is to understand freedom. Choosing the restriction of any ethnic belief expands the issue until it captures your attention within the physical world.*

Different ethnic groups are focused upon the lesson of specific freedom energy. These positive ethnic energy experiences will provide rest for the soul. Other ethnic groups are focused on learning by experiencing the opposite energy to freedom.

There are multiple ethnic families that deal with the elements that are opposite to freedom. Specific elements are important as part of the whole. This selectivity of specifics will create many lifetimes in ethnic cultures to master the overall lesson of freedom for the soul and spirit within.

*The lesson of physical freedom is symbolic of freedom for the soul and spirit within.*

An example of a critical mass belief that restricts the freedom of the soul and spirit within is your belief in original sin. This belief originated from the ego belief of man, not from God. The belief in original sin has become a critical mass belief for many ethnic families.

You are love, truth, and perfection within. Your belief in original sin casts you in the role of a sinner waiting to be saved by God. You were given the power of creation when you were created as spirit and soul energy. When man created the belief in original sin, he created the role of opposites within the Universe. The role of original sin focuses man within the glass jug of his created belief system. The role of opposites creates the dramas of your life.

When we discuss ethnic relationships, we discuss soul evolution, and we discuss growth, change, and drama. The soul and spirit, when it is created, knows that it has many lessons to learn. These lessons are learned within relationships.

Each and every lesson learned is relative to the interaction that occurs in your life. If the interaction between two people is compounded by a difference in ethnic beliefs, the dramas and the traumas image the lessons in a vivid and expansive manner.

*The energy of critical mass is the strongest energy source created by man. Critical mass energy is an energy force within the Universe that is created by the energy of man and his beliefs.*

There is physical interaction, there is soul interaction, and there is spirit interaction. Each of these interactions occurs at different levels of consciousness within you. Each level of consciousness has a different energy force and a different level for you to understand.

It is important for you to realize that the interaction of a lifetime is indeed a choice. In the spirit sense, man is a member of a spirit family. In the soul sense, the soul and spirit move through each choice of life—learning, growing, changing, evolving, and creating.

Soul and spirit evolution is focused upon the understanding and love of self, the truth, and the perfection of the spirit world. Each life that man chooses is his individual choice and how he lives it is his choice. Choice is based upon the level of conscious awareness within the intellect/ego mind.

*The first ethnic family of your world is the human race. The first ethnic group is the individual man.*

The individual does not understand his own uniqueness as a physical being, a soul, and a spirit. He does not understand his power. He does not understand the soul and spirit energy within. Each of you have chosen to be free individuals. You have chosen to learn to love yourself first.

The dramas that you create to learn your lesson of individual freedom are unique within each individual. Man is focused upon his physical being. Understanding freedom as the energy of the soul and spirit will help you understand your choice of lessons. It is the inner energy force seeking freedom that creates the reflection of loss of freedom within the physical world.

No two individuals follow exactly the same path in their soul evolution, not even twin souls. Yet all of man follows the same purpose and that purpose is to BE unconditional love.

***When man loves himself, he can then love his neighbor as himself, and his God as himself. In your choice of lives, loving self with the freedom of self-discovery and total self-realization under any physical circumstance is the important issue.***

It is not unusual within your world for man to commit suicide if he loses his material possessions. He makes the choice of death because he sees death as preferable to living without the physical possessions that he identifies as self. He makes an ego decision to end his life.

Suicide denies man the opportunity to live from the soul and spirit energy of faith. He has no faith in anything except his physical world as he perceives it. This is symbolic of man's strong attachment to the physical reality that he accepts. He cannot see beyond his acknowledged intellectual/ego understanding.

***The act of suicide within the physical world is symbolic of man's fear of understanding and acknowledging self.***

It is the specific lesson of life that determines the ethnic relationship and the ethnic family that you choose. There are certain lessons that are unique to certain ethnic groups. Always remember the first ethnic group, as YOU understand the ethnic group within the energy of YOUR world, is indeed the individual.

An explanation of the opposite energies that ethnic groups have chosen will help you recognize them in your world. For each of these groups, there is a profound lesson. We will not cover all the groups but we will cover some of the lessons. Understanding the lesson will allow you to see the relationship of the lesson to the ethnic group within your world.

The victim energy within your world is a major lesson for many souls. When an energy reaches critical mass it becomes in Universal terms an energy consciousness. The victim consciousness is expansive upon Earth as a critical mass energy.

Not all souls that are involved in the victim consciousness would be recognized by you as belonging to an ethnic group. The individual is the first ethnic group and because of the victim consciousness this is an expansive energy within your energy system. Focusing upon the physical reality denies the freedom of the soul and spirit.

If you have a country that is focused upon war, and HAS been focused upon war for thousands of years, you can understand that the souls who chose to be born into this country are choosing to learn the lesson of the victim consciousness. If you look at Vietnam or if you look at the Middle Eastern countries you will see countries attuned to war. Their belief system supports war.

When a soul chooses birth into a culture that is at war, it is trying to learn not to be a victim of anger and fear. You are trying to learn freedom if you choose to live at war. If you choose to live in the energy of a personal war in a peaceful country, you are trying to learn the lesson of freedom.

In each case the lesson of the victim consciousness has become an issue with the soul involved. This is the personal creation of a mass consciousness energy within the individual soul.

**When an issue becomes a mass consciousness within, it is a Karmic lesson that has been worked with for thousands of lifetimes.**

In the determination to learn not to be a victim of anger and fear, the soul has chosen to view the lesson in the extreme. It has chosen to be born into a country or a group where the victim energy is an issue that will be consistent from the time of birth.

When man is faced with a lesson that he cannot seem to understand within his physical world after thousands of lifetimes, he will choose to experience that lesson in the extreme. This saturated victim experience of the opposites will reinforce the value of freedom on a conscious level.

If man is focused on fear, anger, and hostility for many lifetimes, he will choose to become a victim during a lifetime to attract his own attention. The degree of victimization will determine the ethnic group that he chooses.

This is not a perspective that is understood in your world, yet it is a reality. If you want to live a life of rest, you will choose a very calm and peaceful ethnic group to join. If you want to learn the lesson of abundance, you may choose to join an ethnic group that is suffering in poverty. This is an opposite lesson.

If you are controlled totally by your ego and you control and suppress people, you will choose to come back into an ethnic group that finds itself a victim of suppression. Learning by the experience of the opposites will allow you the choice to be actively involved in the lesson.

During some embodiment in the eternal life of each of you, you have experienced lessons by choosing to be a member of an ethnic group that is different from what you are now. These ethnic experiences and the relationships they create are extremely important in soul evolution.

*For you to choose the experience is an acknowledgement of your own individual difficulty in learning the lesson. You can not learn until you acknowledge what you do not know. Therefore, acknowledgement is the first step in the learning process. The ego of man is inclined to feel that it knows all there is to know. Overcoming this illusion is the first step towards freedom.*

If you are born into a family of extreme poverty, you can learn through your own experiential growth, your own perception, your own understanding, to rise above the creation. You have indeed made the choice and you have created the drama.

There are no accidents within the Universe. Each lesson is a lesson that is essential to your growth. In an ethnic group that is focused upon war, deprivation, fear, and anger, the soul and spirit can become mentally and physically disillusioned with itself. This self-disillusionment will create the choice to rise above the present level of consciousness by learning the lesson once and forever.

Along the path there will be triggers of memory to integrate other soul experience. These triggers will remind you to look at yourself and to see the total creation of you. You will be reminded of all that has been, all that will be, and all that is. You will see yourself in the concept of simultaneous time which is the time of the spirit world.

Your triggers will occur on a subconscious and unconscious basis. You will not have a conscious physical awareness of the integration of experience energy until you learn the lesson. When you learn the lesson, the understanding will begin to fall into place and you will release your attachment to the dramas that you have created.

There are many examples of this experiential learning within your world. The soul and spirit will choose birth into an ethnic group where it will be abused, traumatized, stigmatized, and will live in fear and anger. There will be moments in life when the individual will question their ability to physically survive.

It will be close to impossible for the individual to understand that they are intimately involved in a lesson of choice. Always deep inside the motivation of knowing from the soul and the inspiration to grow from the spirit, will give them a sense of joy in overwhelming adversity.

> *In the most challenging times there will be a consciousness of a tiny, joyful, light within. That light is the vision of hope that shines with total undaunted faith within self to overcome all odds and be successful.*

Despite the level of conscious physical awareness and the "circumstances" of life, the power of that inner hope and faith will allow you to move forward. The soul and spirit will focus on the energy of freedom rather than the opposite energy of the victim consciousness. With your focus on freedom and not on the dramas of life, you can create a new life within the physical world that you know.

> *Freedom is an internal acknowledgment more than an external reality.*

Acknowledging the lesson allows you to change the energy and to rise above the circumstances that you have created for yourself. When you focus upon what you want and not what you feel that you do not have, you will meet your goals. You must grasp the integrated power of the moment and use it to change your world.

In each and every lesson there is an energy that allows you to doubt, to return to fear, to return to victimization, to return to anger, hostility, and rejection. Change creates a threat of survival to the ego.

> *Denying the ego requires an energy of faith that you can create your own reality.*

If you listen to your ego you will remain in the consciousness of the victim energy. Being a victim is a means of ego protection. If you fear failure, you fear trying the smallest change in what you accept as your life. If change would create a new reality for the ego, the ego will live in total fear.

The ego will fear success more expansively than it will fear victimization. The ego sees success as symbolic of freedom. The ego believes in control. All "victims" perceive themselves as controlled by poverty, disease, loneliness, suppression, lack of education, and on and on.

The design of the soul and spirit is created to help you move forward in your evolution. You create your own resistance from the belief systems that you attach yourself to in the physical realm. This resistance will differ in degrees as the integration of the body, soul, and spirit changes.

*As you find yourself growing and opening to new life perspectives, you will find yourself being a victim less and less in your mind.*

In the ethnic groups that choose island life, they are learning the lesson of play in many instances. Their focus might be music or dance. This is a focus upon the positive energy of freedom. It is chosen as an opportunity to balance the soul and spirit within the physical world.

Some will choose an ethnic group that focuses upon art because art is a lesson of the freedom of creativity. Have you noticed that some ethnic groups have great artists, great musicians, great philosophers? Do you see how this works?

In the cycle of soul evolution there is the opportunity for individual design without restriction. This capability creates the opportunity for the soul to be totally involved with its choice of lessons.

*Ethnic groups play an important role in the organizational fiber of the soul evolutionary concept. It is this multiple role experience that presents an ideal opportunity for learning to each of you.*

You can look at ethnic groups as steps on the path of soul evolution. Ethnic groups create a lifetime opportunity to remember lessons that you are working with in the spirit world.

*Understand that in order for man to evolve as a*
*soul and spirit energy, he will at some time be*
*each and every ethnic energy.*

Your perception of the experience offers you total expansion of understanding and coming to terms with the soul and spirit lessons. If your perception is denied or restricted, you will repeat the experience until it is understood.

When you observe groups that are attached to a war focus, to an intellectual focus, to a creative focus, or to a loving focus, you are seeing the evolutionary ladder. Who you are and how you act within the experience, defines your level of lesson in terms of soul and spirit evolution.

*Soul and spirit evolution is focused upon self-dis-*
*covery in the physical consciousness with a total*
*self-realization of your integration.*

Soul and spirit evolution can be compared to your physical educational process. You graduate from pre-school, kindergarten, grade school, high school, and college. Along the path of the process you gradually learn your lessons. As you learn you also absorb your ethnic, cultural, friends, and family belief systems.

Suddenly you are confronted with the opposite of your belief system. At this point the lessons of fear and anger begin with intensity. Fear is a learned belief of the intellect and the ego. Fear is the opposite of love which is an inherent emotion of the soul and spirit. Fear then begins to accumulate in the intellect and ego mind of self.

There is limited opportunity to face this fear and the intensity of fear on a daily basis, unless you can choose an ethnic group that focuses upon that fear with intensity. It is a challenge for many people to understand the expansiveness of the fear within the mind. If you can conceive the expansiveness of this fear energy, you can better understand the magnitude of the soul lessons.

When man reaches the level where he has fear of physical activities, perhaps driving, or perhaps living alone, or going to a job interview, he has focused the intensity of his fear on one activity. He is dealing with the remnants of the fear. He has at this time in his evolutionary cycle, learned a lot of lessons.

Some of these lessons may have been learned in concentration camps, prisoner of war environments, prisons, and multiple other events. They may have been learned as part of an ethnic culture or family that is different than what you are now.

*Always in the history of your Earth there have been different ethnic groups. This is part of the Universal organization that allows the soul and spirit to choose experiences that will be meaningful and directed toward growth.*

Each of these groups exist in different cycles and levels of evolution. As the energy force field of humanity changes, the energy force field of the Earth changes, and this creates change within the energy force field of the Universe. Each change alters the perception and the understanding of man.

*Change creates a constant movement of energy force fields which means that nothing within man, nothing on Earth, and nothing in the Heavens stays the same.*

If you observe your Earth as a whole, the spirits on Earth have evolved through many, many levels. Those who have chosen to focus within ethnic groups where the concept of life is based upon fear are generally "new" or undeveloped souls. All souls were created at the same time. Development is different for each soul. In some instances these souls have been stuck in captive energy for thousands of years. These souls continue to work to move forward one level further in their evolutionary cycle.

When you see a soul who has chosen birth in a fearful suppressive environment and has chosen to change that environment as an adult, you are looking at a soul who has learned a lesson of evolution. They have chosen change from the level of conscious physical awareness. They have acknowledged their lesson.

*It is because all souls pass through these levels of evolution that all souls are indeed equal within your physical world. It is because the soul and spirit as an integrated unit is in the energy of remembering the inherent energy of love, truth, and perfection that you are each and everyone equal in spirit. You each have the God energy within you.*

Where you are in your cycle of soul evolution is determined by the lessons that you have learned. For you to continue growing in your evolutionary cycle, you must search to discover yourself. Look at yourself as an integrated individual.

If you intellectualize your soul and spirit you will be focusing upon ego energy. This is a resistance to growth. You as an integrated individual are unique. When you understand yourself, you will understand the Universe.

For each of you to view the world as a very large classroom would be appropriate. There are levels of awareness which you develop with each lifetime. Each of these levels must add to the other to evolve your soul and spirit self. If you do not learn the lesson that you came here to learn you may experience devolution which is subtracting from soul evolution.

Your individuality of aware consciousness sets you apart in physical perception only. It does not make you superior, it makes you equal. It makes you the son of God, experiencing the identical path that the Christ Consciousness experienced.

*Soul evolution can only be accomplished within the physical world. Your evolution will be physically manifested by the lesson you are learning.*

Leaving the physical world for a new life does not change who you are as a soul and spirit. You will be at the same level in a new life as you were when you left an old life. In the organization of evolution, you must develop a conscious awareness of your own soul and spirit energy while you are in physical form. You must learn the lessons of evolution in physical life with a conscious awareness of what you have learned.

*Once you develop a conscious awareness of your soul and spirit, you must BE who you are in your soul and spirit energy in your physical world. You are responsible for putting your beliefs, thoughts, and words into physical action. When you can put your thoughts and words into action, you have created truth within yourself.*

You have been through many levels of evolution. These levels began millions of years ago. It is the path of the Christ Consciousness that has shown you the evolution within the ethnic group. This is a path which you all follow unconsciously, if not consciously.

For you to be your individual self, which is an accumulation of all that you have ever been and all that you will ever be, is the perfect goal. Within that goal, you will be able to define your own perfection, your own love, and your own truth.

*It is important for you to understand that you are ALL THAT IS. When you pass through the energy of ALL THAT IS, you BECOME everything that exists.*

This is an expansive concept that in many instances is too visionary for the linear mind and your linear language to comprehend. If you do not understand, do not let that concern you. This text is an overview that is planting seeds. With those seeds, we will have germination and full growth with time as you learn to open and discover self.

*Know that this is a concept and understanding which will help you discover who you are externally and internally. Self-discovery is the purpose of man in his evolutionary path.*

Each individual is indeed a group of energies. It is this unique integration of energies that is the first ethnic group. The individual is the primary, the most important ethnic group.

All souls and spirits from the beginning of time have their own accumulation or combination of energies. Understanding that the energies of the individual are forever primary within your world helps you gain focus.

This is not to be misunderstood as an ego self-focus but it is in reality an energy of self-realization. It is when you realize the power of the energies within you that you can begin to understand you.

When you can fully understand yourself, in total self-realization, you will totally understand what the Universe truly is and how it works.

*It is from the energies of the individual that all other energies are created.*

It is because of this energy focus that the individual is the first ethnic group within the Universal system of organization. It is because of the individual's importance and value within your world and in the energy focus of your world that the individual is always primary in all relationships. Being in the position of primary energy gives you the ability to create your reality on a daily basis.

*The responsibility for the accumulation of all energies rests upon each individual soul and spirit.*

When your ego captures your intellect in an energy of unworthiness, you affect yourself and all other energies within the Universal system. Your importance and value to the Universal system are not ego energies which are of external origin and are finite.

*Your importance and value are created by the eternal energy of the soul and spirit. This positive energy that is produced in a humble, caring, and loving way is the energy of evolution that affects you, all of man, the Earth, and the Universe.*

This is an expansive concept that is a challenge to digest in the linear perspective of your intellect. It is helpful if you can open your mind and simply envision yourself as pure energy attracting energy and creating energy.

This will give you a very interesting perception of yourself and the Universe. It will take some practice, but you can indeed accomplish your goal if you are faithful in your practice.

Some individuals will choose a lifetime to be in a certain ethnic group and to be of a certain gender. This experience allows the lessons of gender focus to be perceived in a different way because men and women are treated differently in different ethnic groups.

You choose to experience the opposites in suppression as a female, and dominance as a male. It is within these ethnic groups that these emotions can be more extreme. Gender control is primary in the belief systems of many ethnic groups.

In each and every ethnic lifetime, and all lifetimes are ethnic, you will deal with the belief systems of the ethnic group that you have chosen. The lesson will be found in the creation, the structure of your life secondary to those belief systems.

When you choose a life, you know what the lesson is going to be, and you have chosen it because of the lesson opportunity that it will give you. In your understanding you have a tendency to consider all lives as your life is today. Evolution is not that way.

You will choose lives of great drama. You will choose lives of great trauma. You will choose lives of rest. You will choose lives of focused intellectual education. You will choose lives of suppression, control, anger, and hostility. You will choose lives of greatness and lives of total humility. You will choose lives of infinite variety.

Each life will present to you images of multiple lessons. It is when you have experienced multiple lifetimes learning one lesson, that you begin to see the lesson with greater clarity. As man, you learn best by repetition.

If you look at your ethnic groups as you understand ethnic groups within your world, you will see the variety of lessons that exist within each group. You will see suppression, you will see male dominance, you will see war and killing which is physical dominance, you will see dominance by the country, you will find political dominance, and you will see church dominance.

You will see poverty, starvation, abandonment, death, and disease. You will see all of the members of certain sects living a life of total suppression. You will see mutilations secondary to belief systems, you will see war and you will see killings. You see, the lessons are indeed endless.

Your world will perceive all individuals in these ethnic situations as victims. When you evolve through these ethnic groups, you evolve through lessons of life. As you evolve you will be able to see with greater clarity the lessons that other souls are working upon.

*When individuals choose to come back in groups, such as family groups, they are going through all of the same ethnic incarnations as either family members or close friends together. Continuing the soul and spirit relationship in the physical world gives each individual a subconscious and unconscious support system.*

Souls that repeatedly come back in an ethnic family have not only an individual lesson, but they have a Universal lesson. The Universal lesson, for instance, in the Jewish religion and in the Black race, is the Universal lesson of the victim consciousness. These are not the only two examples that we can use but they are understood examples within your world.

The same victim consciousness exists for other ethnic families as well, because there are multiple elements involved in the victim energy. You will find physical support and an integration occurring among groups who are learning the lesson of the victim consciousness.

*Joining together as groups neutralizes the positive energy of the individual as the group supports the concept of victimization.*

In your world this becomes a massive lesson in energy force. The energy that is produced, both in a negative essence and in a positive essence, will have its impact upon the Universe, your world, and your Earth, as an accumulation of mass consciousness energy.

The uniqueness of the individual serves to support the learning of the lesson. The negative energy that will accumulate in families and groups can be destructive to more than just those that generate the energy. There is always more of an energy impact in large groups because the energy that is produced is of greater force.

In the immediate family where everyone is going through the same ethnic group, the influences from a lifetime are stronger for some than others because of the way they have chosen to perceive the lesson. The time period, the parallel energy, and the ability to learn the lesson are multiple influences that will carry over.

Each individual in a family will have a different image of the lesson. They will work on the lesson from a different perspective. Remember that the individual is totally unique so what each person learns may be similar, but it will be manifested in a different way within your world.

*Loving yourself and listening to the silence within will allow you to understand your individual lessons with more clarity.*

When you love yourself, you will spend more time looking internally at the lessons that you have learned. You should examine your belief systems and find the beliefs that are working for you. Those beliefs that no longer serve you should be released.

Listening to the silence is a way of contacting the inner self and the higher self. In the silence you can listen to your energy at a higher frequency level. When you do this, you must take the time to decrease the noise level from the physical world. You will need some quiet time, but you can indeed focus on the inner self while performing other duties.

When you find yourself being totally open, you will begin to receive more loving energy than you will know how to accept.

You must create a balance within to permit other balanced energy to enter into your life.

Loving yourself is what life is about. It is taking away the restrictions that you have placed upon yourself, and allowing yourself to simply be in peace and joy. You will be able to recognize this peace and joy within your physical level of conscious awareness. You will find that when you wake up in the morning, you are in total joy and total peace.

Peace and joy can be your barometer for measuring your evolution. Learning to love yourself takes a commitment to knowing who you are, how you think, and how you act. When you act with consistency of your thoughts, words, and actions you are living truth. When you recognize the truth within, you will also recognize the love within, and the perfection within your spirit energy.

*As sons of God you have the inherent right to love, to truth, and to perfection. If you choose not to use your love, truth, and perfection within your life, that is the choice you make. If you choose to be love, truth, and perfection in your daily life, then you will indeed be choosing to love yourself. Fear cannot live with love.*

Each of you will create blockages that will be manifested in a physical manner. Arthritic conditions will appear if the integrated self is being denied and suppressed. The ears will become deaf when you choose not to hear. Your vision will be a lifelong problem if you choose not to see clearly. If you choose not to give love, you will develop heart disease. You will develop lung problems if you feel that your freedom of self is being suppressed.

These are examples of the physical manifestation of the suppression of your inner and higher self. There are many more examples that relate to the entire body and the entire realm of mental and physical resistances. What is in the mind will be manifested in the physical body. The mind and body are relative to each other in all instances of physical reality.

*Each time that you want to change your physical, mental, and spiritual energy, you must change your belief system about yourself. All perceptions, all interactions, and all relationships within your life are relative to the image of yourself. All lessons that you are learning within your physical*

***world are relative to the conscious mental percep-***
***tion that you hold relative to yourself.***

It is your image of self that structures your world. The belief systems that you attach yourself to are the belief systems that create your vision and understanding of self. You are your own ethnic human creation.

You are unique in your own special way. Your personal beliefs create you as an individual and they create the lessons that you choose to learn within relationships. This inseparable relationship of self to self makes it important that you discover who you are. The relationship between your body, mind, and spirit energy are inseparable. Discovering who you are gives you control over your life and your relationships.

Self-discovery is not something that you do by snapping your fingers. Self-discovery must be accepted as a responsibility to self. Self-discovery requires a commitment to work toward self-understanding during your waking hours and during your sleeping hours.

When you go to bed if you give yourself permission, you can become conscious of your sleep activity. You can remember what you learn and what you do with other souls and spirits during your sleep period. Your conscious mind will respond to this request and you can be physically conscious of the work that you perform.

As you learn to love yourself, you will attract an energy that is much stronger and independent into your relationships. You will create a challenge of acceptance for yourself. You will be face to face with another resistance to be overcome.

Change requires releasing attachment to the belief systems of your physical world. Let me explain what releasing attachments to the physical world is all about. It does not mean that you must sell everything that you own and become a nomad with a pack on your back.

What it does mean is the understanding within you that you can live without being supported by a person or a physical object. You accept internally that your soul and spirit came into physical life alone, and you can survive alone if you need to. This understanding removes the dependent energy from around you. Once the dependent energy has been removed from your force field, you have free choice in your actions. Your actions will be chosen from the love, truth, and perfection within you.

You have been taught dependency by your cultures, your societies, your ethnic groups, your educational systems, your medical systems, and your families. The belief in dependency has created many problems within your world. This belief affects your image of self and therefore it affects your entire life. Dependency is an ego need.

Releasing attachment means that you understand that your survival depends only upon you and your choice. You can look at physical items as something that can be replaced and something that can be substituted. Strive to understand your individual power of creation, your creativity, your resourcefulness, and your physical abilities. Have no fear of doing what you need to do to promote your joy and happiness within.

All of the consciousness levels, all of the fear, all of the love, and all of the drama of your physical life goes on within your mind first. You create the physical manifestation as an external reality to your thought.

*When you are working to grow in your soul and spirit energy, you will come face to face with the fact that the physical is finite.*

When you choose to leave Earth from this lifetime, you will indeed take nothing with you. You will leave Earth only as spirit and soul energy. Any physical substance, including the body, would create a handicap for you in the spirit world. When you have attachments to material possessions, you are working on this understanding. There is wisdom in learning to release the physical.

*Learning to release the physical possessions around you is symbolic of releasing your fear of death.*

The one physical creation that is important to you within the physical world is the health of your physical body. You must maintain the health of your physical self to be included within the ethnic group of the human race. The lesson of physical restoration of the body is a lesson of being human.

You have become a member of the ethnic human race by the creation of your physical body. Life is your choice now, and has always been your choice. Respecting and valuing your physical body validates your choice to live and learn.

Living longer periods within your physical world gives you the opportunity to expand your learning without as many repetitions of the cycle of development to slow your progress in soul evolution. Living is your commitment to being a member of the human race.

# World
## Relationships

What is a "world family?" Let's begin at the beginning, and look at the two worlds separately. First there is the world that man creates within self and second there is the world that man creates external to self.

Each world is perceived relative to the conscious awareness of self. Your world family, the energy that is close to you but external to you, is attracted to you by the energy of you.

What is your world?

Your world is an accumulation of energy that is created by you and integrated by you into a creation of life. Your world family is your physical self, your soul, and your spirit internally. Your world is the inner world of you. Your physical self is your liaison that relates the inner you to the external you of the physical world that you create.

Your external world family are those individuals who have a similar energy. They are indeed involved with you in the same purpose and with the same type of energy. Your inner and outer worlds are intermingled, interwoven, and inseparable.

When we talk about the external world we must first speak in a singular way about man, because it is man that creates the world. What is man?

*Man is energy. Man is an energy of the Universe that is totally interwoven, intermingled, and insep-arable in all ways from the energy of All That Is.*

The physical body of man is simply the energy of the soul and spirit moving at a slower pace. When the energy slows down it creates physical matter. Once this physical matter has been created, you have what you call a physical body. You have a human being.

*Each of you as humans have chosen to be in the world of Earth in your physical form.*

Earth is an energy that exists within the cosmos. It is an energy, a massive, expansive energy created by individual man as a mass consciousness, just as it was created by All That Is as a planet of healing and cleansing for soul and spirit energy. When Earth was created, it was created as the jewel of the Cosmos. The Cosmos is the accumulated energy of enfinite consciousness.

*Man is an experiment in the world of energy.*

You are being very good experiments because, you see, when God created you He gave you free will. In each and every thought and each and every action you have individual choice.

*You create your physical world, your environ-ment, your career, your relationships, and all of your life by the choices that you make in the en-ergy that you generate.*

It is each individual thought that creates the energy of action and therefore creates your world as you know it. You began as spirit energy and evolved to soul energy, then to the physical energy known as human energy. As man you create an immediate family, that creates a community, that creates a city, that creates a state, that creates a country, that creates a world, and that again creates the Universe.

Physical man has been given the responsibility of expanding self, the world, the Earth, the Universe, and the Cosmos. Man in his physical state generates energy that adds to the energy of all. As man expands self, he expands his world which creates the expanding vibrational consciousness energies that expand All That Is.

*It is always the energy of the individual that be-gins the creation.*

In this energy that you create there are many separate worlds. You can look at the world, the Earth as you define it, and that is indeed one world. In that world you are a Universal family. You are all souls and spirits that have chosen to be on Earth.

You have chosen to be an actor on this stage. Indeed, on your stage you write the script, direct, produce, and act your own creation.

**Everything that you do in your world you create first by a thought within your mind.** It is this energy of thought that creates the reality of your world.

*Man began in spirit energy as a thought form of the Creator.*

The concept of creating your own reality is a challenge for you understand because you do not allow yourselves to visualize your world and yourselves in the expansive energy of your reality.

You see yourselves as victims of circumstances, as pawns of life, as somebody's daughter, as somebody's son, as somebody's mother, as somebody's father, as a worker, as someone who loves to play, and you see these identities as internal to yourself. You perceive your interactions as external concepts, despite the fact that the relationship that you create with your identity forms your world of reality. This is your physical manifestation of your fear of integration.

Believe me when I tell you, NOTHING is totally external to yourself. With your thoughts you create your world in an individual sense, and in each level of energy after that to the Universal sense.

The energy of you is a duplication, a small copy of the energy of the Universe. The Universe in turn is a copy of the accumulated energy of All That Is, which is again all that you are as individuals. Can you envision this cycle of energy?

All that is above is below. The cells within your body are patterns of the designs of energy within the Universal system of energy. All things, all energy is interwoven, intermingled, and inseparable.

> ***Man as man is never alone and yet he is always alone. He is separate as physical matter, but he is one in the concept of energy.***

In the same sense of relativity, you are separate but you are one as a physical being, a soul, and a spirit energy. You as a physical being cannot be only physical because you are interwoven, intermingled, and inseparable from your soul and spirit energy.

Each cell within your body consists of billions of energy elements that function from the same principals of support and expansion, of attraction and repelling of energy that exists within the Universe.

> ***You will need to understand your mind before you can intellectually understand the physical structure of your body.***

Without an open, understanding mind, your belief systems will restrict your level of insight and acceptance. As the energy within the mind changes, the energy within the body changes on an individual basis. This change in energy within your mind becomes a change in the cellular structure of the physical body.

*The energy of the mind is the energy that you
use to create disease, and it is the energy that you
use to heal yourself.*

When you can understand that your thoughts will change
the structure of the cells within your body, you will begin to
understand your power within. This Universal understanding is
a tremendous responsibility for the linear mind of man to accept.

Have you ever known someone who lives in a negative
energy, who speaks only negative words, who conceives, and
who perceives their world always from a negative viewpoint?
This person will continually be involved in one drama after the
other, on a day to day basis in their life. Do you know people like
this? Does this happen to you?

Indeed, YOUR THOUGHTS, the way that you act and react,
your perceptions of your thoughts and actions become the actions
that you focus upon. The energy within your mind creates the
reality of your world.

If you are captured within negative thought energy, you will
be living with depression, fear and anger. This negative energy
will result in dramas, traumas, and disease for you. If you are
joyful within, your world will be joyful without. This internal
joy will remain even during times of stress and crisis in which
you are fully participating.

If you have no concern for Earth, you are going to create
destruction on Earth. Do you see? If you have no consideration
for your family, you are going to create destruction within your
family. If you think a thought and you attach yourself to the
energy of that thought, you create with that thought energy.

You do this by your interpretation of your belief system.
You think that you must act in agreement with what you have
been taught is right. What you are taught becomes the restrictive
influence of what you do.

You learn in many ways. You learn from hearing, seeing,
and structured teaching. You learn from verbal communication.
You learn from silent communication. The behavior of others,
especially in the family unit, will teach behavior without the
benefit of words. You will learn from public media such as
television, magazines, books, radio, newspapers, and speeches.

If a child is beaten, he will beat someone else as an adult. If
a child sees a parent using alcohol and/or drugs, he will use
alcohol and/or drugs. If a child sees parents with multiple lovers,

he will believe in this behavior as correct behavior and he will not understand love and commitment. Do you see how belief systems are created within the mind of man?

If you are told at sometime in your life that you are incapable of learning to drive a car, you will not be able to drive a car. You will not be able to learn how to drive a car because you are acting from the energy of your belief. Your thoughts and the actions within you will duplicate your belief within your external world.

It IS the energy of your beliefs that creates all that is around you, on an individual basis, on a family basis, on a community basis, in a work relationship, in social relationships, in relationships of marriage, or lovers, or sisters, or brothers, or friends. It is YOU, it is your choice that creates your world and your world family.

When you become consciously aware of the thoughts within your mind that restrict you, you have the opportunity to open your mind to change. You will gain insight into the blocks that exist for you.

Once you have insight into your own resistances you can then make a choice to change your beliefs or to remain attached to your beliefs. If the belief is positive for you, keep it. If the belief is restricting your growth, thank it for having served you and release your attachment.

When you were born you chose your parents and you may have agreed to share those parents with other siblings. Each sibling, as they arrive in the family, has chosen these parents as guides, as teachers, as friends in their world family.

You have also chosen your life. You have created a design of what you are going to do and what lessons you are going to learn. You have created this design with other souls and spirits within your world.

When you enter Earth to become a physical body you have already created your life plan. You have told everybody involved, you have consulted with them. They have agreed to the role they are going to play in your world. This includes people in your immediate family, people in your career family, people in your social family, people within the state you live, the country you live in, and the world as a whole.

You see, everything is related. All energy is indeed intermingled, it is integrated, and it is interwoven. This relationship includes the energy of you. But YOU control the energy of yourself. The creation of your life as your world is choice, as every energy within you is choice.

By developing this master plan you have created for yourself a world and a world family. This family is here to help you learn lessons. They are actors on your stage. You have written the script and you are the star.

Each and every person that enters into your physical world plays a role in your life. They are part of your world family on an individual basis and you control the level of the role that you allow them to play within your life.

***You are the star, you are the writer, and you produce and direct the show. Your world is under your control. You have free choice of your will and intention.***

When you look at the dramas within your world, you see that some of you have written some very dramatic scripts. This is as it needs to be, because when you play a drama that is intense it grabs your attention. If it punches your buttons, it gets your attention with more clarity.

When you find that you really are not attached to dramatic scripts anymore, you will know that you are learning your lessons. You do not need the extreme drama anymore to trigger your conscious awareness of your intention.

When you come to Earth and choose to come into a lifetime of rest, you may have no dramas involved in your life. You may be simply BEING, simply resting, simply letting other people take care of you.

There are many roles that you create within your world. You choose the other actors that you want closest to you in this world family of yours. The family that you develop outside of your immediate family, is your world family.

You also must remember that you are part of a larger Universe. As a world family you have multiple levels, starting with you and moving forward in an expansive manner to reach out and include the Universal family.

But your individual world is YOUR nuclear center. It is the center of you. It is your individual stage and the other actors that are involved with you in this world that you create on a daily basis are there because they want to be there. They have agreed to play on your stage in the same manner that you are playing on their stage.

It is their choice to participate and it is your choice to be where you are. When you are no longer comfortable and happy with where you are, or with the role that you are playing in your daily world, you have the opportunity to exercise free choice and to change your world.

What happens when you have someone in your world family, and suddenly they are gone? It is choice, and it is not right or wrong. It simply means that in the role they have agreed to play, all of the lines have been spoken. Their part of the script has ended. When this happens in your world, you simply turn loose of the attachment.

**One of the primary lessons for you in life is learning to constantly accept change, growth, and forward movement.**

You will create daily lessons to help yourself learn not to be attached. Attachment is an internal lesson that is manifested within your physical world as a physical lesson. The lesson of your physical death is a lesson of internal attachment to the finite, external body. The lesson of divorce is a lesson of internal attachment.

Your internal attachment to beliefs is manifested in your conscious awareness as an external attachment in relationships. You find it difficult to release your family and friends in death. You find it difficult to release your spouse in divorce. You find it difficult to change jobs and leave friends. You find it difficult to move geographically.

In the experiential learning of the soul in multiple lives, you learn attachment. Attachment is the opposite of the freedom of the spirit. Freedom is a lesson of physical reality.

Releasing attachment is a physical lesson of freedom. In the spirit sense you remain totally inseparable, intermingled, and interwoven and will continue your relationship despite the physical circumstances.

Releasing attachment is a lesson that the world family plays for you on a daily basis. The releasing action occurs within the world family because it is much easier for you to learn how to release your attachment with people that are not as close to you. Your world family has this fluidity, this constant change, this constant movement as casual acquaintances come and go in your life.

New actors appear on the stage and old ones leave. You create this flow of constant energy movement in your external world, on your stage of life. It is this cycle of change that is teaching you to learn from each encounter to release attachment and to accept the freedom within your life.

Attachment is an ego energy in your world that you have created for yourself that allows your soul to evolve. The role of the actors upon your stage will depend on the strength of the energy attachment of the soul and spirit within you. Each relationship will be relative to your consciousness level of the energy exchange.

In your physical world there are levels of soul evolution. Each member of this world family of yours helps you move along your path of evolution. The energy exchange will be different with your family, your friends, your marriage partners, your lovers, your working colleagues, your casual acquaintances, and your twin souls. Each relationship has its own design of lessons to experience and feelings to define.

Man began in this world billions of years ago. You may not remember the beginning of your spirit energy with your conscious physical mind, but you did indeed enter into this cycle of soul evolution billions of years ago.

Each of you began as spirits. When you began you were focused on the creation of physical presence, the physical world, the physical development of your body and your world.

This was the stage of development in the world of man for many thousands of years. Evolution is occurring for man as a mass understanding and he is now becoming aware of all that he is. Humanity in general has spent many thousands of years focused upon the cycle of development on Earth. Now it is time for change to occur.

**Awareness for man of who he truly IS, is necessary for man because, as energy, man does not stop in his movement and change. Once you reach the level of awareness that you are more than just a physical being, you move forward into other levels of understanding WHO YOU ARE, WHAT YOU ARE, and HOW YOU RELATE to the world and to yourself.**

Once you understand who you are in physical perception, who you were as you developed through your personal world, what you are as you develop, and how you relate in your levels of awareness, you will find yourself feeling full and complete.

When you understand all of these lessons, all of the many thousands of lives that you have lived, and all of the thousands and thousands and thousands of lessons that you have been working on, you will have reached the energy cycle of integration. You will be able to take it all, put it all together, and see the perfection of yourself with total clarity.

When you reach the cycle of integration, you will create for yourself a new world. You will suddenly understand with total clarity that your world is exactly what you create it to be. You will at that time understand the power and the energy within your mind. You will understand your perfect power of creation with total simplicity and humility.

**You not only create your daily existence as an individual, but you create the entire world around you.**

If you looked at the world as it was during the time when you were focused upon the first level of the cycle of development, you would see that you had no clothes, cars, trains, planes, television, missiles, china, napkins or even silverware. You were living as part of nature. You were truly physical beings focused upon developing your physical body, your physical life, and your physical world.

In the beginning your intuitive or instinctive mind was used only to find methods of physical survival within the world. Your instinct or intuition was and is your spirit energy. You were at that level more spirit than physical man. You did not use your intellect and ego in the same manner that you do now. You were unaware of what you could create with your intellectual mind.

Through the years, the thousands and thousands of years as spirit and man, you became aware of your mind and began to develop it. You began to create in the physical sense from your intellect. Your body and your intellectual development expanded. As you learned to use your intellectual mind more expansively, you created within the physical world more expansively using the inspiration of your spirit energy.

**As man created with expanded freedom from the intellectual focus, he began to believe that he created only from his intellectual mind. He began**

*to develop a belief that his intellect was his role to
supremacy. Man began to develop his ego.*

As man's belief in the power of his intellect expanded, he
began to believe that inspiration, motivation, and creation were
one and he saw them as coming from the one source of physical
intellect.

*This perception of creation came to be under-
stood intellectually as a product of the physical
mind because its physical substance was symbolic
of the physical intellect.*

Man began to acknowledge his mind in an external way in
his physical world. He did not at that point remember with a
conscious awareness the three minds within. Man viewed himself as a physical being in tune with nature, during his early cycle
of development. He began to lose his conscious awareness of the
role that the soul and spirit continuously played as an integrated
part of himself.

*In the mind of man the spirit is the inspiration,
the soul is the motivation, and the intellectual
mind is the creator within the physical world.*

All of creation is based upon the integration of all three facets
of the mind within. Man views these three sources of creativity
as his intellectual mind, his rational mind, and his intuitive
mind. No man can truly create in the positive sense of energy
without the integration of these soul and spirit energies.

When the mind reaches an awareness that you are more than
the physical body and more than the intellectual mind, you begin
to understand the influence of your soul and spirit energy.

Suddenly it becomes acceptable that you are a soul that has
been around for a long time. You begin to understand that you
have been creating worlds for thousands of years. You become
aware that the souls and the spirits that are with you today have
been with you since the time of creation.

*You begin to understand that you are far more
than what your physical belief system has allowed
you to understand about yourself from an intellectual perspective.*

As you take down the fences of your belief system, you
become aware of the soul within you that has been traveling

through this Universal energy. Your entire world starts to open just as the rose opens within your garden as it starts to bloom.

You develop an awareness of you that is different from your intellectual perspective. You begin to create something new, something different, something that is expansive within. As this awareness builds, you create a different world for yourself just as you have created a different world for yourself in the physical sense.

You are no longer living as cave men. You now have automobiles, airplanes, computers, and spaceships. You begin to understand what you have learned, how you have grown, and who you are now. As you create an awareness of something else within, you begin to glimpse the expansiveness of you and the power within you. You begin to understand who you are, what you are, and how you relate within your world.

You begin to understand that you are an eternal energy. The word "eternal" becomes a living energy for you, as you begin to see the truth of the action within the word. You know that you have a soul, and that you have with you a soul family within your physical world. When you understand that you are an eternal energy that can create a physical body, you begin to understand how you also create a physical world. You begin to put it all together. You begin to enter the cycle of understanding.

As you understand that you truly are a very superior form of energy, you begin to understand how you create or build within the physical world. The complexity of your energy becomes simple and you begin to understand your power of creation. As you understand how the spirit inspires the soul and the soul is motivated to learn, you see with total clarity how the intellect creates within the physical realm.

In the spirit world we speak of your power of creation and creating your own reality. The concept of these two actions become impossible or overwhelming in your mind. These words have expansive energy that takes them out of the linear understanding of your everyday language. If you choose you can think of creating your reality as: you have the ability to build what you design, and in building what you design you will produce what you build.

Understanding is an integrated response within man. If man denies his soul and spirit, he will not understand his ability to create everything within his world. He will not understand his ability to capture inspiration and motivation to create on an intellectual basis.

*It is the ego of man that allows man to see his creations only as intellectual activity. This is an ego function within man because man judges himself and all other men by this singular function of intellect/ego understanding within your physical world.*

It is the ego of man that focuses on denial of the soul and spirit energy of man, because the ego of man wants to give all of the credit for creation to the intellect. This is the external focus which is a remanent belief of the intellectual/ego cycle of development. When man was instinctively learning to live with physical survival as his focus, his physical energy captured him.

*The humor of this ego belief within man is that during the early part of his cycle of development man was functioning primarily from spirit energy.*

This "I" attachment of the ego to the intellect is the external need to achieve control and dominance. Man has an external physical need for control and dominance of his fellow man only during the cycles of development. The energy of the cycle of development holds man captive in the energy of the physical concept of control and dominance and its opposite energy of submissiveness.

*When man is attached to his physical cycle of development, he is unaware of his own power of creation as an integrated being.*

When you are aware and understand the role of your unconscious spirit energy and your subconscious soul energy in your everyday life, you will no longer be threatened by what you do not know. You will accept, acknowledge, and value all that you are within the inner and higher self and without in the physical body and intellectual mind. Man creates knowledge through the process of soul evolution by experiential learning.

Achieving dominance in your physical world is survival for your ego. In the external world, your lessons are learned by experiencing the opposites. Therefore, if there is an individual need to be in control and experience dominance, there is also an individual need to be in a relationship where the partner is submissive.

*When you understand the eternality of the self
energy, you will understand that survival is not an
issue. It is only within your physical world that
achieving dominance is perceived by the ego/intel-
lect as survival. Dominance is understood as spiritual denial in the spirit world. Man is seeking the
balance of body, mind, and spirit. The body, mind,
and spirit are the physical manifestation of the
Holy Trinity within man.*

You have created spaceships, you have created skyscrapers, you have created airplanes, you have created self, and you have shared in the creation of each other. Despite your accomplishments you do not fully understand your integrated self.

*It is more acceptable in your world to acknowl-
edge your physical accomplishments than it is to
acknowledge the three facets of self in their
equality.*

You can easily view the changes in the development of your world and of your life. You can compare your body to the body of the first man known to you and you can intellectually view the physical stages of development.

You can see the results of expanding awareness and understanding within your mind but you do not relate these changes to the energy of self. You relate change to circumstance, to intellect, to nature, and to others within your world.

*Despite your reluctance to accept the responsi-
bility for your own role in the expansion of self,
the expansion continues to occur.*

You have reached the level of energy vibration where you are integrating all of self. You are integrating your physical body, your intellectual mind, and your soul and spirit that has been with you since the beginning of time.

It is the soul memories that are stored within the energy of the soul. Within your spirit is the spirit energy that is the love, truth, and perfection of the Creator. These energies are resisted and denied by multitudes of men.

*Soul memories are your personal creation of ex-
perience within your numerous lifetimes that remain within you as energy that you can use at will.*

*Spirit energy is the inherent love, truth, and perfection that is within you. It cannot be learned by you. It needs only to be accepted, acknowledged, and valued as part of your natural heritage to be remembered.*

When you integrate this spirit energy of love, truth, and perfection, with the soul energy of all that you have ever been and will ever be, together with the physical energy of your intellect and physical body, you can clearly understand the magnificence of self. In the magnificence of self is the power of creation.

Understanding exactly how you create self, helps you to understand exactly how you create your individual world and your global world.

*Your image of self becomes your image of all other men and your image of the world.*

If you judge yourself, you judge all other men. If you fear yourself within, you fear all other men without. If you are angry with yourself, you show anger to all other men. If you dislike yourself, you will dislike the world that you have created.

The image of you is reflected back to you from other energy sources. This does not mean that the world is angry, fearful, judgmental, or unhappy, but your energy reflects that image back to you. That is the way in which you create your world from within yourself.

Your friends will perceive the same physical world that you share according to the image of their own reflection. There will be a unique individualism to the interpretation of the image or perception of life, dependent upon the energy of the individual.

This reflection of energy can best be understood by understanding the children within a family unit. Each child will perceive the family unit from their own reflection of energy. Therefore, each child will feel differently about their childhood and the parenting they received despite the similarity of the environment. Each child will be following its personal path of evolution.

When you create an integrated energy of body, mind, and spirit, you have created a balanced energy of self. As a balanced, integrated energy within the world of self, you can create a more balanced and integrated energy in the world around you.

You will understand your relationship to Earth. You will understand your relationship to the Universe. You will understand your relationship to each other. You will view self with enlightenment. You will value self.

*It is when you understand, accept, acknowledge, and value self with the love, truth, and perfection that is within you, that you are able to create a new world and a new energy around you. The world, as you know it today, is a creation of mass thought.*

When you have negative energy in your world, that negative energy will expand and expand and expand by the negative thoughts of the individuals focusing upon that specific consciousness energy, until it reaches a point where it explodes. The energy breaks apart and creates a crisis within your physical world.

*This negative energy that is created by individual man in turn creates natural disasters, wars, killings, and other negative dramas within your world.*

Your world is the creation of the individual and the energy the individual radiates his thoughts and his actions. When man can understand how he creates his world by the family that he gathers around him, by the energy that he brings unto himself into his own force field of energy, he will understand when he needs to change that energy. When he changes the energy within himself, he will create change within the energy of his world.

*The energy within the physical world is a reflection of the energy within man.*

When you have wars in your world, they first begin with the energy of the thoughts and actions of multiple individuals. All that is within your world is your creation.

The responsibility for this creation is overwhelming for you to consider, is it not? When you think, "I am the creator," you suddenly realize that you alone have the power to change yourself and your world individually and globally.

*When you change YOU, as an individual, you change your world as a whole.*

The soul family that you attract in your world is the energy of you. The electromagnetic energy of you attracts a "like" electromagnetic energy from the same force field. If you are attracting negative energy and YOU change, you will begin to attract a different energy. You attract according to what you are.

This is an expansive concept for you to understand, because you attract from all sources of energy within. This energy may exist outside of your conscious awareness of the energy. All energy will create an image.

Understanding images is understanding the creation of illusions. This IS the way you have chosen to learn your lesson. It is not right or wrong. It simply IS. It is profoundly effective within your physical world because it allows you to see the energy of yourself in others.

Indeed, this was the lesson of the Christ Consciousness as He lived on Earth as Man. He allowed you to see your own spirit, soul, and mind energy in the energy of Him.

The image of the Crucifixion creates within you according to your individual belief system. Man saw what he believed that he saw. Man created the image from his individual belief system. He created and saw an illusion or a vision of self. If man saw himself as suffering within his physical world, he viewed the Crucifixion as Christ suffering upon the cross.

Christ was completing His lesson of unconditional love. These were His thoughts and His actions. He was BEING truth in His own drama of love, truth, and perfection. The image that man perceived within the reflection of self was dependent upon his understanding of self.

Christ was releasing His attachment to the physical world. He was BEING Unconditional Love. He chose His method of learning as a message to the world. It was a message of joy and peace. The world continues to view the Crucifixion as an image of self.

*Therefore, many souls view the Crucifixion as suffering and dying on the cross in the same way they view their life and all of life as suffering and dying on the cross. This view of life as suffering is a reflection of your view of self and your life as suffering. This view of life creates a negative focus in all of life.*

How do you understand what you are doing in the physical sense?

You must go back into your world family, your relationships that are around you now, and the relationships that you have experienced in this physical life. You can look at each individual person and understand why you chose that person to be within your world.

Why did you choose your parents? What lessons were you learning from your parents? Did you learn that you cannot be happy if you fight all the time? Did you learn love? Did you learn independence? There are multiple lessons to observe.

You see, each event in life IS a lesson. If you saw your parents constantly fighting, then you learned what you do not want to do. You can learn lessons by reflecting either a positive or negative image.

Each and every lesson is an issue for the soul within. The way that you choose to learn the lesson is up to you. If it is a lesson of many lifetimes, you may choose to surround the lesson with drama to capture your conscious awareness of the lesson.

If you are married, is your marriage good? Are you happy? Do you wake up in the morning full of joy? Do you communicate from your soul and spirit energy? Does the presence of your spouse motivate and inspire you to new ideas and new understandings?

This is your world. Your life is the creation of your world by you. If you are not happy, what is the lesson you are trying to learn? Are you trying to learn to be patient? Are you trying to learn that you really matter and what you feel is more important to you than anything else? Are you trying to learn to balance out those energies within? What are you trying to learn? Are you trying to learn who you are so that you can love yourself?

Marriages are an ideal energy force in which you have chosen to learn. Marriages within your physical world are primarily created out of physical attraction. This is an image, an illusion of marriage that has been created from the belief system of man.

Marriage in the eyes of God is the integration of two spirits committed to spirit growth. Love is the spirit energy within. Love is also an integrated spirit energy with truth and perfection.

Because of the integration of love, truth, and perfection, they are one and cannot be separated within the marriage itself.

Therefore, marriages are created by you to be physical examples of love, truth, and perfection to the world.

Marriages are symbolic of the power of creation, therefore, you can create children within marriage. You can create family unity, as love, truth, and perfection. This is the creation of commitment. You can create love in all of its many levels.

The energy of love, truth, and perfection is the energy of the spirit and it is true inspiration within you. The soul energy that is shared by the partners will provide the motivation. The spirit energies will provide the inspiration. The intellect of the two partners will create within these energies exactly what they wish to create within their world.

The closer the energy of the soul and spirit within a marriage, the more motivation and inspiration there will be to inspire creation within the mind. If the soul and spirit energy is not activated by the partners, the marriage will be a physical union that will deteriorate with time into boredom and apathy.

Your world of today has a strong belief in physical attraction which is the impulsion for many marriages. It is this impulse activity that creates divorce within your world. The physical body will change with time and deteriorate. Your soul and spirit will expand if you give it the opportunity. It is for this reason that good marriages are committed to the soul and spirit growth of both partners.

Soul evolution is the purpose of life. If the physical focus stays as consistently within a marriage as it was when you first met, the marriage will not survive.

The changes of the physical or external self and the changes of the internal self will create separation between two partners focused within the intellectual/ego world of judgment. Without the commitment of the spirit and soul, change within the physical world will be judged as unacceptable.

When you create your world you can create it without an awareness and an understanding of what you are creating. But as you become aware and as you understand self, you have the power to go back and to look at each relationship within your world family. When you understand the lesson, you can heal what was by changing your perception to the positive image through the understanding of why you created the experience.

In each and every relationship within your world there is a specific lesson for you to learn. The true lesson will always be a positive lesson for you because it is of your own design. You would not have accepted that member into your world family if there was not a lesson designed into the relationship.

*Changing the reflection of the image that you see will change the energy of the relationship. This is true in all aspects of life whether it is individual or global.*

As souls and spirits you are focused on your own evolution. In your world this is called the "Stairway to Heaven." This is literally a spiral of lives with each life created by multiple experiences.

"Heaven on Earth" for you is understanding your world and understanding the family relationships within your world. This understanding will create within you the vision to understand yourself.

As you think about the people that you know or the relationships that you have had, you can easily see some of your lessons. In each and every instance these lessons will be yours, not the other individual's.

*The other individual agreed to play a role in your drama. The lesson they learn from playing a role in your drama is individual to them, and it has nothing to do with you. Indeed, their image of the reflection of the relationship will be unique to them. It may in no way resemble your own image.*

This difference in image within relationships can be seen in the difference in the understanding of a relationship at the time of separation or divorce within the physical world. The perception of each individual is focused on the lessons they are actively working upon. These two individuals will not communicate because they are speaking about separate visions of reality.

The path for you is different than the path for any other individual. The script may not seem to you to be written in that way, but believe me when I say that it is.

If you look at relationships and you try to figure out what the other person was learning, you are like a car stuck in the mud and your wheels are spinning. You will not be able to remove yourself from the rut that you are in. It is outside of your realm of energy. The energy of YOU is what you must deal with.

**Your energy is a beautiful, powerful energy that you need to learn to love, appreciate, honor, and USE!**

You are the love, truth, and perfection that is your God-self. The Godself is the God energy that is the inherent right within each man.

If you do not SEE love, truth, and perfection within each man, do not attach yourself to that image. Understand that you create the image or the illusion from the energy of self. Focus your energy in another direction and allow yourself to be all that you can be, because it is only you that you control. It is YOUR energy that impacts upon you first. It is your world family that is there to help you. But no one is there to BE you.

### All of man is forever responsible for himself.

The church is not responsible for your soul. You are. Are you good? Are you loving? Are you truthful? Are you perfection? The inherent energy within your soul and spirit are all of the above.

The medical world is not responsible for your health. Your body is your temple that you live in and YOU are responsible for it being healthy. You are responsible for your body each moment that you live.

If you abuse your body and go to a physician to give him the responsibility for making you perfect, you are going to be very dissatisfied, because he does not have the power to create perfection within you. YOU have that power. He can put a bandage on you and give you some medicine and make you feel better temporarily.

Indeed, it is perfectly fine to use help to bridge a challenge on a temporary basis, but YOU ARE responsible for self on a daily basis.

The schools are not responsible for your education. When you go to school, YOU have to study, YOU have to be the one who learns. If you fail to accept your responsibility to study, you will fail to learn.

The school is a facilitator. The physician is a facilitator. God is a facilitator. YOU are responsible for self. YOU create YOUR reality in YOUR world.

When you focus your life and create your world into an energy essence that causes you sadness, you will give yourself disease. If you create stress in your life, you have chosen to be stressed for a reason.

You alone have the power to change your world. And ONLY you can change your world by changing yourself first. Your spouse, lover, or friend cannot change your life for you. Your mother cannot change your world for you. NO ONE can make you change. No one can develop your awareness and understanding except you.

When you develop this awareness and understanding it will be reflected within your life and your world. It will be reflected in the world family. It will be reflected in you physically, mentally, and spiritually. You will have created change within yourself and you will have created the opportunity to change your world.

You are the creator of your world and your world family. When you think of the world as being Earth, you create all that is. You create the world around you, the energy around you, and the people around you by the energy within you.

Do you understand how powerful you are?

**You have total choice and total control of your world.**

This is what is referred to in your world as the "golden ring." The energy of you forms a golden ring within the Universal energy. When you grasp the energy within you, you can move the golden energy of you in the direction that you want it to go. Your golden ring of energy is your "Heaven on Earth."

When you choose to use all of the energy that is available to you in your daily life, you will find your life full of new creations, new ideas, new inspirations, and new understandings. Your world will change for you as you change within it.

**You are what you create, and what you create you are.**

Understanding your power of creation that creates the reality of your life and your world, allows you to understand who you are, what you are, and how you relate as a physical being on Earth. Understanding self gives you the power to create your world so that it works perfectly for you.

*TODAY*
*I AM*
*NOW IS*

# Universal
## Relationships

*Tomorrow is illusion*
*of the MIND*
*The time and space*
*of another Universe*
*in rhythm with*
*BEING*

When we speak of Universal relationships we speak of another aspect of reality. We have been discussing you and your relationships, and how your physical relationships structure your experiential learning on Earth.

Now I am going to explain to you as simply and concisely as I can the relationship of each of you to each other within the Universal energy of relationships.

Remember as you read, this dialogue can only be an overview. Explaining the concept of Universal relationships in detail would require volumes of books. Maybe someday we will focus on that but for the purposes of helping you to understand yourself in this moment of your reality we can be much less expansive.

The Universal reality is a world of energy that exists with a far more expanded level of consciousness than your physical world. Consciousness is energy and energy exists in multiple levels of consciousness. The consciousness levels on Earth are different for each person on Earth. Consciousness within man is a point of energy.

In Universal relationships there are many families and there are many cultures. A Universal relationship is created by a focus of energy. When two points of energy come together within the Universe they create an expanded energy frequency.

Earth is part of the Universe. You are part of the Universe. Man is the sum total of all consciousness energy. He does not acknowledge this energy within so he does not use the energy within. Man has chosen to focus his energy consciousness within physical matter to allow him to function as part of nature on Earth.

We have discussed man as energy throughout our books. If you have been able to understand that man IS energy within the physical world, then you should be able to clearly understand that man as energy originates within the spirit world.

Families and relationships are developed in the spirit world by focusing energy. Energy attracts like energy. The identical pattern is repeated within the physical world when you focus your physical energy into developing relationships. Try to expand your perception of the energy that you devote to nurturing a physical relationship.

When a spirit is attracted to an energy field in the spirit sense of energy, it becomes one of a family of spirits that is focused toward that energy. Do you understand?

In the same way that in the physical world you choose a profession, in the spirit world a spirit focuses on what he "likes" in spirit energy. If you choose to become a nuclear scientist, an artist, a dress designer, a secretary, or any other profession within a lifetime, you will focus your time and your physical energy toward your goal.

You can call this energy attraction by many names, but I call this psychic association, counterpart association, soul association, or family energy. They are essentially all one. You have chosen to mingle and interweave your energy into the mass energy of that specific focus.

There are indeed many levels of spirit relationships. Group or family focuses are developed within the spirit world and each of them can be changed at any time. Free will is clearly understood and used within the spirit world.

Changes occur because as the spirit expands and changes, the focus of energy will be changed. Not all energy will evolve or change to the same level at the same time. This same phenomena occurs within your physical world. As you grow and change, your friends will grow or you will change friends. The energy focus will be maintained at a level of similarity. If the focus for two people on Earth changes, the relationship will change between the people.

As spirits, you may be in a family as counterpart energies and you may stay in that family for thousands of lifetimes. For reasons of learning and experience you may choose to join another family. You will at that time change your focus of energy.

In the spirit world when you change your energy focus it creates a different reaction than when you change your focus in the physical world. The spirit world is not involved in fear, drama, and trauma as man is. In the physical world you do indeed change your focus many times in a lifetime. Each change of focus will create physical effects.

In the spirit world you deal with only positive energy. Illusions are created for physical man in transition but this too, is done in a loving, positive energy. When you die on Earth with a belief in Heaven, the illusion of your belief will be created for a short period to allow you to move from one world to the other world without disappointment or fear.

In the Universal concept of energy the spirit will change its focus a few times, perhaps several times in the concept of total soul evolution. So you see, what you do in a spirit lifetime is repeated in a physical lifetime. This is a focus of expanded spirit energy in the physical sense.

At some point in your physical sojourns you may have been a member of a soul and spirit family where you focused on painting, music, writing, sculpting, or other artistic creativity. At another time you may have changed your focus and you may have chosen to serve mankind. Another time you may have chosen to be spiritual.

These are only a few of the energy focuses that are available within the spirit world for manifestation within the physical world. Changes in focus will expand growth. Your relationships in the physical world are created by the attraction of energy focus.

You may live many lifetimes with the same counterpart energies, and you may have lived many lifetimes before with other counterpart energies. When you have a focus the entire family could be focusing and changing their focus simultaneously in spirit energy. There is a flow, a fluidity of spirit energy that allows a harmonious, balanced movement and change to naturally occur.

In any one period of soul evolution you would be traveling through this entire evolutionary process with souls that you are familiar with as spirit energy. The degree of involvement with each other within the physical world will depend on the life design that you each have created.

Counterpart souls can also focus upon spiritual teaching. My conduit is one of a group of counterpart souls that has come to Earth to focus upon spiritual teaching of the masses. This is very important in your world today. There is a very large family of counterpart souls within your world that is focusing upon teaching the masses.

This teaching is part of the evolutionary design of the Universe to create an awakening in the physical energy of man. As this evolutionary design begins it must begin with the individual. As they teach the energy of those involved will create the expansion through an accumulation of energy forces.

*All of man teaches and all of man learns. As you learn you must move through the steps one at a time. Movement in soul evolution is remembering as well as learning.*

There is a creative balance that is maintained within the Universal energy that allows man to teach and to learn at the same time. The balance is only compromised on the physical level by the individual when there is resistance to learning and therefore, there is resistance to teaching.

*Openness to learning is an important point of energy power within your world. When you learn, you also teach and when you teach, you will always learn.*

Until an individual can evolve, can focus, and can understand this Universal energy of evolution, he will not be comfortable with his inclinations, his inspirations, or with his intuitions. He will not be comfortable giving up his belief systems of the physical world.

*It IS when man understands, accepts, acknowledges, and values who he is and what his intentions are that he becomes inspired, motivated, and creative in this intentional energy.*

It IS through the acceptance and acknowledgement of who you are that you begin the process of Universal unity. All of the counterpart souls that are involved in understanding self are souls and spirits that are walking the path of evolution.

When the internal energy within man expands sufficiently, it will reach a point of critical mass. When this energy reaches a state of critical mass, all of man will suddenly understand and accept. What you know, what you understand, and what you accept will suddenly be understood, accepted, and acknowledged as truth by all of man.

Critical mass energy is a gravitational pull of energy. All energy is relative to all energy. Once the critical mass has been reached it will become as fact to the intellect of man. It is at this time that all members of the counterpart family will come together. They will be the wisdom of higher learning for man.

All other spirit energies will understand the teachings of spirit energies such as I AM. This is a time that is not far in the future of your world, as you understand your future. We will not give specific dates because the energy itself will determine the dates in your time.

If you are reading this book it is valuable for you to know that you have within this Universe millions of counterpart energies. These millions of energies are there supporting and helping you within the energy of your unconscious or spirit self.

Indeed, the spirit energies themselves are not unconscious. It is man that does not have a conscious awareness of the spirit within himself or of the spirits external to self.

### *The spirit energy within all of man is totally aware of all other energy.*

This Universal family of counterpart energies that is now on Earth is focused upon teaching man to understand himself. As man understands himself within his physical reality, he will at last begin to understand his relationship to his Creator.

This family is a spiritual family of advanced soul energy. This spiritual energy is the God energy which you share. As man, it is time for you to understand the true relationship of self to the spirit world.

### *It is your attachment to your physical world that creates denial within your ego of all other energy.*

You should value, acknowledge, and understand self as an integrated energy of the spirit world. UNDERSTAND the value of self, the value of what you are doing, and what your individual participation means.

This is an energy "whose time has come" because the energy of the physical and the energy of the intellectual are now seeking balance with the energy of the soul and spirit.

Balancing the energies within man is necessary for man to be productive, creative, and harmonious within your world. Being productive, creative, and harmonious allows man to balance himself, the world, the Earth, and the Universal energy.

There is much work to be done to teach man about the Universal energies, and man's role with this Universal energy. In physical lives you have lived as counterparts before as you live as counterparts today.

There have been many "past lives" where all of you have been in that creative physical energy, that experiential learning, and in the roles as counterpart Universal families. This soul and spirit association is a relationship that has served you well.

There have been lives where you have not been focused on the spirit energy. But at this time in your life the focus is identical in millions of people. In the spirit world as in the physical world there are many paths to one destination.

Your souls are evolving through the cycle of development. The energy is perfect for further evolution for man, if he will accept and acknowledge evolution. If man denies and resists evolution, he will remain captured within the physical energy. As energy you must move and change. If you move and change without understanding that movement and change, you will create crisis within your physical world.

In your physical world it is a challenge to understand that you are not all of the same PHYSICAL family, but you are all of the same SPIRIT family.

In physical life you do, indeed, choose your physical parents, and your physical families. In the spirit world the spirit family is created by the focus of energy. All spirits and all of man are sons of God. As spirits you choose a family of specific energy focus or counterparts. They are then your spirit family.

***Families are chosen by your energy attraction in the spirit world, and by what you must learn in the physical world.***

You cannot always learn the most efficiently by being in the same family. The focus could be so intense and the similarities so profound that your physical experiences would not teach you new insights.

Because of this need for experiential learning you will choose opposite physical families or different physical families. This creates a more expansive intermingling of energies on the spirit level and on the physical level. This broadens your capabilities in the physical understanding.

You will make your choice despite the fact that you are one spirit family. Understanding this energy of life design is the energy that allows you to understand that you are eternal. It is for this purpose that it is important for each of you to understand the Universal family relationship.

***If you were finite beings there would not be a Universal relationship.***

You would simply be born in the physical world of a mother and father, and you would cease to be at the time of death. That is a belief system within your world that has no validity. This same belief system destroys the understanding and hopefulness that man is seeking in his physical life.

**When you understand the expansiveness of your own energy, you can then understand the creativity of your energy, the abundance that you can produce, the miracles that you can create, and the power that you live with.**

As long as you are focusing on positive energy, you will be creative in terms of abundance. When you allow negative energy to enter into your reality, you allow your positive energy to be neutralized and you allow the energy to become stuck. You will in essence stop the rhythm and flow of the energy. You will block the harmony of balance.

The Universal energy is truly magnificent. It is a glorious, expansive energy where you have traveled through the energy realms of this Universe with millions of other spirits. In the expansiveness of the energy of the spirit family you have many different relationships and capabilities.

The counterpart is someone who has traveled with you. They may have energies that are slightly different, the focus is slightly different, but the goal is the same. The focus for both of you may change paths as you grow but it will return to the original focus with growth.

**In addition there will be soul mates. Soul mates are those souls of the opposite sex that you have spent many lifetimes mating with.**

They have been mates for you in the physical world as your souls evolve. This will be a role which they have played for you regardless of the role they are now playing. This role has created for the two of you a close, intimate, physical relationship that allows you to produce your dramas within the physical world. The energy of these soul mates will be of great influence within your physical world regardless of the present role.

You will also have your twin soul, the spirit soul that you share. This twin soul energy is the other half of your soul and spirit self. This does not mean that you do not have your own soul and spirit. When God created man and woman, He created them from one spirit energy.

Your twin soul is the one soul and spirit within the Universe that is closer to the energy of your soul and spirit than any other spirit and soul of the Universe. The twin soul is the energy of closest attunement with your energy. It is the energy that will integrate with your energy with perfect harmony and balance. It will enhance the soul and spirit energy within each of you which will allow for infinite motivation and eternal inspiration.

When the Creator divided man to make woman He created twin souls within the Universe. It is with the energy of this twin soul that you evolve in the Universal system of energy. In the spirit world you are one, in the physical world you are separate. Balanced, harmonious marriages within the physical world are frequently physical unions of twin souls.

God created for man the "buddy" system when He divided the energy of the spirit to form a twin soul. It is this "buddy" or "twin" energy that is there to give you strength, love, and support when you need it the most.

Adam and Eve were created as twin souls. Mary and Jesus were created as twin souls. Each and every soul within the Universe has a twin soul.

In times of great revelation and transformation within the physical world many twin souls will unite to give strength to their purpose in life. This is the Universal support that can always be used within the physical world.

The twin soul energy provides the support of infinite commitment and unconditional love. It creates a physical climate for maximum use of the motivation of soul energy and the inspiration of the spirit energy. When the energy of the soul and spirit are combined with the energy of the intellect, man will far surpass his accepted physical creative abilities.

When you meet your twin soul for the first time in the physical world, your reaction will depend upon your attachment to the physical world and the degree of resistance and denial that you have towards the soul and spirit world.

Many times you will dislike this soul the most because it will be so close to your own energy that if you do not like yourself, you certainly will not like the other soul, the other half of your spirit and soul.

As each of you evolve, the energy will change for both of you. This energy change may go through many transformations before you see each other with total clarity.

It is within the energy of the twin soul image that man is allowed to see himself with the utmost clarity. The image that you see is your own individual illusion of self, but that will not keep the illusion from punching your buttons.

In terms of souls, souls themselves can indeed be more than one, and yet they are one. This is called "fragmented souls" by some people, and this is a fairly understandable way of describing what this means.

You are all that you have ever been or will ever be in terms of energy. These energy points remain always as they are which creates for each of you multiple lives within each micro-second of your physical world. In using the word micro-second, I am using a word that you can more easily understand. In the spirit concept a micro-second is a lifetime within the physical world but in the spirit world micro-second has no meaning because there is no time.

You could say that as physical beings, when you have children you fragment, and when a soul goes on to another focus, it can fragment. So you will have an intermeshing, an intermingling, an interpenetration of all of these energies.

It is man's belief in the singular focus of the physical that prevents him from understanding the multiple points of energy within himself. Compare these multiple points of energy within the spirit and soul self to the multiple activities that you accomplish within a day of your time.

In the variety of activities that you undertake, you may function as several different people. You may start your day as a wife, progress to being a mother, suddenly become a teacher, go to a fund-raiser as a volunteer, dash off to class to be a student, and on and on with your day.

*The spirit and soul within you is capable of moving from one activity to another very rapidly. Your spirit has the freedom to keep the energy growing in all of the lives that you have ever been, are now, or ever will be. The fragmentation of your physical activities could be compared to the fragmentation of your soul and its activities.*

Have you ever noticed that the female is more capable of fragmenting her daily life than the male is?

The female accepts a more expansive integration of the soul and spirit energy. The male is focused upon the physical. The physical focus does not allow for harmonious fragmentation of energy.

Have you ever met a man who felt that if he got out of bed and worked all day, that he could do nothing else?

This is symbolic of physical attachment within the physical world. When a male becomes a father, he will feel this physical attachment more intensely. This physical attachment will create a greater need for sex, and less involvement with other activities. He will continue to work usually but all other activities will be focused upon the physical body through sex, sports, and physical activities.

The exposure to the soul and spirit energy of the child threatens the physical ego of the male, if he is not comfortable with his own soul and spirit energy. The soul and spirit energy is very strong in infancy and diminishes with growth.

Some parents will feel differently in relationship to the child as the child grows beyond the conscious focus of soul and spirit energy. Both males and females can react to the child from their male energy within. In this case, the parent will relate better to the child as they reach the second Law of Sevens. Child abuse occurs when the parent is strongly attached to the physical cycle of development and is in total denial of the soul and spirit energy.

This ego threat will be seen in the male as jealousy, anger, an increased need for attention especially in sexual activity, resistance to participation with the child, and all physical indications of rejection.

The male will not want to give up his dominance and control, his place of supremacy to a child. The ego may become so rejected that it will purposely seek solace with another woman where the attention will be directed specifically on the "wonder" of him.

The threat of the soul and spirit energy of the child creates the illusion of the fear of survival within the physical ego energy of the father. The ego faces the possibility of its own demise if the soul and spirit of the child attracts the soul and spirit within the father. Indeed, there is a dual purpose in the creation of physical life for man. He continues the physical cycle of energy or humanity, but he also gives himself the opportunity of triggering his soul and spirit energy.

The more focused the parents are in the physical ego energy, the more important it becomes to have children to trigger the memory of the soul and spirit within. If the parents resist parenting, they resist exposure to the soul and spirit energy of the child because the ego is captured in the illusion of death.

Energy creates illusion within the physical world. Misunderstandings occur because you think in linear concepts rather than in the expansiveness of the Universal energies. Think of yourselves as a star and when you look at the heavens you can see all of the stars around you. These stars are your energy points. Do you see how expansive you are?

In terms of the physical world, you relate on a spirit energy basis without your conscious awareness. You do this unconsciously with known soul and spirit energies. With your twin soul you will be attracted to the energy whether or not you like the person in the physical sense.

This is seen in the attractions that develop between males and females in your physical world. Have you ever been attracted to an energy and not understood why? Have you ever found yourself focused on a relationship and had no logical or intellectual reason for that focus? Have you found yourself attached, obsessed, and totally confused by this attraction?

The soul energy of soul mates will create a magnetic energy force between two souls. In many instances this magnetic energy force allows old Karmic debts to be repaid. You have designed this meeting into your life plan.

When this happens to you, you are dealing with energy that you have known in the spirit sense and that you do not understand in the physical sense. You can also develop a strong physical attraction for someone who does not have the same family energy in the spirit sense.

When this happens it is because you have at one time been in a counterpart energy, and the memory is retained in the spirit energy. In your physical world it will help you if you can focus on attachments with those of like energy. These energies will be closer counterparts and closer Universal energies for you to relate with.

In your physical world you speak of opposites attracting. That is not the way spiritual energy works. In the sense of true twin soul energy, you will find an energy that is so closely focused in the same area that yours is focused that it will surprise you. It may also terrify you, because you will see a mirror of self with total clarity. You may not see the twin soul but you will certainly see your reflection in their energy.

*It is important for man to understand himself and to love himself. Man cannot love the spirit energy of his twin soul until he can love the spirit energy of himself.*

Indeed, man will find a challenge in loving any spirit energy if he cannot love himself. If man views his relationships only from the physical perspective of physical attraction, his challenge will be in maintaining the relationship and growing at the same time.

*It is good to remember that the male and female energies enter the atmosphere of Earth as physical beings with totally different focuses. The male focus is towards the external physical, intellectual, and ego energy of the cycle of development. The female energy is focused toward the internal soul and spirit energy in the cycles of awareness and understanding.*

The male energy is manifested in the external world of possessions, identity, intellect, and ego beliefs. The female energy is manifested in the feelings and emotions of the heart. Because of the opposites in energy focus, the thoughts, the perspectives, the concepts, the words, and the actions of these male and female energies are totally different.

This difference in consciousness levels creates two people who do not in effect speak the same language. This difference in energy focus has created a problem of communication for man since the beginning of physical communication through speech.

Thoughts, words, actions, and understandings all exist on a different level of conscious awareness for the male and female.

In relationships this communication challenge becomes extreme. Women, in their efforts to live with the challenge, focus their growth toward the intellectual and physical world. Men in their challenge to survive with women must look internally at their emotions and feelings.

You can easily see how this challenge has been accepted by your physical world when you see what you call "role reversal" occurring.

*The male and the female have all energies within self. It is the resistance to using these energies in a harmonious balance that creates the challenge of understanding self, and surviving in committed relationships.*

It is also apparent within your world that change is easier for women than it is for men. The male is attached to the physical belief system and the ego that creates an expansive internal tug-of-war at the concept of change.

This attachment to the physical holds the male captive from internal growth. This reluctance to release the physical attachment creates devolution in the male and multiple repetitions of similar experiences in other embodiments.

As the female focuses upon the physical and the intellectual world she is creating male embodiments within her soul path. She is creating "role reversal" with her twin soul energy.

This swinging of the pendulum acts as a focus for the next lesson for you. The perfect challenge is the challenge of balance. Balance within the physical realm happens when man discovers himself. This self-discovery allows man to use all facets of self, the energy of the intellectual, rational, and intuitive mind equally.

*Using all facets of the mind in a balanced energy is self-realization. Self-realization creates an unconditional love of self.*

It is when you love yourself that the energy can exist in truth and perfection within and will then be imaged without.

*If you do not love yourself, you will find yourself in constant judgment of all other men.*

It is when you love yourself that you can know who you are. Knowing who you are allows you to recognize the soul and spirit energy of another.

*If your energy on a physical basis is intermingled with other energies on a physical basis that do not focus in the same direction as yours, you will tend to neutralize your own energy.*

If you have two energies that come together in the heart or spirit energy, but their understandings of that energy are not equal, you will develop resistance. Resistance will either neutralize your energy and you will be stuck, or it will short-circuit your energy and you will be drained.

When resistance occurs within your physical world you will begin to feel boxed in. You will not be able to be expansive in your creativity and in your learning. If one energy is focused upon the physical, there will be resistance to the soul and spirit energy from one source and resistance to the physical focus from the other source.

Because of this resistance factor that occurs in relationships on the physical level, it is more productive for you to form your relationships with individuals who are closer to your level of conscious awareness.

The consciousness of man is an energy force. If the consciousness of a friend is focused upon the physical and you are focused upon the feelings and emotions of self, you will create an unequal relationship that will not last.

Being with the same or an equal energy force is the ideal relationship from the spirit and soul energy as well as the physical energy. When you choose to develop a relationship in your physical world with a person of a different conscious awareness, you will be exposed to the physical elements of fear which will be manifested by the ego in its fear of survival. This ego fear energy will create apathy, depression, stasis of energy, anger, judgment, resistance, and denial.

Understanding the consciousness level of man is easier if we return to the dominance and submissive energy. Male energy is focused upon the dominant physical energy. Female energy is focused upon the submissive feeling, caring energy.

If a man meets a woman that he feels is as intelligent or more intelligent than he is, his ego will be instantly threatened. A man who is functioning from ego energy to the point of survival of the ego, will not be a compatible or equal partner for a balanced woman. A relationship with a person of this consciousness level will be one of dominance and submissiveness. If you as a female enjoy being submissive and dominated, that is your choice. If you prefer freedom to be you, you will not survive in the relationship.

Know what you want in loving yourself. The example given could work the same way with the genders reversed. The gender is not as important as the understanding of the consciousness level.

If the consciousness level of man is focused upon the physical, relationships will be more compatible if they are focused upon the physical. An individual with an expanded consciousness level will have a happier relationship with another person with an expanded consciousness level.

An equal consciousness level creates better communication with words, thoughts, and actions. The energy will be welcomed by each participant.

If you look at your world with discernment you will see the challenges that are created when relationships develop between people of different consciousness levels. The dramas, the traumas, the unhappiness, the murders, the divorces, and the abuse is daily reported in your various news media.

Consciousness is an energy from one, two, or three facets of the mind. Each individual facet of the mind has multiple levels of consciousness. It is your consciousness level that controls your daily life, your physical life, your world, your Earth, and your Universe. Your consciousness is the energy of you. It is the energy from which you create your reality.

In the cycle of development you are functioning from the first facet of the physical mind. When you begin to realize that the physical mind is not all there is, you will begin exploring the other facets from an INTELLECTUAL perspective. You will look beyond hesitantly, and only with the understanding of the physical intellect.

When the soul and spirit information does not satisfy the judgment of your ego/intellect you will create resistance, denial, and disbelief. Many of you are now looking at the spirit and soul of self with your intellectual judgment as your guide. You explore many paths in your efforts to discover yourself.

Your ego would like to find a way to satisfy your search without giving up the power that it has over you. You will explore all the props on the stage in your efforts to find your soul and spirit energy. Your soul and spirit energy cannot be found in stage props.

Your soul and spirit energy dwells comfortably inside your mind whether or not it is accepted, acknowledged, respected, or valued. Your soul and spirit energy is in effect being held captive within you by the control of your ego self.

Your soul and spirit are too lofty to be judged by your ego because your ego is not coming from the energy of freedom. Your ego cannot think, conceive, accept, understand, or believe expansively enough to comprehend the energy of your soul and spirit self.

When you are ready to welcome the soul and spirit energy of you into your world you must do so with faith. Faith is the loving energy of your spirit self.

**Faith defies judgment by the ego or the intellect because it cannot be understood or examined by your physical senses in your physical terms.**

Faith cannot be measured, qualified, quantified, analyzed under a microscope, frozen, dissected, and/or studied in any known physical manner.

**Faith is the beginning level of soul and spirit consciousness energy. In your world it is manifested in the spirit energy of love, truth, and perfection. If you do not have faith, you have not yet accessed your soul and spirit energy.**

Integrating the consciousness energies of self into one cohesive energy will allow you to reach a level of self-discovery that will astound you. In discovering yourself you will discover a new dimension in your relationships and in your world activities. As you grow you will attract into your energy force field the counterpart energies of the spirit world.

These Universal family energies are the most important energies in your physical world, because they are of the same focus, they are supportive, they are creative, and they are imaginative. These are pure energies of motivation and inspiration.

The integration of spirit energies will expand for you beyond what you can expand for yourself, because they will enhance, they will extend, and they will motivate your own energies to greater and greater heights. All counterpart or family spirit energy will enhance the energy of each other.

There is unlimited power in the attunement of like energies. The energy point of the twin soul energy doubles and creates a vortex of inspirational and motivational energy when twin souls recognize and understand the soul and spirit connection.

When the physical self, the intellect/ego, can acknowledge the twin soul energy, it has taken a giant step forward in allowing it to find the proper attunement within your physical world. The twin soul energy adds a like force that enhances the physical world of intellect, work, play, and love.

If you find yourself in a purely physical relationship you will find yourself without enhancement of your energies. Indeed, you will find an opposite energy to be draining to you after a period of time. You do not want to drain your own energy reserves. In the physical world with your physical focus, you drain your reserves by creating for yourself daily drama, tremendous trauma, anger, and hostility. Indeed, you show more concern for your ego needs than you show for your physical body.

Create your relationships from the same energy focus. Spend time exploring your own consciousness level as well as the consciousness level of your partners in relationships. If your interests are similar, your beliefs are not in opposition, you share the same goals and purposes of life, and your consciousness of life is similar, you will be more compatible to each other. Your energies will be in harmony. They will work in unison. They will expand. They will not box you in. You will find yourself bursting with joy within your physical world.

When you can understand the Universal energies as they pertain to you within the physical world, you will be able to work with more clarity and more understanding in your entire life. You will find yourself being in harmony, being in happiness, and in BEING love. Suddenly you will realize that you have created for yourself this world of harmony and balance.

In a world of balance, you will be using not only your intellectual mind to capacity, but you will be using your soul memories to capacity, and you will be using the spirit energy to capacity. You will have this expansive funnel of energy that will come down into your physical body and allow you to be WHO YOU WANT TO BE.

The energy of the Universe and the energy of your large Universal family is always there. It is always there and it is always supportive, protective, loving, and expansive. It is the energy of true creativity and enhancement. It is within these like energies that you need to look for your physical partners.

The energy of the mate in your physical world should always be one of enhancement and growth. This enhancement and growth allows you to be all that you can be, and your partner to be all that he or she can be. If you are fortunate and have designed a life with your twin soul, you will find pure inspiration, motivation, and creativity your constant companion.

The energy of a soul mate is an energy for partnership bonding. It will be an energy that expands you. It will not box you in, because it allows you to live in total freedom within.

I am not speaking of total freedom with other individuals in the physical sense such as other lovers. I am speaking of love that is committed to physical enhancement and soul evolution.

When you find your true energy partner from the Universal energy that surrounds you, that partner will enhance your life. You will be better than you were before the partnership. You will be joyful, happy, and productive within your physical world. You will look at your partner and you will see the Universe of the soul and spirit energy that surrounds you. You will expand your concepts of who YOU are, who THEY are, and your relationship to the Universal energy.

Sharing soul and spirit energy in relationships is living in Universal energy. Sharing enhances the energy of loving self that will help you understand yourself and the Universe as you relate to it. It will strengthen and expand and enhance. You will never feel lonely or feel the need to search again. Your love and joy will create a different energy around you.

Know that you are perfect just as you are, because you are a Universal spirit. Understand that the energy of you is complete. You have no needs. You may have a LIKE of enhancement, but you have no needs, because you ARE complete. You ARE a spirit energy from the Universal realm.

*All of man searches for the perfect partner. This searching is created from the spirit energy within that misses the energy of its twin soul. The absence of the twin soul in the physical world creates a sense of incompleteness within the spirit energy. The energy is then manifested within the physical mind and the search is conducted within your physical reality.*

This sense of incompleteness was part of the design by God to remind man to search for a perfect partner for the purpose of completion. This is an inherent trigger of memory that was designed to perpetuate the human race by the human race.

Man has focused himself singularly into his physical energy. Therefore, the energy sense that began as a spirit energy for attracting a mate, is manifested as a physical energy focused upon physical attraction within your world.

Some of you search consciously, some of you search subconsciously, and others of you search unconsciously. When man lives his life searching for a physical partner, or a spiritual partner, he should always look for the energy of enhancement.

It IS this energy of enhancement, of pure joy, and peace that will allow you to understand and identify within your physical world a compatible energy. The Universal energy that is perfect for you in this lifetime is not the only alternative for you. There will always be another harmonious energy which will usually be found in a counterpart with a like focus.

*If you as a physical being find the twin soul counterpart in your advanced state, you should know and you should recognize from the energy of that soul exactly what your relationship is. This should be for you an opening into soul memory, into spirit understanding. This crossing of energy points will trigger "past life" memories or in my terms it will expand your consciousness level to remember all that you are, have ever been, and will be.*

This magnetic force will be different than physical attraction. This is an energy of Universal relationship that is duplicated in the physical world. It is indeed an energy that you will like if you are attuned to your soul and spirit energy.

The lessons of the relationship will be clearly delineated in your physical understanding. Your challenge will be to accept, acknowledge, respect, and value what you have found within your physical world. If you focus upon the intellect/ego judgment, your opportunity will be ignored. To ignore is to live in ignorance.

The energy of the Universal family that you share is an energy that you should be proud to be with. It is an energy that has been in existence from the beginning of time as you know it. It is moving, it is evolving through the Universal families and it is the energy that is important today upon your Earth. This advanced energy is here on Earth to help with the healing and cleansing of the planet Earth.

See your spirit self as you believe it to be, and as you understand it to be in the Universal energy of the unconscious self. Allow this spirit self to flow together in total harmony, allowing the positive to neutralize all negative energy. Now you have a very rhythmic flow of energy.

This flow of energy is the flow of love, truth, and perfection of the soul and spirit within you. Allow this love, truth, and perfection to move as a river into your physical body and intellectual mind. The river flows in total calmness and peace as it brings harmony to the intellect. Understand and love yourself to live in happiness and joy on Earth.

It is the Universal consciousness energy that creates families from consciousness levels. Allow your intellect to be at the consciousness level that you would like it to be. Resistance to growth is the negative energy within self. It is not external to you.

Nothing is completely external to you. The physical, intellect/ego is external to the inner and higher mind only because of the energy focus of consciousness. The energy of you creates all of your world and the world is your physical creation.

*The Universal energy within is God's creation. It can be denied, resisted, and ignored, but it continues to exist internally as an integrated energy of you.*

You are integrated as an energy force. You have a spirit and soul that is supporting you and loving you despite how you imagine yourself. It is this unseen force within you that is your Godself. You cannot separate yourself from this force, no matter how hard you try. Your Godself understands you and it is unconditional in its love for you.

It is the consciousness of man that creates the world of man. It is the consciousness energy within the Universe that creates the Universe of man. In each and every respect, the energy of one is dependent upon the energy of the other. The way to focus the Universal energy is to focus the energy within yourself.

When your energy is focused upon the consciousness level that you choose to be, it will influence the consciousness level of the Universe. Your consciousness level will bring to you the consciousness level that will enhance you as a physical being.

The relationships that exist upon the Universal level, continue to exist upon the physical level. The spirit within man has total freedom and moves freely between the spirit realm and the physical realm. There is no time, there is no space. NOW IS. For spirit energy NOW IS, is a Universal reality.

When the spirit energy is residing within the body of you, it travels during your sleep periods and in micro-seconds of your time while you are awake. Spirit relationships continue despite all physical relationships or physical circumstances. It is the freedom of the spirit to be who it is that maintains the balance within the mind that you enjoy. When the spirit energy is resisted and denied the struggle increases within your physical mind.

In your physical world you will spend just over 40 years in your cycle of development. In the last period of the Law of Sevens, you are moving forward into the cycle of awareness and understanding. In your terms you would say that you are living on the edge. This period of soul and spirit awakening creates a period of physical crisis within your life.

Your physical crisis is developed by your ego/spirit tug-of-war that is raging within. It is at this period that you will focus your physical energies upon the supreme physical sense. The supreme physical sense within you is your sexuality.

Sexual crises are frequent during this period of your life. You will struggle to remain attached within your physical world. This "physical need" to remain attached to the physical you is being triggered by the spirit within that is seeking balance.

This crisis period is more significant within the male of your world than it is the female because the male is focused within the physical world. Indeed, many males will feel they are losing all attachment to reality.

This sense of loss of reality will focus their consciousness on the eternal world of God and the external physical world of the ego self which is ruled by their sexual ability. This will be the physical manifestation of the ego/spirit tug-of-war within.

*The more balanced the male or female is at the time of transition from the cycle of development to the cycle of awareness and understanding, the less noticeable the ego/spirit tug-of-war will be in the physical world.*

This sense of loss of reality will trigger dramas of youthful marriages, adultery, affairs, divorce, suicide, financial disasters, career changes, depression, mental and physical illness and many other reactions.

*This period of transition from the world of physical attachment to a world of awareness and understanding in the life of a male, is the crisis period of struggle for ego survival and understanding self.*

All reactions will have a sexual basis whether or not that basis is apparent within the physical world. If the struggle is expansive, you will find a profound physical manifestation of sexual crisis and religious crisis both as the tug-of-war increases internally.

The male that is balanced internally will not be physically conscious of a serious struggle within. The female will more willingly begin her search of self-discovery at this period of her life. The conscious resistance of the male will be an indication of the consciousness level within.

In some of you the spirit influence will be totally accepted and acknowledged within your life. You will gracefully make the transition from the cycle of development at any age. Indeed, if your mind remains open to the soul and spirit influence, you will be living the cycles of awareness, understanding, and integration in total unity with your cycle of physical and mental development.

This balance of energies can occur in both the male and the female early in life, although in your physical world the male will find it more of a challenge because of his belief in his life role. When you can accept the spirit and soul as an everlasting presence, you will become comfortable with its influence.

The spiritual relationship that you maintain internally with yourself is of unlimited value to you within the physical energy of your world. It can help you maintain health of the body and mind.

*Health of the body and mind is the path to being human. Acceptance and acknowledgment of the soul and spirit within, is the path to being spiritual.*

In understanding your relationships with others, you will understand the intricate web of energy that exists on the Universal level. If each and every relationship within your life could be viewed without a physical body, you would see the energy of the Universal relationships within your physical world.

When you create harmony and balance in all relationships within the physical realm of Earth, you will create harmony and balance in all Universal relationships.

The energy of Universal relationships exists on all the infinite levels of consciousness energy. Therefore, what you create within your physical world is manifested in the Universal energy of the spirit world.

The Universal energy is the governing energy of the physical world that is created by the accumulated energy of the spirit of man. Create your Universe as you want it to be.

# Celebrating
## Relationships

Celebrating relationships is a physical manifestation of the joy within you. If you have no joy within, you will not be celebrating the relationships within your world. If you love yourself and your life, you will find joy in everybody and everything each and every day of your life.

> *The joy that you need to celebrate relationships is not a joy that is given to you through the relationship. It is a joy that is inherent within you. It is the harmony and balance that you enjoy when you love yourself.*

Loving self creates a cyclic energy within you that reflects within your life to your family, your friends, your colleagues, all of man, the world, and the Universe. Love is the energy of you. You are one and you are inseparable.

Your life is indeed a celebration. Life is a celebration of all that has been before for you as a soul and spirit, and all that life is now. If you can perceive life today as a continuation of your spirit energy you will be able to appreciate the value of each day when you wake up. The spirit as an eternal energy is living that energy in a state of joy and happiness, a state of constant celebration.

Appreciating this continual celebration may appear a challenge for you at times within your physical world. Imagine with an open mind that no matter where you are today or what is happening in your world, you are exactly where you want to be.

You are where you are because it is part of your life design. You are searching to learn lessons that will help you in your spirit growth. You are experiencing through the energy of physical life your soul evolution.

The design that you have created may not always seem pleasant from your physical perspective but it is the path that you have chosen.

> *Life is a celebration of spirit energy in physical manifestation.*

Understanding and appreciating this spiritual celebration will allow you to perceive life in a joyful way. You will see the wisdom and ingenuity of your life design, and you will appreciate you.

As joy and happiness become part of your daily energy, you will find yourself expanding. As you expand, grow, and open, you will know that you can do whatever you want to do. You will recognize your own power of creation.

You must know what you want to do or you will be challenged to focus your energy with the proper intensity to accomplish your goal. If you cannot focus and if you do not know what you want to do, understand that this is your level of conscious awareness at this time.

You will many times live an entire lifetime and feel that you have not truly found your path of life design. Accept that some life designs are focused upon rest within the physical world. This focus upon rest is a focus upon self-understanding. If you do not come into life to work upon a global issue, a world issue, an Earth issue, or an issue of intention, then you have designed personal work into your path of learning.

When you create the design of your life, you build into that design multiple alternative paths. These paths are created by your level of motivation and inspiration needed to understand them. If you consistently choose the simple physical way of life you will never reach your ultimate goal of growth in this lifetime. Challenges of alternative paths are defined as risk-taking in your physical world.

> ***All paths change in physical character as you open and expand or as you become more restrictive in your life.***

This could be compared to starting out on a physical journey in your car. You have not consulted a map but you understand the direction to turn onto your super highway when you leave your house. Each time that you come to a new exit in the highway, you make another turn. Within a few hours you are totally confused as to the direction that you are heading.

You continue to make turns and take different roads as your confusion increases. Making the turns is easier at the moment than trying to find new information that will tell you where you are and in which direction you are going. Before many hours have passed you are feeling helplessly lost. Just ahead of you is a large sign that says, "Dead End."

You turn your automobile around and you retrace your path. Now you are alert to finding help. An energy of desperation and fear overtakes you as you drive down the lonely country road.

You watch carefully for a gas station. You realize that you need to make contact with a knowledgeable human being. You know that you need a relationship. You know that you need help to discover where you are and how you find your way to your destination.

Many times the easiest path is not the best path to our destination of growth and expansion. When you do not know that another path exists or you fear to take a path because you believe that it is heading in the wrong direction, it is time to look, to listen, and to find guidance.

It is easier for you to seek guidance when you lose your physical way than it is to seek internal guidance when you fail to see your spiritual path clearly. You are less willing to share your feelings of the heart than you are your observations of the physical world.

OVERCOMING THE FEAR OF RELATIONSHIPS IS OVERCOMING THE FEAR OF SELF.

**When you understand the beauty and wisdom that is within you, you will choose to share it in your relationships. Sharing the beauty and wisdom within you is celebrating your relationships.**

You create the energy of relationships and you create your own conscious awareness of that energy. When you experience events in your world that appear to you to be negative, try to perceive them in a different energy. Look for the positive message.

Ask yourself, "What am I trying to learn?" "What am I teaching myself?" "Why am I celebrating this event as part of my life?"

*You created the design. You created the event. It is your consciousness of the event and of the creation that will allow you to look within and change the energy form of the event.*

As an example, have you ever had the privilege of being fired from your job?

When you are working in a position that does not give you the joy of celebration on a daily basis you should not be there. Many souls will focus on the commitment that they made to the job or to their boss. This commitment becomes their responsibility to stay with the position, despite the energy of the boss or the position.

If your values are different than the values of the company or of your immediate supervisor, you will become a threat to their belief system and to their activities. Your difference in values may not be physically understood but the energy of who you are will be reflecting to your other relationships within the company.

Your energy punched ego buttons that created your dismissal. You became a risk, a threat to someone within the company. The company and the personnel involved were not able to change so they chose the easy path of removing you from their presence.

For you this is a reason to celebrate. You maintained your commitment and your responsibility was fulfilled. You exposed the energy of your value system to others which created risk for you in maintaining the relationship. You developed a relationship that had a potential of working, if all parties involved within the relationship could risk a new internal path.

The joy of testing your value system in an opposite energy is that it allows you to see the love, truth, and perfection within you. Seeing the opposite energy validates within you that you are following the perfect path for you.

It is the knowledge of self that you could see imaged in this event that gave you multiple reasons to celebrate. When you find that your consciousness level is higher than others whom you are in relationship with, you face the energy of devolution if you step down to their level. At this moment in your life, you choose your own path based upon your conscious physical focus of self.

When you find joy, peace, and happiness within from your decision, you create the energy of celebration within your life. The event itself will be perceived in relationship to the consciousness level of each person involved.

**The energy within you is only affected by your perception of self.**

In each and every event of your physical world there is a celebration that is hidden. It is hidden from your conscious view by your own resistances to learning the lesson. Celebration is inherent in learning. Learning is movement, change, and growth.

If you were studying math and you hate math but you have a tutor who is trying to teach you to understand the basic principles of math, these principles will not absorb within your mind. You cannot grasp what it is that makes the formula work.

Sharing: Self Discovery in Relationships

Someone suddenly comes into the room and presents this mathematical process to you in a totally different way that relates it to your world. Suddenly your entire understanding of math changes because you are presented the lesson in relationship to all past knowledge.

If you do not learn the lesson you will continue to create and recreate the same circumstances with a different image form. If you want to create something positive in your world, you have to make the commitment, you have to accept the responsibility, and you have to produce the physical work to create the event within your physical world. Once you set the stage the Universal energies will then be able to allow this energy to flow in a harmonious rhythm.

When you perceive your world with a positive, joyful, and creative energy, you do not have to effort in the physical sense. It is through the creation of relationships, events, people, and actions that this energy builds, and builds, and builds to create for you your chosen goal. The responsibility is always yours because the energy that you expend and radiate is your responsibility. The design of your life is your responsibility.

Discovering who you are, accepting the responsibility for who you are, and for what you do is the most joyful energy within man. This energy creates a daily celebration of life and living. It creates a daily celebration with those who share your world.

Always within your world, people have resistances that prevent them from appreciating and accepting the joy that is found in relationships. If you are focused upon yourself in a self-centered, egotistical manner, you will not have a conscious awareness of the relationship that reaches beyond the focus of yourself.

You will look at the relationship and you will judge it by what it can do for you. You will reflect your image of need to the relationship and you will judge the reflection that is returned. Your judgment will be focused upon your own energy reflection, not upon the relationship as it is.

You will not see the value of the interaction. You will not see the giving and the receiving. You will not care if you are contributing to the joy and happiness of another. Your focus will be on self. You focus upon self because you fear sharing self. You fear the risk of survival if you give anything away.

***If you are afraid that your survival is at risk if you share any part of yourself, you have an extremely limited vision of yourself.***

If you fear sharing yourself, you will find very little in your physical world that you will want to celebrate. You will not find the occasion to celebrate because you do not perceive life and self as being "worthy" of celebration.

***In the spirit world the opposite to celebration is depression. Depression is an energy of mourning or grieving for the unworthiness of self.***

Life is created by you from your perception of self, relative to your level of consciousness. If you find yourself unworthy, then you will see all relationships as unworthy of you, and you will see your life as unworthy of you. This reflection of unworthiness is from self, and your judgment is of self.

***The level of consciousness within man is created by man secondary to his willingness to be open to self-discovery. If man loves himself he invites self-discovery. If man fears himself, he fears and denies self-discovery.***

If you do not know who you are, you will judge yourself by your belief system. Judging yourself in relationship to your beliefs creates unworthiness. Judgment is the opposite of unconditional love. If you judge yourself, you are not loving yourself. Your judgment of self creates a standard of belief that you know you cannot meet. Therefore, you attach yourself to your vision of unworthiness because you cannot meet your own vision of belief. Do you see the destructive cycle of this negative energy?

Your belief in your unworthiness depresses you, which in turn decreases your ability to function in your work activities, in your relationships, in your love life, and in your play. Your withdrawal from life interferes with your entire world and creates a cycle of negative energy. As the negative energy becomes predominant around you, your judgment tells you that the world has validated your belief in your unworthiness which intensifies your depression.

Understand that depression is your choice of emotion. You fear knowing who you are so you choose depression as the easy path. Depression allows the ego to literally wallow in self-pity. It is easier to think positively than it is to think negatively.

*The reason that controlling your thoughts be-
comes a challenge for you is that you do not have a
conscious awareness of the fact that you create
your reality by your thoughts, words, and actions.*

Discovering the joy of self and life requires a commitment and a responsibility to be open to risk, to change, to learning, and to changing your perception of self.

If it is your choice to become an actress, you must commit yourself to hard work, dancing, singing, drama classes, experience, practice, and tremendous self-discipline and responsibility. This is the vision and the reality of learning to become an actor or actress.

None of this commitment assures you that you will someday become rich and famous. But if you have the commitment to try, you will discover whether or not you can truly act. But you must live what you want to be. Acting requires an openness to the energies within you. Living requires an openness to the energies within you.

If you want to enjoy your life and see each moment as worthy of celebration, you must commit yourself to hard work, studying, schools, life experience, practice, and a tremendous amount of self-discipline and responsibility.

You must not fear to be you. You must not judge your abilities. You must live what you want to be. You must accept yourself and the world without judgment and you will be love in celebration.

You will find that you have no time and no space in your life for depression. Depression does not survive in an active life that is filled with positive relationships.

*Depression is an emotion that is fostered by inac-
tivity and boredom.*

How can you be depressed if you are working hard to help someone else? Would that make you feel unworthy?

Unworthiness and depression are created in self-centered, self-focused, and lonely people. Unworthiness and depression are choices of the ego that is reacting to fear. The ego chooses depression when it feels the inevitable ego/spirit tug-of-war within you.

*Depression is an ego survival technique.*

You can relieve depression by understanding that you are judging yourself, and then creatively seeking activity, self-understanding, creativity, relationships, and play. As you do this, you will find yourself releasing your attachment to the ego judgment of unworthiness. You will quickly begin to understand that you create your reality.

### *Your spirit will choose to celebrate, if you let it.*

You do not focus on celebration enough in your world because you are focused upon the emotion of fear or its elements. Anger is an emotion that creates expansive dramas within your world. An angry person will move mountains to seek revenge. Revenge is seen by you as a way of proving yourself right as you prove someone else wrong.

Focusing your energy on revenge will require most of your life energy. Revenge will expand the negative energy of the event and validate the importance of the attachment within your life. Validation provides a sense of justification which allows you to proceed with negative energy forces.

### *Revenge will serve you better if you choose to focus on the positive energy of you. Live well, be happy, celebrate, and allow the energy of the attachment to be released.*

Anger is an emotion that affects only the individual that creates it. If you carry your anger to the extreme and create physical or bodily harm, then you have created punishment within your world. Punishment is another negative energy that is attracted by the anger.

Negative energy becomes cyclic within you. If you value yourself, you will change the energy to a positive force. The Universe will help you celebrate by sending good energy to you. Your gifts of happiness and joy will astound you.

### *People have resistances. Resistance and denial are the physical process of energy blockage that allows you to become uncomfortable enough to capture your attention.*

You are taught by your belief system to depend upon physical processes. You feel that if you do not do something in the precise way that you were taught, you will not be successful. It is interesting to see how you maintain your beliefs throughout your energy spectrum.

*You create the energy of judgment around your life event. It is the energy of the belief in failure that creates failure. It is the energy of the belief in the process that creates resistance.*

The intellect and ego energy within you can be utilized to help you, and to help you understand. You must not restrict yourself with beliefs of negativity and judgment. There is no perfect way to do anything within your world. The energy of you and the event is different than any other energy. Look within yourself for the path of soul memory rather than the way of the physical process.

*Within you is the joyful spirit that is celebrating every moment that you live and grow. Peace is the emotion of the soul, and joy is the emotion of the spirit.*

You must remember that the spirit within you is eternal. It began its Earth form millions of years ago. The soul is learning. You have developed. You have created a new level of physical body, a new level of awareness, and a new level of understanding.

The spirit energy within you is the inspiration within you. Your inspiration is seen in your physical world as imagination and is immediately discredited, denied, and resisted. If you cannot imagine, you cannot be creative. All great works of art began with imagination.

*Through the energy of imagination that began as inspiration you create a new experience.*

If you allow yourself, the soul memory, the spirit energy, and the intellectual mind to have their freedom to fly with wings, you will be using inspiration. You will accept this inspiration as imagination from the intellectual mind. Your physical work will then bring your imagination into your reality as creation.

If you insist upon focusing upon physical process alone that has been learned through the ego and intellect, you will never produce the positive energy to expand, to grow, and to build. You will not be able to accept the faith within yourself that will allow you to understand self. Faith allows you to grow internally as you grow externally.

You can accomplish these energy points within your life by the energy exchange of giving and receiving, caring and sharing, speaking and listening, and by loving self and others within your world.

When you are open to loving other people, your energy will automatically expand. As your energy expands, the energy of your world will expand. Loving is giving and receiving, sharing and caring, and speaking and listening as an exchange of loving energy within all relationships. Each of these relationships is a gift of the soul and spirit when you give of yourself.

> *A gift of self is a validation of the respect and value that you feel for the other person.*

Celebrating the love of self is not celebrating a self-centered focus. It is celebrating self-realization. It is celebrating the love that you feel for yourself, other people, your world, your Earth, and your Universe.

Who you are is not just your physical body. You are all that is. You are inseparable from ALL THAT IS. You are inseparable from all the spirits and souls within the Universe and you are inseparable from the energy of the Universe.

> *Knowing who you are creates the joy to celebrate who you are. Self-discovery is a path of learning. It has no beginning and it has no end.*

You begin as an open and loving soul and spirit in infancy. You learn to constrict and deny who you are in your cycle of development. As you follow the path of self-discovery, you begin to wander back into the energy of self that reaches beyond the physical belief system that you were taught.

Who you are is the inspiration of the spirit within. You must live within the physical world as spirit energy in order to grow, to expand, and to evolve the spirit energy. The spirit path requires that you learn to balance your physical life and integrate your physical life with the internal self.

Balance and integration utilize all that you are in each facet of self. You give of the self within the opportunity and the challenge to be all that you can be as a total, joyful being.

> *It is the isolation that is taught to man as a physical process that creates the resistance to integration within the mind of man.*

For you to be all that you can be, you need to understand yourself. You need to integrate each and every facet of yourself. You need to admit to yourself that you are more than just a physical body, an ego, and an intellect.

If you were nothing but a physical being, then each of you would live only one life as a physical organism. At death you would return to dust. You would be as finite as some of you may believe that you are, but that is not the reality of the energy of man. Neither is it the reality of the energy of the spirit that is within you.

The belief in one physical life is a belief that influences you from the beginning of your life. This belief was created by man to control the actions of man. When the belief was created, most references to the story of continual soul evolution through countless opportunities of physical lives was purged from your historical records.

Your purging began more than 500 years after the life of Jesus of Nazareth. Some writings continue to remain within your world that tell another story. The decision to make these writings public is of concern now as an economic issue.

The belief in only one physical life creates a sense of hopelessness and helplessness within you. It creates an energy that says, "No matter what I do, no matter how hard I try, I will ultimately die and be forgotten."

*The belief in only one physical life supports the belief of unworthiness in you. It supports and values the perspective of guilt and sin in you. It creates hopelessness and helplessness as a daily reality for you.*

*WHEN YOU DO NOT HAVE HOPE, YOU DO NOT HAVE FAITH.*

You are eternal as spirit and you will eternally live multiple physical lives until you reach a state of love, truth, and perfection. In your physical world you have been given countless opportunities in each lifetime to learn.

What is above is below. In the same manner that you may choose to marry 10 times in one life, you may choose to return to Earth life 10,000 times to learn the lesson of marriage.

The lessons of the spirit world are manifested within your physical world by symbolic events. Not even man limits himself to one chance at any one thing. Would God be less giving than man?

If you came to Earth only one time, you would not have the opportunity to grow and to improve the self that is made in the image of God. The Christ Consciousness showed man "the way" in multiple embodiments. He showed you the path of self-discovery as it moves forward to self-realization.

Believing in one life removes responsibility from you for your own growth. It allows you to imitate God in the belief system that you are taught, without accepting the responsibility of being what you believe. You give God the responsibility of saving you.

This perspective of life is a lesson in accepting responsibility. Failure to accept responsibility for self is a form of the dependent personality of you as humans. Many of you will return to Earth multiple times to learn this lesson. The imitations of God have multiple energies among you with multiple versions of belief that exist as illusion. All of life is a lesson, the lesson of religious belief is no different.

The eternal soul and spirit of you is the celebration within you. As you see yourself grow there is joy and happiness in your own accomplishments. You are not captured by a belief system other than your own soul and spirit energy. You are willing to expand and enjoy the physical world around you in the love, truth, and perfection of you. You are willing to accept the responsibility for your own soul evolution.

When God created you, He gave you the power of creation by the energy of love, truth, and perfection. In this power that He gave you is the freedom of choice, will, and intention.

Because of the gift of free choice, free will, and free intention, you create your own belief system within each life. The beliefs that you create are not as important as the attachment that you create to the beliefs.

*When you are attached to beliefs they create walls of resistance and denial within your life. It is the walls that you must overcome in your world.*

Look at your life. Do you live with a continual sense of joyous celebration? Do you live in depression, guilt, sin, and fear?

Only you can feel the emotions of the ego and spirit as they strive to balance and integrate you within. Only you have the free choice to know yourself.

Knowing yourself is loving yourself. When you love your-self, you will love the God within you, and you will love all of mankind.

The wall that separates you from loving yourself is the wall of forgiveness. If you find yourself unworthy, fearful, guilty, and overwhelmed by sin, forgive yourself. That too, is your respon-sibility.

Loving yourself gives you permission to love all of man. It creates the peace and joy of continual celebration within your life. You see the value of you in the image of love, truth, and perfection. In seeing, you can then Be you.

All relationships will create dramas of interaction that will challenge you to grow. Each relationship will present your dramas to you in a different perspective or image. The interaction with family members and friends will be different, for instance, from your interaction with lovers or spouses.

Despite the difference in the relationship, your response to the interaction will be from your understanding of your con-scious awareness. You will respond to all drama from the basic emotion of love or fear that exists within you.

Your response will mirror your understanding, and the other party's response will be coming from their understanding. Do you see why communication is a challenge within your world?

It is for this reason that you must listen carefully while focusing your attention on what your friend is saying, not on what you are thinking. Even when you listen carefully you may find yourself giving an answer that your friend does not want to hear.

An example that perhaps you will all understand, using male and female lovers. The male asks the female to help him understand why he has heartburn. The female, in trying to answer the question, may remind her friend that he had two hamburgers, french fries, and several bottles of beer.

This answer may produce a response of "I don't want to hear that. Why can't you just tell me how sorry you are for me and hold me?"

The question that was asked was the question that was answered but it was not the answer that was wanted. This response could then trigger a discussion about not wanting a teacher but wanting someone to love him.

*Most of you consider yourselves open to learn-*
*ing, but you have a tremendous resistance to being*
*taught.*

You will look at information and casually say, "I know all of that. I've read it a hundred times before."

The words will be familiar but putting those words into action and integrating them into your lifestyle become a different situation for you. Truth is the consistency between words and actions. When you acknowledge knowing everything there is to know, you acknowledge your intellectual gathering of the facts. You do not understand that the truth in knowing is in doing.

*You intellectualize facts but you learn very*
*slowly. The method of learning on Earth is through*
*repetition which is your highest order of learning.*

Learning is controlled by the belief system. If you have a belief system that doubts what you are hearing or seeing, your learning will require many repetitions to overcome the beliefs. Because the soul and spirit within you understands your resistance to learning, your life design is created by the use of drama which provides you with the repetitious experience necessary to attract your attention.

Indeed, you repeat the same experience countless times in your life before you realize what your lesson is. Recognition of the lesson will gradually become obvious to you but you may have spent 50 years repeating the experience over and over again. Chances are that while you were repeating the experience, you have been blaming everyone else for the outcome of the event.

*Failure to accept responsibility for self and your*
*world creates many false illusions within your life.*

In relationships you will mirror to others your own beliefs, emotions, and resistances. Have you ever had a spouse say to you, "Stop teaching me. I didn't marry you because I wanted a teacher?" His resistance to learning, to being taught is being mirrored back to him. You may have had no concept that the statement that you made would be perceived as teaching.

Always within relationships there is a giving and a receiving that continues regardless of the conscious awareness within the partners. The giving and the receiving may be coming from positive energy or it may be coming from negative energy depending upon the focus of the individual.

This interaction will be present in all relationships regardless of the Earthly connection. The interaction within the relationship affects the life of each and every individual. It is the responsibility of the individual to focus his energy upon love and caring.

Relationships within the immediate family are the most important relationships within the life of the spirit and soul upon Earth. These relationships should focus upon the celebration of the love that exists.

Each person within a family has a spirit energy of unconditional love. Allowing that love to be openly expressed will allow you to want to spend time with each other. Spending time together as a family is the physical safety net that you can offer yourself and each family member that is involved.

When a family member marries, you have accepted the marriage partner into the physical family unit. The member is already a spirit family member in most cases. Many marriages in your world today are focused upon Karmic relationships that you are working through.

Karmic relationships frequently are focused upon the lessons of the physical, ego self. These lessons will be seen as physical attraction, dominance and submissiveness, dependency, attachment, and self-worth. Lessons of this magnitude require thousands of repetitions within your physical world to be understood.

In some embodiments, a soul and spirit will choose to work through all lessons within one physical life event. This happens when the soul is advanced and is trying to clarify Karmic issues for the last time. The knowledge is there for the soul and spirit but the integration within the physical energy needs clarification.

*Celebration of life, self, family, lovers, marriage, and all other relationships is controlled within the mind of man by his belief system. Your life minute by minute, day by day, should be lived in the energy of celebration.*

Understanding the lessons of life will give you the "key" to understanding yourself. If you are going to walk through a door and the door is locked, you will need a key. You need to be able to open that door. The key for each and every one of you to open the door to joyful celebration is understanding and self-realization.

Looking with total openness at each event within your life will allow you to understand the lessons of your life. Understanding the lessons of your life will allow you to become self-realized as a perfect Being. Within the multiple events of your life, you find your key.

Your triggers to understanding will be found in the repetition of life events. Each repetition will look slightly different from the physical perspective and the image will appear slightly different. But if you continue to look, you will find the core of the lesson to be identical.

You are painting for yourself a panoramic vision of the lesson in all of its images so that you can at last focus in with total clarity on who you are. When you understand who you are, you will have balanced the intellect and ego with the soul and spirit within.

Your intellect is impatient with repetition which is amusing in your world if you stop and think how you created your world. Everything within your world is repetition. Your work is repetition. Your life is repetition. Your play is repetition. Your relationships are repetition.

*When you find that you resist repetition, you are resisting the lesson that is there for you.*

*If you think in terms of reading or reviewing your life events, the repetition will either annoy you or escape you. Annoyance, impatience, and avoidance are the human methods of ignoring an issue. Ignoring issues is the survival technique of the ego. Ignoring issues is resistance to learning.*

It is by the repetition of your world that you learn and you relearn. When the ego becomes annoyed and impatient with repetition, it is because the ego feels that it knows the subject to ego satisfaction and it is not open to relearning from a different perspective.

*The ego focus is to avoid balance with the soul and spirit. True celebration occurs only when the soul and spirit are balanced with the intellect and ego. Without balance the ego of man fears celebration.*

Your peace and joy are found in the soul and spirit of you. The soul and spirit within are the motivation and inspiration for celebration. Creation of celebration within the physical world is accomplished through the balanced intellect and ego.

*Be open to learning in all your relationships. Be open to learning from teachers and guides. Listen to the silence and be open to hearing and seeing the soul and spirit within you. These are the ways to balance self in the physical energy of life. This is the physical action of celebration.*

With this balance of self man will automatically celebrate self, life, family, marriage, lovers, friends, and all other relationships. There will be no fear of BEING self within all events of life and living.

*When you love yourself, you are willing to share the "you" that you love with other people. SHARING IS A CELEBRATION.*

*Loving self is the energy of self-realization. Self-realization is a joy to celebrate each day of your life.*

Learn to be open to friends, to play, to yourself, to your family, to love, and to BEING. Life is the ultimate celebration for man, because it is the choice of man. If you fail to celebrate life, you are failing to validate the wisdom of self in choosing life. Acknowledge and accept your ingenuity and wisdom.

Love yourself and you will love life. Love yourself and you will eternally celebrate living.

Be in peace and joy.

# About The Author

Kathy Oddenino is a practicing R.N. with more than 35 years experience in the fields of TB research, kidney transplant research, nursing administration, nutrition, intensive cardiac care, emergency nursing, and preventative health care.

A graduate of St. Vincent De Paul School of Nursing in Indianapolis, she has worked with Georgetown University Medical School, the National Institutes of Health, the Naval Medical Research Institute, the Uniformed Services University of Health Sciences, and other major medical centers.

**Sharing: Self Discovery in Relationships** is Oddenino's third book to be published since 1989. Her work has received wide recognition and praise for its unique perspective on man's responsibility to understand himself, who he is, what he is, and how he relates to self and others within the world. Her work focuses on man as a total being of physical, soul, and spirit energy that creates eternally in an integrated manner, whether or not the union is consciously acknowledged by the intellect. Her books are written in a simple, easy to read style that relates to you and your life as an individual.

Oddenino's work has guided many thousands of people in discovering and understanding the love that is within themselves. She delivers lectures, conducts seminars across the United States, and frequently appears as a guest on radio and television talk shows.

Oddenino has six adult children and six grandchildren. She was born and reared on a farm in Salem, Illinois as Kathy Heskett, the second child in a family of five children. After graduation from nursing school she moved to Arlington, Virginia. For the past eleven years she has lived in Annapolis, Maryland.

## DATE DUE

| | | | |
|---|---|---|---|
| 12/10/94 | | | |
| ILL 5593409 7/28/97 NOV 11 1998 | | | |
| ILL 9180570 8/1/01 | | | |
| ILL 4299786 3/11/02 | | | |
| OC 23 '02 | | | |

Demco, Inc. 38-293